Boys Who Have Abused

Forensic Focus Series

This series, edited by Gwen Adshead, takes the field of Forensic Psychotherapy as its focal point, offering a forum for the presentation of theoretical and clinical issues. It embraces such influential neighbouring disciplines as language, law, literature, criminology, ethics and philosophy, as well as psychiatry and psychology, its established progenitors. Gwen Adshead is Consultant Forensic Psychotherapist and Lecturer in Forensic Psychotherapy at Broadmoor Hospital.

other books in the series

Ethical Issues in Forensic Mental Health Research
Edited by Gwen Adshead and Christine Brown
ISBN 1 84310 031 2
Forensic Focus 21

Personality Disorder
Temperament or Trauma?
Heather Castillo
ISBN 1 84310 053 3
Forensic Focus 23

Violence and Mental Disorder
A Critical Aid to the Assessment and Management of Risk
Stephen Blumenthal and Tony Lavender
ISBN 1 84310 035 5
Forensic Focus 22

Working with Sex Offenders in Prisons and Through Release to the Community
A Handbook
Alec Spencer
ISBN 1 85302 767 7
Forensic Focus 15

Forensic Psychotherapy
Crime, Psychodynamics and the Offender Patient
Edited by Christopher Cordess and Murray Cox
ISBN 1 85302 634 4 pb
ISBN 1 85302 240 3 hb
Forensic Focus 1

Challenges in Forensic Psychotherapy
Edited by Hjalmar van Marle and Wilma van den Berg
ISBN 1 85302 419 8
Forensic Focus 5

A Practical Guide to Forensic Psychotherapy
Edited by Estela V. Welldon and Cleo Van Velsen
ISBN 1 85302 389 2
Forensic Focus 3

Forensic Focus 24

Boys Who Have Abused
Psychoanalytic Psychotherapy with Victim/Perpetrators of Sexual Abuse

John Woods

Foreword by Arnon Bentovim

With a contribution by Anne Alvarez

Jessica Kingsley Publishers
London and New York

First published in the United Kingdom in 2003
by Jessica Kingsley Publishers Ltd
116 Pentonville Road
London N1 9JB, England
and
29 West 35th Street, 10th fl.
New York, NY 10001-2299, USA

www.jkp.com

Copyright © John Woods 2003

Library of Congress Cataloging in Publication Data
A CIP catalog record for this book is available from the Library of Congress

British Library Cataloguing in Publication Data
A CIP catalogue record for this book is available from the British Library

ISBN 1 84310 093 2

Printed and Bound in Great Britain
by Athenaeum Press, Gateshead, Tyne and Wear

Contents

Foreword

John Woods is the ideal psychotherapist to write about a psychoanalytic approach to therapeutic work with young people perpetrating sexually abusive behaviour. As an experienced child psychotherapist, he has worked for many years with the generality of young people with emotional problems to help contextualise his specialist interest in young people who abuse sexually. He has a training in group analysis, and is interested in the way that groups function, whether in residential contexts, or in applying the principles to develop group work with a group analytic orientation. He has worked in a variety of out-patient and residential contexts, and with young people of all levels of ability, and of complexity of presenting problems. Importantly, he has also worked with colleagues with a wide range of orientations, whose major aim has been to create a therapeutic climate for young people, to help them develop an abuse-free life so they can achieve their potential, and to protect the community. He has kept the banner of psychoanalytic thinking aloft, yet he has absorbed and understood the approaches associated with his colleagues' thinking. He respects the impact of different approaches, and has attempted to understand both when they are indicated, and what are the shortcomings and value of both their approaches and his own.

He has brought a broad range of current thinking together and has considered how his psychoanalytic approach needs to be modified to meet the needs of young people, and to balance the intimacy and confidentiality of the psychotherapeutic encounter, with the need for maintaining a systemic, open approach to communication. This ensures that a young person is managed safely and benefits from a broad range of interventions.

John Woods processes the research and clinical experience which now confirms the malign effect on young people growing up in a climate of violence. Through detailed work with young people, he has described the impact of violence on the child's sense of self, his potential to attach and his emotional life. Concepts are used which are embedded in psychoanalytic thinking. Winnicott's development of a false self to help cope with the traumatic impact of such experiences forms an important building block in his thinking. He also describes the way that exposure to repeated patterns of violence create an atmosphere of never knowing when violence is to be expected. Aggression is then used in order to protect a self that is felt to be under attack without warning, a response reinforced by the growing brain. Using Fonagy's concepts of the way identification is built, he sees that to be an object of abuse in someone else's mind builds an identification on that basis. Attacks on the thinking capacity of the other can be understood as attempts to escape from the intolerable thought of the way one is seen by the other. The focus is on the body which becomes a refuge from intolerable feelings of fear and pain. Such feelings are then divested from the self through the abuse of the other, a response which becomes addictive, and a process which needs to be confronted through re-parenting and through the operation of therapeutic approaches, which can modify this dangerous process.

The model of trauma organised systems is developed to consider how a therapeutic approach can be focused on such dangerous thinking patterns. A systemic field is described associated with abuse, secrecy, silencing, oppressive control and unreliability. This helps to understand the way the young person feels, and the way his responses connect with the environment he has been living in, and the way that this is reflected in residential and alternative care contexts. A systemic approach is required to shape the way that a psychoanalytically orientated therapist can work with colleagues using other approaches to achieve a satisfactory outcome inclusively rather than idealising one approach over others.

The book ranges widely, describing long-term work with individuals which demonstrates the unfolding of the processes associated with abusive behaviour. Change achieved both through the committed relationship offered by the psychotherapist, and the range of understanding through appreciation of transference and countertransference responses, and the support of supervision to de-construct the way family contexts associated with abuse may re-enact within the therapeutic situation.

John Woods calls on his group-analytic background to devise a powerful group approach, which he contrasts to current cognitive behaviour approaches which advocate a structured way of dealing with a succession of topics. He introduces an approach which focuses on communication, openness in a context of safety, maintaining firm boundaries, the use of the therapists' selves, and the exploration of themes. A succession of powerful role plays are described which enable young people to explore the issues associated with abusive behaviour and its origins, and finding a resolution at the same time drawing in young people into an effective therapeutic process.

One of the topics which has been little described in working with young people who are behaving in a sexually abusive way is the issue of the gender dimension of self concept. Female identification is a not uncommon response to being sexually abused and living in a climate of violence, as an alternative to taking on a dangerous identification with the aggressor. Finding a refuge in feeling oneself as having a female body rather than a male one becomes a way of avoiding dangerous behaviour, but yet with its own considerable risks. The value of a psychoanalytic approach is the openness to themes which are not ordinarily perceived as part of the curriculum of even an extended cognitive approach. The value of allowing such themes to emerge and to be worked with is demonstrated as a helpful approach to this often un-addressed subject.

Using Laufer and Laufer's work on body identification as a mode of identity formation in adolescents, John Woods describes a lengthy intensive treatment with an adult who commenced in adolescence increasingly sado-masochistic abusive behaviour with young boys. Although he was not convicted, the therapeutic work had as its condition that any abusive action had to cease; this ethical position demanded that any revealing of specific action would lead to the termination of therapeutic work. A safety network was established within the clinic to ensure that there was no organisation of the therapeutic approach as a way of maintaining abuse under the cloak of respectability. This introduces an essential restraint to the therapeutic work and was one of the factors which helped in the examination of whether the sado-masochistic pattern of relatedness set in motion in adolescence was permanent or could be altered through therapeutic work. This is an important issue in dealing with those severe perverse conditions commencing in adolescence. Other current approaches to therapeutic work with adults helping them achieve an abuse-free life also emphasises the essential role of self-control, and community control when required, and an examination of the pathway leading to abusive action and its reinforcement. The development of a coherent narrative which makes sense of experience and action is an essential component of any therapeutic change. A psychoanalytic approach to achieving this coherence is an important contribution to the current debate on therapeutic effectiveness and approach.

A contrast is introduced between abusive actions, associated with severe traumatic experiences associated with living in a climate of violence, and those which arise from distorted relationships, which result in less serious forms of sexual violence. John Woods shows how his building blocks of thinking can lead to a successful, more traditional form of psychotherapeutic work with these individuals. He shows how different family relationships emerge within the therapeutic encounter, and the way in which change can be facilitated. Anne Alvarez uniquely contributes a chapter on supervision of work in this field, and the importance of creating a team to assist the psychotherapist in understanding and managing risk, and to capture as Alvarez states 'budding new feeling states' as well as to face pathological and highly disturbing states of mind.

There is an increasing number of publications introducing approaches to working with young people who sexually offend. It is recognised that they represent about a third of those responsible for the sexual abuse of children and young people. Therefore they are a significant risk group, for perpetrating a form of abuse which is increasingly seen as representing a public health risk because of the frequency of abuse, and its long-term deleterious effects. Intervention is essential and we are very early in knowing what is effective. At this stage, to state that one approach is going to meet all needs is not supported by clinical experience. These are young people who are at a key stage of their development, and it is essential that we take a broad approach to finding effective therapeutic approaches. John Woods has shown the value of a psychoanalytic approach to therapeutic work, and the way such work can be integrated with other approaches to form a powerful systemic field. He is beginning to tease out how such an approach can be introduced as a vital component of a successful programme of work. In my view, this book is essential reading for psychotherapists who wish to work with young people showing sexually offending behaviour, and for all therapists who are struggling to work with these young people and need to deepen their understanding of this complex field.

Arnon Bentovim,
Psychoanalyst, Honorary Consultant Child and Adolescent Psychiatrist,
Great Ormond Street Hospital and Tavistock Clinic

Preface

I would like to acknowledge the following people who have helped in many ways: Gwen Adshead, Harold Behr, Arnon Bentovim, Al Corbett, Earl Hopper, Dorothy Lloyd-Owen, Mannie Sher, Jake Spencer, and colleagues at the Portman Clinic, Respond, and at S.W.A.A.Y., though of course the views expressed here are mine and are not necessarily representing those organisations. I am particularly indebted to Anne Alvarez, and honoured by her contribution of a chapter on supervision. And most important, for her constant support and encouragement, Marie Zaphiriou Woods.

As a study of clinical work, this book draws upon many case examples. To protect confidentiality the names and details have been changed. Where possible, the permission to publish has been obtained. In some cases this has not been desirable; in these cases any information about individuals has been so modified and combined as to represent not particular people, but to bring alive the general problems of dealing with abused and abusive behaviour.

Heaven lies about us in our infancy!
Shades of the prison house begin to close
Upon the growing Boy

Wordsworth

CHAPTER 1

Psychotherapy with Young Abusers

WHAT DO WE MAKE OF YOUNG PEOPLE WHO HAVE COMMITTED SEXUAL OFFENCES?

Sexual abuse by young people evokes intense and contradictory reactions. There is the desire to punish, based on a fear perhaps that the young perpetrator must be deterred from becoming a habitual and dangerous sex offender. This intention can sometimes backfire; as a convicted adult paedophile once said to me, 'Society has taken away my moral choice; I will do whatever I can get away with.' This man had used his punishment as a justification and also a stimulus for further acts of abuse. He was caught in a pattern imprinted on him by the abuse he suffered from the earliest age, in children's homes. At the other end of the spectrum society may recognise that offenders are not born but created through a history of neglect and violence (Gilligan 1996). Some repair may be attempted for the emotional damage the young perpetrator has inevitably sustained, in his personal history (Hodges *et al.* 1994), and will continue to suffer, if nothing changes. Both sets of responses produce their own difficulties; condemning the perpetrator reinforces his identity as an abuser, whilst attending to his emotional needs as a *victim* may be perceived as condoning the crimes. One boy, for example, was reported by his counsellor as having done such good work on his experiences of being abused he was now all right to share a bed with a younger brother, with disastrous results.

An eminent psychoanalyst Christopher Bollas describes 'that familiar sinking feeling' whenever he hears from a new patient the beginnings of a tale of abuse (Bollas 1989, p.179). Professional burn-out, which is sometimes very evident in teams and individuals who have long been dealing with such cases, tells us something about the nature of trauma and abuse; and despite their training analysis, psychotherapists are not immune. The relentless similarity of the case histories, the mind-numbing uniformity of accounts of abuse, the sense of helplessness in workers when abuse seems to go on and on in certain families, while abusers evade justice – these processes conspire to produce a sense of defeat in the professional helpers. This is especially so when working with those who have not only been abused but are becoming abusers as well, since these young people seem to represent the continuation of the cycle of repetition. At adolescence, as the adult personality is created, there may well be opportunities to interrupt the continuation of patterns of abuse. This moment is often lost, however, because it seems that in our caring systems there is little optimism for these cases. The emotional strain on those who work with sexual abuse is beginning to be documented (West 1997; Erooga and Masson 1999, pp.225–34). Professionals of all disciplines need to be able to find hope in themselves that change is possible. The aim here is to identify those elements that can facilitate change whilst maintaining an awareness of factors that tend to perpetuate the abused/abusing of some young people.

The abused/abuser produces complex reactions and for the therapist the challenge is to use these emotional responses in the most constructive way. As Anne Alvarez (Chapter 10) notes, there comes a point when the therapist makes a chilling observation that the abused/abuser is holding on to his abusiveness because *he enjoys it.* The therapist, who may well have been more used to helping the traumatised victims of sexual abuse, is bound to be affected by meeting a perpetrator. Horne (1999, pp.348–9) reports that some therapists are reluctant to treat such patients, fearing that their sense of outrage at what the young person has done might get in the way of working with the patient. The worst development perhaps is that the therapist becomes in effect an abuser to the victim in the patient. However, given the right conditions, as Horne goes on to show, it is possible to guard against such repetition of abusive relationships, and work with these dynamics. Technically this means both differentiating and combining the duality of victim and perpetrator. The clinical commentaries that make up a large part of this book are attempts to explore these questions in more detail. There was to have been a separate chapter on countertransference, but in the writing of each section it was clear that this aspect was a constant feature that required attention. To hold in mind these equal but opposite aspects of the person who needs help means being able to sustain the contradiction implied in our own feelings which are aroused.

WHY TREAT THE YOUNG SEX OFFENDER?

A naïve question perhaps, but given the paucity of such efforts in general it is important to note that adult offenders, who would on average each commit hundreds of crimes (Becker and Abel 1985), usually begin their offending in adolescence (Hodges *et al.* 1994). Some, but not all, juvenile sex offenders will become adult repeat sex offenders, but there is little certainty about what characteristics predict those who will persist into adult sex offending (Beckett 1999, pp.205–7). The difficulty is not only in knowing which young people need help but also which ones may be treatable. There are factors however which produce a more hopeful picture. One of the most significant beneficial indications that can be identified is the consistency of a sufficiently good attachment relationship (Bentovim and Williams 1998, p.104). Even though the efficacy of long-term psychotherapy itself may be hard to prove, it will at least contribute to the provision of an appropriate placement. If there is a consideration of the young person's needs, something psychotherapy naturally tends towards, then the network moves away from primitive reactions against the perceived 'evil' of the offender's acts. As will be seen from the treatment cases described, the placement of a young person is crucial in considering whether he may be helped by treatment. If he is in treatment, then he is at least less likely to be lost in the system, as happened for example in the case of Dominic McKilligan.[1] The model of psychological treatment proposed here is inextricably bound up with the young person's social situation.

TOWARDS AN UNDERSTANDING OF ABUSE

Forensic Psychotherapy has helped our understanding of what drives people to abuse: Gilligan (1996) for example has worked with prison populations and shows how the aggressor comes to feel that violence is necessary for his survival in a hostile world. We can easily see that perpetrators of violence, even against defenceless victims, usually feel perfectly justified: 'evil' does not operate as an abstract entity, but as a process that happens between people, a complex series of 'interlocking roles' (Bentovim 1995, p.44), which binds victim and perpetrator. In the international context we see perpetrators and victims all the time, and on all sides, whether they be Palestinians and Israelis, Serbs and Croats, Russians and Chechins, Irish Republicans and Unionists, Hutu and Tutsi, white and black Africans, the West and the rest, justifying their actions by blaming the other, both locked together in a state of mutual projection; and as each stage of conflict develops, then the creation of a new wave of violence is bred. Today's perpetrator was yesterday's victim, just as today's victims, or their heirs, will become tomorrow's perpetrators.

In her influential text on trauma Herman (1992) has shown how society requires, and selects, scapegoats according to social class, colour, gender, or other more behavioural criteria. The need to preserve our norms ensures that we condemn the breaching of them in others. What we are is defined by what we are not. As a result of this, as well as for other more specific and personal reasons, the 'offender' often feels that he is the victim of society. His identity is constructed by internalising the experiences to which he has been subjected. However, the therapist can, in principle, seek a wider view, and acknowledge the 'offender' as a product of his social situation, not to negate his responsibility, but to mobilise both the forces within that individual *and his environment* toward change.

The individual's external world is only half the story, however; and from its psychoanalytic orientation this book is concerned with the interaction between a person's external and internal reality. Prominent among the psychodynamic theories referred to is Glasser's idea of the 'core complex' (Glasser 1964), which illuminates the intrapsychic process by which an individual becomes resistant to any positive changes in his environment. From many years of clinical experience at the Portman Clinic London, Glasser showed, among much else, how sexualisation is employed to control the object and protect against fears of engulfment and abandonment. Working analytically with those infantile fears was seen as providing the means to change the structure of the abused/abuser's personality (Glasser 1988).

Being labelled a 'pervert' is possibly the worst nightmare of the young person who has abused someone sexually; but the psychoanalytic theory of sexual perversion promotes the therapy in valuable ways. It was to infant development that Freud first looked in his exploration of the perversions, from the 'Three Essays on the Theory of Sexuality' (Freud 1905) to 'A Child is Being Beaten' (Freud 1919). This book will not attempt a great deal of theoretical discussion of complex questions about perversion as such, but will draw upon these concepts to illuminate clinical work. Rosen's (1964 pp.42–75) introduction to the theory is extremely useful and there he mentions some key factors for ordinary therapeutic work. He shows for example how McDougall explored the quality of compulsion and fixity in perverse sexuality, a feature that will crop up in the following pages. However, as to the essential nature of perverse sexuality, Rosen (p.46) directs attention to the work of Stoller, especially in *Perversion: The Erotic Form of Hatred* (Stoller 1975b). It is the presence of aggression in sexuality that both enables us to define perversion and also to understand its manifestations. The specific knowledge about an individual's need for such aggression that emerges from the work of psychotherapy is that which often determines the outcome of the cases that will be discussed.

WHAT KIND OF TREATMENT?

The recent appearance of *Psychoanalysis and Developmental Therapy* (Hurry 1998), has given a new way of conceptualising the psychological needs of the more seriously disturbed and damaged patient, and informs many of the considerations here made about the treatment of this particular patient group. Developmental therapy has put a framework around the already existing practice of many child and adolescent psychotherapists who have seen that interpretations of unconscious material may be unhelpful or even damaging to certain patients (Hurry 1998, p.37). These therapists will have been helping young people to name feelings, and parts of the body, to control wishes, and impulses, rather than enact them, to think of and see others as having feelings, and taking an active part in play. This theoretical development, catching up, as it were, with practice, will be very valuable in dispelling outdated and stereotypic notions about psychoanalytic psychotherapy.

Within this context a number of clinicians have applied and developed psychoanalytic ideas to work with adolescent abusers (Lanyado *et al.* 1995; Campbell 1994; Horne 1999). Clinical work with this patient group has been enhanced by other conceptual developments; to take an example, the importance of shame was highlighted in the work of Campbell (1994).

Young abused/abusers in treatment continually bring this theme to mind because of the prominence of such intense shameful feelings in the work. The faces behind which they strive to hide, and gradually come to accept as their own, are sometimes shown in drawings produced in the course of therapy. (Some of them will be reproduced here.) Campbell (1994) shows how some adolescents feel forced to deal with the experience of victimisation and defend themselves against traumatic fears by becoming a perpetrator. However, in treatment this traumatic shame that had been the source of terror can be transformed into a creative and productive experience, used to support mature development rather than to hinder. For this to happen there needs to grow an emotional bond between patient and therapist, a complex relationship that has negative as well as positive qualities.

WHY PSYCHOANALYTIC PSYCHOTHERAPY?

Where, it will be asked, is the evidence of the usefulness of the psychoanalytically based approach of this work? It has to be said at the outset that I make no claim to prove the effectiveness of a particular kind of therapy for any or every patient bearing this kind of problem, nor indeed for therapists of other orientations. What is clear, however, is that patients have responded in certain ways that illuminate the meaning of their difficulties, and which moreover show what they need to develop in a new direction. As a result of this psychoanalytically informed therapy they seem to get better, and not only in terms of the social demand that they stop offending. What is difficult to measure is the personality changes that we expect are necessary for someone to be much less dangerous to others and themselves in the future.

This may seem unscientific, but the relevance of empirical certainty for the complexity, variability and irrationality of such human problems may also be questioned. Take for example the often held conclusion from research into the treatment of delinquency: '*We know* that psychoanalytic psychotherapy is ineffective in the treatment of conduct disorder' (Bailey 2002, p.4, my emphasis) – and yes, that does seem to be so if we attempt to look at the results of psychotherapy in isolation. However, the contention on the pages of this book is that psychoanalytic psychotherapy may be applied effectively to what may be described as a type of conduct disorder, sexually abusing, if it is modified in terms of an offence focus and adapted to specific management issues. Under these conditions such treatment has produced results, at least in these cases. Where it has failed, I try to see what can be learned. Generalising the findings is more difficult. Does this mean that the clinical work is worth nothing, beyond the haphazard gains of a few individual patients? Not if we can learn, both from our own experience, and from that of others. Perhaps as Bateman *et al.* (1996) put it, 'every new patient is a new research project.' This becomes much more possible if the broader view is taken, as in that of the textbook on forensic psychiatry by Gunn and Taylor (1995): '...some form of psychotherapy is an essential adjunct to all the other forms of treatment...' (p.559).

Empirical research, far from providing proof of evidence for the effectiveness of psychoanalytic psychotherapy on its own, is instead a valuable source of information that informs clinical practice. For example, Clulow *et al.* (2002) have showed how psychoanalytic interpretations may be confirmed by information from the Adult Attachment Interview. Attachment theory is in the background to all the treatment cases described in these pages. Another important feature of the work represented in this book is the focus on offending behaviour, since there have been favourable indications from the literature devoted to treatment if it is focused on the specific effects of abuse (Finkelhor and Berliner 1995, quoted in Bentovim and Williams 1998, p.105). Whilst the clinical work represented in this book cannot claim to be scientifically validated, nevertheless evidence from empirical studies is drawn upon to help create the conditions for a meaningful therapeutic endeavour.

Psychotherapy is being validated by knowledge from a new source: neurological research. It is now clear that early deprivation and abuse have observable effects: 'Any deprivation of optimal developmental experiences (which lead to underdevelopment of cortical, sub-cortical, and limbic areas) will necessarily result in persistence of primitive, immature behavioural reactivity' (Perry 1997, p.129). Extensive study has been made from the neurological perspective on the effects of trauma and abuse. Dissociation has been identified as one of the protective devices employed by people with a history of abuse and neglect (Mollon 1998). *The Diagnostic and Statistical Manual of Mental Disorders IV* (American Psychiatric Association 1991, pp.484–7) describes dissociation as the 'separation' (i.e. splits) of ideas, feelings or identities that would normally go together. There is a wide spectrum of this disorder, but it has been used to make sense of otherwise inexplicable actions and mental states of people with trauma. Morrison (1997), for example, observed that the motivation behind the killing of the child Jamie Bulger seemed to have arisen from the terror in the minds of the two young killers of being punished by their parents. Their desperate need to remove evidence of their having abducted the child produced an unawareness of the far worse crime of murder. The slow and painful process of undoing the dissociation of feelings through the emotional attunement of the therapist can now be claimed as an important aim of all types of psychotherapy (Schore 2001b, p.302). Far from being a purely subjective, or self indulgent exercise for the 'worried well', psychoanalytic psychotherapy can now be seen as addressing those most important effects of emotional damage that contribute to the perpetuation of trauma.

Whereas difficulties during therapy might once have been thought of as failings of the treatment, they may now be seen as inevitable production of defensive patterns that must be worked through systematically and over long periods of time. Mollon (1998) has explored the 'bipolar reaction', identified by Koss et al. (1995), Nijenhuis and Van der Hart (1995), and observed even in small infants (Perry et al. 1995). In this formulation the traumatised individual is seen to oscillate between hyperarousal and dissociation. Such 'mood swings' are frequently evident in young abusers and may be misinterpreted, either as 'out of control' behaviour, contrasted with 'denial', as if they were consciously determined. Mollon (1998, pp.27–28) goes on to show that the bipolar traumatic reaction is linked with attachment patterns and with the difficulty presented to the infant by the need for closeness with a caretaker who may be also be abusive, or profoundly neglectful. Thus, early formative experiences of abuse and neglect will lead to all sorts of faulty development such as disorganised attachments and an impaired self-regulatory system. Indeed Friedrich (1995a) has set the main aim of emotional self-regulation in his work with abusing boys. Glaser (2000) in a comprehensive review of the evidence for changes in brain function in association with abuse, points toward a positive outcome being achieved by 'the construction of a coherent account by the child of his or her experiences' (p.110), something that is well within the province of psychotherapy; and telling the story reawakens the emotions connected with the past experience.

Zaphiriou Woods (2003) draws upon the work of Schore and other neuro-scientists to suggest that a therapeutic relationship can act as growth-facilitating environment, 'which cannot erase trauma, but can provide a context in which higher, i.e. regulatory and reflective structures can develop'. The difficulty in practice is that an attachment relationship such as that offered by a psychodynamic therapist is bound to evoke the same traumatised reactions, such as dissociation, hyperarousal, and the tendency to fixed perverse patterns, that were established by the blueprint of the original abusive attachment bonds. Thus, there will always be a struggle with, (and within), the young 'abuser' between the need for change and the powerful tendency to revert to pre-established templates of cognition, affect, and behaviour. As the Post Traumatic Stress Disorder responses (Mollon 1998, p.28) are managed and reduced, so the underlying intense and disturbing affects will emerge in the therapy; for a time the young person will seem to be (and may well feel) worse. The cases presented in this book are stories of this fundamental conflict, played out in different ways, with young people of various kinds of problem, and with various kinds of outcome.

However, while the scientific dimension may support and validate what we do in terms of psychological treatment, for a deeper understanding of the abuser's state of mind perhaps we need to turn to artistic expression. Harold Pinter's (1984) play *One for the Road* is a brutally convincing portrayal of a torturer, one who gives the orders, not dirtying his own hands. His rationalisations, quasi-patriotic, -religious, -moralistic, are insignificant when it becomes clear that there is an overriding need to relish the power he has over his victims. He is as habituated to this as he is to the whisky he keeps pouring himself in this short play. His fragile masculinity underlies his hatred of others; he glories in his power over a political prisoner whose son is contemptuously referred to as 'the little prick!', and is casually killed. With unerring perception into these states of mind, Pinter shows how a torturer is compelled by his own emotional damage to inflict that damage on others. Bea Campbell, Annie Castledine and Judith Jones (2002) have also explored the mindset of the abuser in their play *And All the Children Cried*; the character Myra (based on Myra Hindley) says, 'They cannot destroy us, *we are* the evidence.'

Just as the aim is for the 'offender' patient to be able to see beyond his abuse and abusing, so the therapist needs to see beyond the symptomatic behaviour, to the human being at the centre of it. For an understanding of abusive behaviour we must draw upon a great range of resources, from both science and art; for this purpose psychoanalytic psychotherapy, of an interactional kind, with its emphasis on the emotional aspects of relationship, is the most flexible instrument available. The theory also provides room for the rediscovery of a healthy form of desire for these young people. By their abuse and abusing they have all but destroyed what should be, and perhaps still can be for them, the source of greatest value and fulfilment, a healthy sexuality.

CONCLUSION

Coming from abusive family and social conditions, up against the limitations of professional structures, burdened with the internal fixity of their own defensive systems, some young people seem destined to become offenders, and thereby victims of society. But this book is also about adolescence as a time of hope. Winnicott (1958a) wrote in the 'Anti-Social Tendency' about delinquency as an act of freedom, a step toward the creativity needed for the formation of the mature adult personality, moving away from early trauma and deprivation. He frequently observed how the adult world overlooks the intrinsic value of the adolescent's protest expressed in the anti-social act. Instead, young people who transgress are defined as criminals by a social system that needs perpetrators. Looking for containment and acceptance, all they often find is rejection, bitterness and, worst of all, the justification for further offending. Whereas in Winnicott's time delinquency may have taken the form of petty theft, or vandalism, anti-social behaviour today seems to be more extreme and violent, involving assaults on the person rather than property. Such acts may also be seen as communicating something about society's attitude to the body that has changed since the time when Winnicott wrote. Eroticism, desire, instant gratification, and violence as the answer to conflict are pumped by the mass media into everyone's home, and the more so into the more deprived. It is no excuse for an offender to say that he is a casualty of society, but it makes sense of the dangers he represents to, and for, us all. Clinically this balance can be achieved by the attitude created by the therapist; whilst recognising both the real perpetrator and the genuine victim in the young person, the therapist is taken over by neither to the exclusion of the other. Instead, the young person is presented with a third alternative, that of accepting help in thinking his way through to a state of integration and maturation in his personality

Though its method may be unscientific, and the result inartistic, this book represents the author's clinical enquiries into the intersubjective world of the young abused/abuser. Whilst it is not possible to be neutral on questions of child abuse, it is an axiom here that our attitude in dealing with those who have abused is crucial both to their fate, and to reducing the number of future victims. Therefore, the accounts are based on the central psychoanalytic principle of transference and countertransference. Although primarily a study of technique and the practicalities of psychotherapy, this book is also an attempt to convey a sense of hope. Therapeutic work demands much in the way of specifics, what to do, or say, and when, and so forth. This book is not intended as a manual with predictable programmes of work, or as a substitute for intensive training requirements, especially that of supervision, or indeed training analysis. Rather its aim is to draw attention to a field in which there are too few psychoanalytic therapists, partly because of practical and historical problems but perhaps also because of countertransference difficulties of our own. However, it is also one which, given modifications of technique, offers rich opportunities for exploring some universal human problems presented by the young abused/abuser.

NOTE

1   This 17-year-old was sentenced to life imprisonment for the abduction, rape and murder of a 10-year-old boy in March 2001. And as was widely reported in the papers, he had been psychologically assessed as 'highly dangerous' when he was 14, but due to his many temporary placements around the country, did not receive proper supervision or treatment (Reed Business International Nov. 01).

CHAPTER 2

Psychotherapy in a Systemic Context

INTRODUCTION

Practitioners in this field do not currently have a shared set of ideas derived from an integrated theory with which to address some fundamental questions, such as 'Why do some people abuse?' Nor is there an agreed set of aims based on concepts of desirable change. In this country we are in a state of professional fragmentation, as a survey of recent publications on adolescent abusers shows (Woods 1999). This state of affairs has admittedly much to do with longstanding rivalry and division between various schools of mental health workers, but is given an extra emphasis by anxieties in the professional helper who might be held responsible not only for his or her client or patient but for potential victims of his client, should the management and treatment fail.

What is needed is the kind of integration and consensus that can be seen in the work of Ryan (1989; 1998b) and Ryan and Lane (1991). Gail Ryan and her colleagues are eminent American practitioners in the treatment of juvenile sex offenders, and they describe a process of change in the interface between adult and adolescent offender work. Treatment provision for young people in the US had originally drawn from the predominant philosophy in work with adults, which was heavily influenced by theories of the criminal personality, eschewing psychoanalytic concepts, concentrating on the observable results of behavioural change. This tradition relied on techniques first of all from behaviourism and, latterly, from cognitive behavioural therapy. The aim was to change the way the offender thinks, not to delve into early childhood for possible long-term causes. Work with young people, however, demanded recognition of the offenders' developmental stage, their attachment relationships, the representations of which led naturally on to considerations of their inner world, and to questions about the development of a capacity for empathy with others. Only through these factors could there be any confidence in achieving the cognitive, and behaviourally defined goal of relapse prevention. Ryan (1998) has observed how practitioners with adolescent offenders are developing their work in the direction of these psychodynamic ideas previously characterised as subjective, unscientific, unproven, and, therefore, worthless.

In this country, however, it is still unfortunately the case that professional groups are split, over questions of theory and practice. They exist in separate organisations conversing only in their group of like-minded colleagues. Treatment programmes rarely combine professionals from different groups. Publications from each school either ignore or dismiss work that does not come from familiar or 'proper' sources: for instance Hoghughi (1997) and Howitt (1995) seem to come from a world where psychoanalytic psychotherapy does not exist. Events such as conferences are conducted on a kind of tribal basis, each one an exclusive arena for discussion only between those with shared basic assumptions. Differences in customs between them was highlighted for example at a conference attended by this author, which included professionals from judicial, law enforcement and statutory agencies, as well as treatment services; the proceedings began with one of the main speakers introducing her qualification to speak on this subject, including her own history of sexual abuse by her father. How unlikely and inappropriate that would have seemed at a psychoanalytic gathering!

TOWARD THE COMBINATION OF TREATMENT MODELS

At one point early in my own involvement in this field I asked my outside consultant if I should agree to a request to see a boy for psychotherapy whilst he was still participating in cognitive behavioural therapy. She said, 'Why on earth not? This boy needs all the help he can get' (Anne Alvarez, personal communication). I had been under the sway of my training, which dictated that change could take place only through a distinct and discrete transference relationship with the therapist. Through subsequent years I have allowed the work with young abusers to bring me closer to other professionals, and though of very different theoretical orientations we are united by the common purpose. Cognitive behavioural therapists of my acquaintance become very interested in the psychodynamic perspective, and in practice we find that young people benefit from a combination of treatments. A psychodynamic session provides a very useful opportunity for a young person working through material introduced in cognitive behavioural therapy. I have attempted to describe elsewhere the interplay between different modes of psychological treatment (Woods 1997). Far from being necessarily in competition with other treatments, psychodynamic psychotherapy can occupy a valued place, as long as it is integrated with other provisions, and not taking place in isolation. It is sometimes difficult to know if divisions between the schools of therapy are really to do with a realistic or even a theoretical incompatibility or perhaps more to do with a felt need to compete for the resources of the marketplace

The credibility of psychoanalysis is still suffering from its failure to acknowledge the reality of child sexual abuse. Despite revelations from earlier work with female hysterical patients, Freud came to believe that these reports were untrue and to maintain that symptoms were derived from fantasies and not from real events. In other words the memories of being seduced by the father were the expression of the typical Oedipus complex in women (Freud 1896, p.168). Despite attempts at reinterpreting psychoanalysis by, for example, Chodorow, Alice Miller, and J.L. Herman, (described in Sanderson (1991, chapter 2), this limitation has led many to mistrust a model that has been seen to place responsibility for abuse in the child rather than in the perpetrator.

Within psychoanalytic psychotherapy there is another polarisation: between those who place trauma at the centre of the therapeutic endeavour, and see aggression as a reaction to experiences of victimisation, as against those who regard aggression and destructiveness as innate. This controversy does not inspire confidence in other professionals. As was heard from a senior psychoanalytic therapist in a recent clinical discussion, 'all right this patient was abused as a child, but what was her part in it?' Clearly this was unpalatable to those from other disciplines, as it was also to some from psychoanalytic psychotherapy. The gulf between psychotherapists and others seems, at least in some areas, to be widening.

The post-war years have seen much debate; family therapists and theoreticians have argued for abuse to be seen as a failure of the family, whilst those in sympathy with the feminist school have characterised this as a covert attack on the role of the mother, another example of the power structures in our society that permit women to be blatantly abused by men. It was not until the early 1980s that Finkelhor (1984) proposed his model of four preconditions for abuse to take place, which is a comprehensive description of the context of abuse. This model (to be discussed in more detail later) directs attention on to the abuser, and bridges the gap between the sociological and the psychological.

The image of psychoanalytic psychotherapy has also been tarnished by a reputation for lengthy treatments producing little improvement. It is hard to refute the steady erosion of confidence in psychoanalytic psychotherapy described by Lousada (2000). There has been a tendency, therefore, to dismiss the whole school of thought, as happens in less than a page in a book on therapeutic work with young abusers by Hoghughi (1997, p.25). It is not hard to see how such misapprehensions arise. Take for example the work of the psychoanalyst Joyce McDougall who accounts for the development of perversions by pointing to developmental problems such as '...overwhelming castration anxiety stemming from Oedipal conflicts ...faced with the need to come to terms with the introjected image of a mutilated body...' (McDougall 1995, p.181) If this is accepted, it follows that treating this underlying psychopathology will relieve the need for sexually perverse behaviour. The likelihood is, however, that the indefinite length of intensive analytic treatment needed will be of little use to someone whose main aim is to alter their own, or in the case of a social agency, another's dangerous behaviour; but, the psychoanalyst will argue, the main aim is not to alter, or to control behaviour, but to understand, and increase self-knowledge. Thus it is that those agencies and professions whose task it is precisely that – to alter and control behaviour – have turned away from psychoanalytic psychotherapy.

This rift has meant that both sides lose professional effectiveness. Those responsible for the care of young people are frequently perplexed by the contradictions in the behaviour of their charges and keenly seek guidance as to the meaning of what is going on. Campbell (1994) discusses what happens sometimes when a young abuser apparently complies with treatment; in these cases there may later be unwelcome revelations that induce a sense of betrayal in the worker. There is then a powerful temptation to give up on the young person. 'Treatment programmes that do not take into account the abused/abuser's inner world of deception and counter self-deception are likely to be victimised in the same way that the child's victims are' (Campbell 1994, p.322). Listening as the present writer has, over several years to referrals of offenders, there are frequently references to previous attempts at counselling that have fallen foul of the adolescent's secret continuation of his abusing. It becomes apparent that these treatments did not engage, either at an individual or at a systemic level, with the abusing that was known. The child was either seen as a victim or the treatment was regarded as separate from 'outside' concerns. These failed treatments inevitably compound the problem for the abused/abuser because they repeat the rejection and the triumph of the psychopathology that underlies the abuse.

Abusive actions arise from a number of causes, including the emotional effects of deprivation, traumatic sequelae such as dissociation, as well as faulty cognitions, character disorders and neurological phenomena. Psychoanalytic interpretations such as that of McDougall above may be true as a comment on the defensive function of perverse or antisocial behaviour, but have only limited relevance, depending on the orientation of the professional worker. The vast bulk of the current literature on adolescent abusers shows a preoccupation with case management and behavioural control, rather than a concern with the therapeutic work as such. There is little reflection on the internal world of the young abuser. Attempts at working with the young people get caught up in professional splits that are re-enactments of the dynamics of abusive families; therapists may become identified with the victim, and statutory agencies can take authoritarian or neglectful roles. These processes have been explored by Davies (ed) (1998).

Again a comparison with the US shows that the combination of social and psychological problems that abusive adolescents portray has led to a greater interest in combined treatment and its research (Shevrin 1996). It may well be that a group of theories rather than a monolithic entity provides a more accurate view of complex psychological and social reality. Some psychoanalysts are tending in this direction: 'Heteroglossia, not monoglossia is the natural state' (Pines 1999, p.162). Group analytic psychotherapy is another source of questioning assumptions about the concept of an individual who exists with an intrapsychic reality separate from social reality (Dalal

1999). In the field of adolescent abuse a recent collection of papers demonstrates that there should no longer be any need to defend one school of thought against another (Pithers *et al.* 1998). Whilst there is little evidence that any one treatment is more effective than another, Multi-Systemic Therapy (MST) is presented by these authors as a combined treatment, a way of addressing the social, educational, behavioural, and psychological aspects of a young person. The multiple needs of a young person who has abused provide us with an ethical imperative for professional partisanship to be put aside (Swenson *et al.* in Pithers 1998). As Crittenden (1997, p.25), said, 'what is needed in this field is a 'purposefully integrated form of eclecticism'. Without any one overarching psychological theory there is nevertheless increasing empirical evidence to demonstrate the effectiveness of MST (Pithers *et al.* 1998, p.356). As a flexible and individualised approach to a wide range of problems MST is proving to be a very significant and non-partisan way forward with psychosocial problems of the more severe kind (Rowland *et al.* 2000).

So, if psychoanalytic therapy can no longer convincingly hold centre stage, what is the rightful place of intrapsychic theories? What for example can psychodynamic theory contribute to our understanding of why only some who have been abused go on to abuse, and some, (the majority, in fact) do not? Studies show the high incidence of victimisation in the life story of an abuser, though the reverse is not true; only a relatively small proportion of the abused (12–14%) show signs of developing into abusers, (Bentovim and Williams 1998, p.102). It may be possible to predict those young people who are more likely to become or remain abusive by formulating and applying a risk index (Watkins and Bentovim 1992, p.231). Certain features have been noted, e.g. the relative severity of physical abuse, neglect and rejection of the child, the witnessing of domestic violence; and sexual abuse by mother seems a particularly significant factor. Other predictive factors in the child's own behaviour include other delinquent traits, and features such as cruelty to animals or encopresis. However, it should also be noted that many well-established adult paedophiles show no other criminal behaviour, and there may be little observable trauma in that offender's history (Howitt 1995, p.64). Again, there is the dilemma of weighing up the relative significance of internal and external factors. The classic statement of Stoller (1975) that 'the act of abuse is the realisation of a fantasy of mastery over childhood-induced trauma' (quoted in Finkelhor 1984, p.38), is one to be treated with caution. It may or may not be relevant in a given case. The great variation of individual differences among sexual offenders is lost in statistical analysis. Internal factors do not feature in such research, but they do provide possible answers as to why different children respond in different ways. With some it seems that early sexualisation may be the crucial factor, though it is the element of fear of coercion in another. How can the effects of neglect and deprivation be measured? It is hard to measure the kind of fixed expectations of the abused, that the world is hostile place, and that satisfaction can never be found. The internal representations of attachment patterns, characteristic defensive patterns, and the impact of these on emerging sexual identity can all be assessed and evaluated for treatment only on an individual basis.

The complex interaction of risk factors in the child's life suggests that beyond the observable facts the child who becomes abusive has done something different internally with his experiences of abuse. He, or she, has transformed the experience into the opposite of that of victimisation, so that the compulsion exists to be instead the victor. It is not enough for some, it seems, to find safety from abuse; perhaps they have given up hope that this would be possible. Safety is found, for these young people, in reversing the role into that of the abuser, but for different reasons in each individual case. The subjective meaning of abuse, and the response to that experience, is the crucial variable. Changing that meaning is what can lead a person to make different choices in his behaviour. But we cannot look at the individual in isolation; abusers do not spring into being. First we must examine the context for that individual, the foundation, the substructure of the abusive environment.

THE TRAUMA ORGANISED SYSTEM

It is axiomatic for a psychotherapist that a child affected by an abusive environment cannot be helped by psychotherapy alone. If this were attempted it would be like a train signal 'Passed At Danger', and disaster might well ensue. Systems theory has addressed the context in which abuse takes place and develops. Arnon Bentovim has been in the forefront of the UK child abuse field for many years. His *Trauma Organised Systems* was revised in 1995 to incorporate ideas from the feminist movement and constructionist family therapy. An abusive act in this model is seen as one event in a network of interdependent elements, not as part of a simple cause-and-effect chain. Certain families take on a particular role in relation to a social matrix that gives permission, indeed exerts pressure on members of the family, to continue in abusive relationships. This happens through socio-economic conditions, through gender roles and the particular history of that family. Bentovim draws on the work of Goldner *et al.* (1990) to show how males have a need to define themselves as *not* being the victim of traumatic events, and under certain conditions will instead develop relationships where the victim is found in the *other* sex, i.e. 'not me'. The male's need to be powerful and dominant is exacerbated in families where there is deprivation, and where the boy has been forced into submission to abuse. He will then find women who are predisposed through their own traumatic experiences to take on roles of subservience and collusion. They will then produce or otherwise bring in children who are sometimes literally 'born to be abused'. In a different version the pattern may also be seen in a certain exploitative kinds of homosexual relationship (see Chapter 8).

Kinston and Bentovim (1980) describe the *intersubjective meanings* that become the *dominant narratives* of abusing families. The function of the Trauma Organised System is to silence the victim by a process of blame and disqualification. Through this experience the victim comes to blame him – or herself. Thus, the abuser exploits the dependency and fear of separation in other family members. The victimiser blots out those thoughts, actions, or statements that threaten to destabilise the structure that perpetuates the abuse, just as the traumatised individual fends off awareness of a traumatic past that nevertheless persists in the form of symptoms. Any family member who threatens to disrupt the protection against change faces exclusion. The abusive family creates an impermeable barrier against the outer world and all discourse is devoted to maintaining its interior stability.

This schematic diagram (Bentovim 1995, p.47) shows

the common patterns associated with the establishment of sexual abuse within a family. The arrows bending back on themselves show how those communications to father (F) or mother (M) that would signal distress or anger, which should modify the actions of the other, are re-labelled as the child (C) deserving abusive action and rejection.

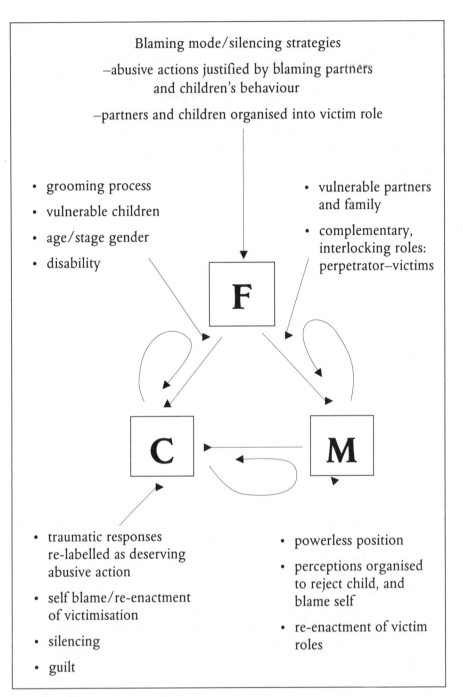

Blaming mode/silencing strategies

–abusive actions justified by blaming partners
and children's behaviour

–partners and children organised into victim role

• grooming process

• vulnerable children

• age/stage gender

• disability

• vulnerable partners
  and family

• complementary,
  interlocking roles:
  perpetrator–victims

F

C

M

• traumatic responses
  re-labelled as deserving
  abusive action

• self blame/re-enactment
  of victimisation

• silencing

• guilt

• powerless position

• perceptions organised
  to reject child, and
  blame self

• re-enactment of victim
  roles

Figure 2.1 The Trauma Organised System

Note: Figure 2.1 originally appeared in *Trauma Organised Systems: Physical and Sexual Abuse in Families* by Arnon Bentovim (1995) published by Karnac, London.

These unconscious assumptions about each other are powerfully held and constantly turn back on themselves in a reflexive and internalising way. The telling of stories that blame the victim, justify the perpetrator, and perpetuate secrecy against the outer world are challenged in therapeutic work with families. A technique known as *externalising conversations* is then a strategy for the therapist. The 'stories' that perpetuate abuse by protecting the role of abuser are replaced by those that enable victims to speak out, that allow victimisers to accept responsibility, and that will create an open system that is connected with the outside world.

This particular conceptualisation of an abusive system arises from a family therapy perspective and is primarily intended for application within a family therapy intervention. The orientation of the present discussion however is toward treatment for the young person. The family of origin cannot be ignored, though opportunities for working with the family as such are limited by the fact that in many cases the family has in effect disintegrated. Individual work with a young person does not ignore the family context: Campbell (1994) for example integrates the family perspective in his discussion of assessment. However the Trauma Organised System model can be developed through its relevance to the inner world of the child who is the product of such a family system.

The Trauma Organised System can be applied as a virtual map of the child's inner world, a template which limits and controls the child's experience, interactions, and ultimately, if nothing changes, his fate. The father is represented as a corrupt superego impervious or hostile to anything that might spring from the child's real emotional needs, substituting covert permission for continued exploitation and abuse. The internal mother is powerless to provide nurture or protection so that the young person is unable to conceive of care or concern being shown him. If such a gesture should be made by the environment, it is then intercepted by the internal father and cynically interpreted as another opportunity for advantage. The child self absorbs punishment, and is silenced by what he believes to be the upper hand that is identified with the abusive father. Often the real target of sexualised aggression is unconsciously the mother against whom attacks are felt to be justified because of her perceived failure. The internal mother figure is projected on to some outside person or organisation, such as therapeutic community, hospital, clinic, or group such as 'the social workers' or 'shrinks'. Thus, denying himself any nurture or hope of change the child self is wedded to the destiny of victimisation. These inner dynamics can be inferred from events, and they are reinforced, time and again, by the adolescent's patterns of behaviour in placements. In sessions he may alternate between the roles of victim and abuser, whilst at the core the maternal image is fixed as failing, hated, and neutralised. The repetition of spoiling and rejection by some children from abusive families is often a mystery to well-intentioned workers or foster carers seeking to provide a good environment. The Trauma Organised System and its internalisation illuminates this malignant process and is also a means by which psychodynamic work can intervene at the appropriate level. Whereas systemic thinking can influence interventions in the external world, the achievement of the internal change, necessary for some, depends on the application of these principles in psychodynamic work. As the therapist listens to the child's communications, so the landmarks of this internal map become evident, and through externalising conversations their power can be questioned, and rectified.

THE DOUBLE VALENCE OF TRAUMA

It has been the struggle of psychoanalytic thinking to comprehend the social as well as the personal meaning of trauma, a struggle which sometimes has failed, according to many (Herman 1992, pp.7–32; Sanderson 1991, pp.33–5). The dynamics of trauma have to be at the centre of any discussion of treatment for child abuse, including or perhaps especially for that of the perpetrator, since it is impossible to understand the cycle of abuse and abusing without investigating the effects of traumatic states of mind. Finkelhor's traumagenic model (Finkelhor 1984) has been very influential in the systemic field and it is now generally established, and accepted, that abusers have a history of their own abuse and neglect (Beckett 1999, p.210). What we mean by trauma is something that by its nature stretches the use of language because of its essential quality for the individual who is, or is threatened with, being overwhelmed with states of mind that include pain, fear, anxiety, with feelings that are experienced as 'too much to bear' (Horne 1999, p.268), and may be also 'too much' to articulate. Just as physical pain can produce a mechanism of cutting off into unconsciousness, in the same way the mind may self-protectively fend off unbearable stimuli, driving it away from awareness. However, this mechanism operates at the cost of an array of symptoms that have been described as the Post Traumatic Stress Disorder in DSM IV 427–429 (American Psychiatric Association 1991). There is direct neurological evidence (Perry 1997) about very young children traumatised before communication is possible. There may be no conscious memory, but the effects of the past are demonstrably retained and continue to be expressed in feelings, behaviours, and bodily states. Psychodynamic ideas about defence mechanisms now become more relevant because it is impossible to account for these clearly observable phenomena without concepts such as the unconscious, repression, or repetition compulsion.

Therapists may be wrong-footed by the perpetrator's use of his trauma, perhaps through (conscious) justification of his actions, or more unconsciously as a defence against awareness of anything that might be connected, including his own actions. The existence of trauma, although real enough, is not sufficient to account for the continuation of the cycle of abuse. Indeed, if it were the only or the main preoccupation then treatment enters the cul de sac of justification and denial of responsibility, that are classically the hiding place of the abuser. Recasting the perpetrator as victim is hardly better than resorting to unthinking punishment, if abusing is not to continue. The real facts of the aggression in the acts of the perpetrator have to be kept in focus, but the person who was abused has also to be brought into the foreground because he too carries responsibility for the continuation of abuse. Cognitive behavioural group therapy comes into its own here, since the group knows well the techniques of evasion among its members. However, cognitive behavioural therapists acknowledge that not every offender is fitted for 'the programme', and this is especially the case with adolescents who may present a more complex picture than that of most adults. Cognitive behavioural therapy often seems to lack a more complex theory of mind. For instance it may be that a perverse sexuality is a necessary defence against adolescent breakdown. Behavioural symptoms, particularly in adolescence, may mask '…primitive anxieties of annihilation, abandonment, disintegration…' (Horne 2001, p.4). Prepared programmes of work, even the most excellent – for example, that developed by Bentovim (2000) – will fail to meet the needs of young people who find it impossible to be with themselves, let alone with a therapist making them aware of their feelings.

ADOLESCENT DEVELOPMENT

Puberty is a crucial stage for the development of the individual in relation to their family, giving possibilities of maturity, change and independence, even from the kind of family to be described, that may be organised for the perpetuation of abuse. An important aspect of adolescent development as outlined by the Laufers (1984, pp.36–49) is the relationship the adolescent has to his own body. They describe the growth of a sense of ownership of the body, the lack of which can be seen in many disorders of adolescence. This ownership comes about in normal development through a process of separation from the early relationship with the mother, in stages which are recapitulated in adolescence in order to form a sexual identity. The notion of responsibility is intimately bound up with the sense of ownership. Many adolescent abused/abusers convey little responsibility when they first come to speak about their actions: 'It just happened,' they say, in a similar way it seems to the way 'it just happened' to them. However, as treatment develops the young person expresses astonishment at his discovery of the true meaning of what has happened, or of what they made happen. Change for the abused/abuser is a constant struggle to regain 'ownership' of actions, and of the body that is the agent of those actions. Lack of responsibility is enabled by a disconnection with the body, which leads to the adolescent danger of losing command of himself. In one aspect this is an evasion, but it is also expressing a psychological truth. Hence the mystification and feeling of injustice that often transpires when an adolescent is forced to accept the painful consequences of their acts. Without understanding anything except that he is once more the victim, the abused/abuser nurtures the grievance that will ensure his continued perpetration as soon as he feels he can get away with it. Only in psychoanalytic therapy can the question begin to emerge, and begin to be addressed: if the young person does not 'own' their body, then who does?

GENDER ROLES

It will be evident to readers of the clinical chapters of this book, as it will be to anyone working in the field, that the vast majority of perpetrators are male. In the various specialised settings where I have worked there have in fact been no such referrals of females. Of course women and girls may become abusers, but by certain measures they seem to be fewer in number

(Masson and Erooga 1999, pp.6–7). It may also be that females choose different and less obvious ways to express their aggression. Welldon (1988) has explored the ways in which women may take their own body and the children they can produce as vehicles for perversion or sexualised aggression. These manifestations come much less to the attention of society until some particular crime cannot be ignored. It seems then that the outrage against the offender is magnified because she seems to have done more than the particular offence; she has broken a mythical idealisation of femininity.

The social construction of masculinity has made violence much more openly the province of men and boys. Gilligan (1996) has shown how the fear of shame and dishonour is equated with a fear of being emasculated, and how the reassertion of masculinity is intricately bound up with complex feelings about violence. Some young people are taught, by the most effective means, that is by direct experience, that violence is the way to achieve power, domination, and thereby safety from vulnerability to attack. The following picture was produced spontaneously by a 15-year-old boy who was telling me with some distress that he felt his hands were perhaps really those of his father. He felt unable to touch himself while washing because these were the hands that had abused children, just as his father's were when they were touching him sexually. His anger came out on paper as he depicted the perverse delight in the face that is at one and the same time victim and murderer. The disembodied hand is both his own and the father's that has removed the head and the ability to think. The perversion of a masculine sense of identity is discussed in more detail in Chapters 7 and 8. Where Gilligan (1996) develops his thesis to propose social policies that reduce the sense of humiliation and powerlessness in certain sections of the population, the therapeutic orientation here is on a much smaller scale, though perhaps no less ambitious; the task is to find a way through the persecuting sense of shame in these soon-to-be-men, in order to achieve an identity that is less fragile and less dangerous.

Figure 2.2

THE DEVELOPMENT OF SELF

The work of Fonagy, Target, and others illuminates the defensive role of aggression and provides the means of application of this understanding to a therapeutic process. In 'Aggression and the Psychological Self' Fonagy *et al.* (1993) draw a distinction between the pre-reflective or physical self, developing from the earliest months of life, and a reflective, or psychological self, slower to form, that is, or should be, taking shape over the first two years. This reflective capacity is acquired by the child through an intersubjective process, and it is modelled by the child on the thoughts perceived as coming from an adult caregiver about that child. An example is given of the child who may be pleasurably banging his cup on a fine piece of furniture. A parental figure could react to this as if it were intentionally aggressive, and therefore to be punished. An alternative parental model is to substitute another physical object for the child to playfully explore an aggressive impulse, which is seen as essentially innocent. This has the function of demonstrating to the child an adult's ability to think of the child as not inherently hostile. The child in this environment grows into one who has faith in his existence in the mind of another as someone who has value, goodness, and can experience pleasure. By contrast, what of the child who has no experience of a parental figure who considers him or her even as a person with thoughts and feelings? What of the child who has been for these adults nothing but an object of abuse? 'In time aggression may become an organising influence on the construction of self and take the place of emotional relatedness and concern for the other' (Fonagy *et al.* 1993, p.482). Such a totality of abusive environment is found in the background of those young people who come to abuse (Beckett 1999, pp.210–11). However, with many young abusers there is a compartmentalisation that permits an ordinary or false life to be lived. Winnicott's conceptualisation of the False Self, discussed by Fonagy *et al.* (1993, p.475), shows how the 'the crushed essential being of the infant' is protected by such structures. Aggression, as well as compliance, may be part of the False Self. This is where long-term detailed analytic treatment comes into its own: the multiple and sometimes paradoxical layers of meaning that underlie abusive behaviour can find their containment and can be worked through.

The work described in the following chapters aspires to Winnicott's therapeutic model, in which the traditional emphasis on the analytic therapist's interpretation and the patient's insight is put aside in favour of something like, though not the same as, re-parenting. The stance of the therapist as 'real', or as 'developmental object' (Hurry 1998, p.35) supplies an emotional need of the young abused/abuser. Therapists in this view need to use their own emotional responses with careful judgement, not to condone or to condemn, but to show firmness as well as understanding where appropriate. However, the classical notions of transference/countertransference remain as important mainstays, especially when the therapeutic relationship is overloaded with residues of the abusive history.

The above is a brief account of the kind of integrated theory which opens up avenues to the inner world for therapeutic work with the young abuser. However, sometimes these opportunities are less than welcome in the care system around a child, introducing as they do further complications – for example, the management of regression to these earlier states of development, or the emergence of problems not previously envisaged, such as depression, self-harm and suicidal impulses, or conflicts about gender identity. Through a variety of therapeutic casework I hope to illustrate the necessity for many of these issues to be included in the treatment for abusive behaviour. In these cases the therapist needs to engage with the systemic context and be at times almost an advocate for the young person, towards an understanding of their inner world through their treatment needs. This will be possible usually only when other professionals are assured that the offence focus remains. Interacting in this way also confirms for the therapist the overall structure of the offence-focused work.

SUMMARY AND CONCLUSION

The experience of many workers in the field (for example, Ryan 1989; Calder *et al.* 1997) proposes that adolescent sex offenders be, first, held responsible for their actions and, second, given offence-specific treatment. A therapist subscribing to this agreement modifies the psychoanalytic approach in two ways: first, there are changes that arise from the context of child protection in which the treatment takes place (external considerations) and, second, the therapist has constantly to bear in mind the sex-offending behaviour (and its internal meaning) that has brought the adolescent into treatment. Some of these requirements will go against the grain for psycho-analytic therapists who will be trained in a non-directive stance. A truly spontaneous unfolding of a transference relationship becomes much more possible if the offender/patient feels himself to be safely held in a context that actively militates against abuse. The case studies to be presented are intended to illustrate the effectiveness and functioning of this combined approach.

Splits exist in the practice and provision of treatment for young abusers, which can be seen to arise partly from a dichotomy in the thinking about victim and/or abuser. In the legal system it is clear that a young person can take the position only of one or the other, but this seems to extend mistakenly into other services. Certain agencies gather around the cognitive behavioural-therapy orientation on the offending behaviour whilst other professionals focus on the victimisation that underlies the offence. It is contended here that such polarisation impoverishes the work in general and severely limits what is offered the young abused/abuser.

Nevertheless, the integration of psychoanalytic psychotherapy in a systemic context both brings benefits as well as problems; a wealth of concepts becomes available to a wider network rather than being the jealously guarded property of an isolated therapist. Certain information can be shared by the therapist that will ultimately be in the patient's interests. The complex task is to preserve a sense of privacy and safety for the young person in treatment so that he can confide personal and painful feelings without fear of further shame or humiliation. This has to be achieved without falling into the trap of secrecy. However, such communication that the therapist has with others may also represent the young person's emotional life in a beneficial way, especially about the defensive function of abusive behaviour, or the possible meanings of repetitive and self-destructive actions. The otherwise inexplicable actions of a young person become issues that other professionals can see and understand. When an intersubjective model is employed the therapist can demonstrate to both child and carers that the abuser/victim interaction are two sides of the same coin. The capacity of the child to speak out depends on a willingness in the adult to see and hear. Both therapists and other professionals should concur that the child who has been victimised needs to be heard in order to become less dangerous. Openness of communication throughout the system of carers is the antidote for the kind of closed structures that perpetuated abuse.

What psychoanalytic psychotherapy gains from this kind of integration is the social perspective, both at a technical or practical level as the treatment is supported, and also at a theoretical level. The systemic concept of externalising conversations releases psychotherapy from the straitjacket of misplaced confidentiality that becomes secrecy. These conditions allow the young person to create a new narrative of his life of abuse. Offence-focused work makes it possible for the psychoanalytic therapist to choose from a vast array of psychodynamic concepts; these need not be limited to the problem that has brought the young person into treatment, but may well lead on to the perhaps deeper problems that he brings to our attention.

CHAPTER 3

Common Themes in the Psychotherapy of Young Abused/Abusers

Thus far I have been arguing for an approach that integrates elements from systemic, cognitive behavioural as well as psychodynamic theories. This could perhaps be described as a 'post-modern' orientation, since there is less emphasis on explanations of an 'objective' reality, and more on the function and relevance of the belief system represented by theory. The position of the observer and his involvement with the clinical problem is central to this perspective. New philosophical ideas have been applied to child psychiatry, for example by Timimi (2002), who makes a plea against the imposition of theory in the practitioner's mind, and *for* an openness to the child's story, and that of the family. In subsequent chapters I will present detailed case histories that, in effect, deconstruct the image of 'young abuser'. Here in the ensuing, briefer examples I endeavour to present stories of the interaction between the young person and his therapist in order to reveal some of the forces that have brought both to the present point.

BULLYING AND BEING BULLIED

The young 'abuser' may well feel forced to attend appointments, especially to begin with, or for an assessment. (This question is dealt with in more detail in Chapter 7.) However, it may also emerge during treatment as a transference relationship takes hold and develops.

> 'Hussein', 14, and physically big for his age, had forced his 7-year-old sister to submit to genital intercourse; this happened only once, so it seemed, since she showed her mother that she was bleeding. He was cautioned by the police and removed from home. He had experienced early separations from his family due to their refugee status, and was very distressed at his being taken into residential care. There seemed to be no history of his having been abused. He soon became arrogant and threatening to residential social workers. I was asked to assess whether he could return home and/or whether he could be helped by psychotherapy. When I first met him he was full of grievance complaining bitterly how he had been severely punished for a one-off mistake, which he accepted was a very bad thing to have done, but which would *never* be repeated. Why did no-one believe him, he asked. What could he do to convince people? It was so unfair! Clearly he felt himself to be the victim, and when I asked him if he felt himself to have been more abused by what had happened than his sister had been, he glowered and glared at me so that I felt I might be physically attacked. I asked if he felt I was just getting at him and he said yes, that he felt I was being sarcastic and went on to say that of course it was completely wrong to have done what he did but that he could not understand why it had happened.

We went on to discuss in detail, not 'why it happened', but *how he came to do it*, a simple but crucial difference in this dialogue, which I have found it useful to repeatedly emphasise. The former question is usually unanswerable, at least in the early stages of work, whilst the latter provides more useful information about the context, and therefore the meaning of the abusive act. Hussein's threatening look appeared again, and I heard also that he could be aggressive to his social workers. He was able to make some links with his fear of father, but more deeply a sense of being abandoned and unprotected from past events that had seemed to have affected his parents more than himself. This was not of course a smooth process since he would also at times feel again attacked by me and would react automatically in an aggressive way. There were links to his having taken on, resentfully, some of the denied trauma of his parents. He came to see that this dominating manner, the need to impose his will, for fear of being vulnerable, was connected with the abuse of his sister. His assault on her was therefore no longer an isolated, and incomprehensible, event, but something which he could own, and which could even lead to change in his personality. Communication between these different parts of himself (see the Trauma Organised system above) was set in motion by a transference response to the presence of the therapist, seen as the abandoning (and thereby abusive) parent figure.

My recommendation that he should not return home before he had done some therapeutic work was far from welcomed by him, and it returned us both to the potentially abusive relationship, where I was seen as bullying him into submission. Nevertheless, over the ensuing months he came to realise that I was also able to hear his painful feelings of inadequacy, socially, intellectually and sexually. As the bully in him was restrained and contained by a legitimate authority outside himself, so he could find that the bullied self was recognised.

Although this treatment did get under way, and eventually had a good outcome, that initial phase of refusal, and the flash of aggression when defences were touched, is not untypical of other cases with less positive conclusion. Denial, the first line of defence of the abuser, and which is to be found in various forms, and to varying degrees, always sets up this bully/victim pattern. The therapist is immediately presented with a choice, either to accept the evasion, or minimisation of responsibility, and therefore be perceived by the young person as having been successfully neutralised, or to challenge it and thereby become, in the young person's eyes, a persecutor. The dilemma cannot be entirely avoided, certainly not by such conventional psychoanalytic techniques as therapist 'neutrality', or having no contact with agencies outside the therapy. The transference will ensure that this fundamental abuser/victim dyad is played out, one way or another, in the treatment relationship.

> 'Rick', 11 years old (discussed in more detail in Chapter 8), went through a phase in his therapy of swaggering into the session and putting his (often muddy) shoes on my desk. After asking him not to do this, and being ignored, I felt rather helpless and said that I now had a sense of what it must have been like for him being abused, and no-one helping, or hearing him. He was angry at this because he had tried to insist that I should say nothing about abuse. (My interpretations had

become in effect a form of abuse.) He then further tested my tolerance by going out of the room and hiding in corners around the clinic. With the help of supervision, however, I began to see that these provocations usually occurred after a missed or very late session, due to sometimes inadequate escort arrangements. I commented therefore to him that he *should* be brought reliably and on time, and perhaps felt powerless when things went wrong. He might also be angry with me for not making sure that he was not messed about by the escort arrangements. This had the effect of calming him and re-establishing our channel of communication in the session.

When under attack there is a temptation for anyone to retaliate, and for a therapist to use interpretations defensively. The history of these young people has often made them adept at wrong-footing teachers, residential social workers, and other carers, into replicating the sado-masochistic partnership of abuse. The therapist's task is not to avoid such conflicts, but to meet them, hopefully, in a different way from the one the child has previously experienced. The principal of equal rights has to be communicated to the child or adolescent, in order to convey not equality of status, because that would be false, but a sense of mutual respect. Over a period of time then the young person will have an experience that mitigates the previous pattern of grievance and powerlessness.

THE BOUNDARY OF THE THERAPEUTIC RELATIONSHIP

Shortly before a summer break 'David' (aged 15, and small for his age,) withdrew under the couch with his packed lunch, gloating, 'you can't get me!' He jeered at me that the chocolate in his mouth, was 'nicer than a boy's penis'. I said that he was going to be away from me for a while and was seeking to fill the gap perhaps with chocolate, or perhaps with a boy's penis. He came out from under the couch and said more seriously that he was worried about a boy at his (boarding) school who was making what sounded like sexual overtures. 'He keeps asking me to go to the woods with him.'

As he told me more I felt increasingly concerned that this was something that was beyond the bounds of the therapy and so I said that his social worker needed to know about this. David protested that he wished he had not told me, that it was a lie, that he had been exaggerating, that the other boy would beat him up, he would have to go through 'those awful police interviews', that he would be thrown out of the school, and so on. He pleaded with me not to tell, but I explained the reasons why I felt that others needed to know. He threatened to refuse therapy from now on and left angrily. I spoke to the social worker in the week and there was some action taken. David allowed himself to be brought to the following session, and acknowledged that he did need help from adults to avoid being drawn into a sexual situation that he did not really want.

By this point in his therapy David had formed an attachment that was important to him. This was his second long break. He had been steadily distancing me and going into a perverse world under the couch. I had already been feeling excluded and somewhat disgusted by his triumph at what he could put in his mouth. I could well have been relieved not to see him for a few weeks! When he said that there was a boy who wanted to take him into the woods for sex, this could be seen as his way of fending off a sense of being abandoned by this 'Woods', turning the separation instead into a sexual invitation. When I refused this, in effect, by saying that we must defer to external reality, he tried to reverse the situation by marching off and threatening to reject me; I was now to be the one to be left.

There is a question about the therapist taking his concerns outside the session; should he not have relied upon interpretation of the meaning of David's communication within the therapeutic relationship? David's anger with me and sense of betrayal would seem to suggest that the issue of the other boy should have remained within the session. On the other hand, David had been told at the beginning of treatment about the limits of confidentiality, and that any issue of child protection would be referred to a social worker. It is therefore quite possible that in telling me about his vulnerability to more abuse, he may unconsciously have been mobilising the network of adults around him to provide the holding he knew was needed. He also could thereby create a situation in which his anger at me for going away could be more directly expressed than by sealing himself off in the perverse world under the couch.

The modifications to psychoanalytic psychotherapy proposed in the previous chapter work against the perversion of the therapeutic relationship which can exploit privacy and confidentiality into the kind of secrecy that enables abuse to continue in certain families and other systems (like the children's home in which David was again abused after being ejected from his family). The relative openness of the treatment functions in the same way as the 'externalising conversations' of going against the fixed and interlocking roles of the 'Trauma Organised System' (Bentovim 1995). The incident might have had a very different outcome had the therapist not been prepared and known how to respond. I would have been left with a great deal of anxiety at having been drawn into a repetition of abuse and abandonment. Not to have acted would have been another abandonment of David to the dubious comforts of perverse sexuality.

The topic of limits and boundaries to the treatment is of course a more pervasive one than this situation, involving many instances of testing out by the young person. For a more detailed discussion see especially the case of 'Rick' in Chapter 8.

SEXUALISATION IN THE THERAPEUTIC RELATIONSHIP

'Robert' (16) asked for 'extra sessions' in conjunction with his cognitive behavioural treatment in the residential unit, because of his bad dreams, and flashbacks to his own abuse. Once in psychoanalytic psychotherapy, however, he recounted masturbation fantasies in such a way that continued to gratify his fascination with the erect penis. A masochistic element was evident in his imagined submission to the powerful phallus. He set up situations on a daily basis; the other boys in the therapeutic community detested and scorned his constant staring at their genital area, and sexualised talk. This meant that he had little in the way of constructive or social experience. In the session he also became transfixed on my genital area, and it became clear that he was creating for himself an erotic experience, something that was much less possible in his 'other' therapy. Discussing this with his cognitive behavioural therapist I found that such behaviour had been disallowed, but that the therapist was beginning to feel he could get no further with Robert. In discussion with several other staff members, we came to the formulation that the sexualisation of all Robert's contacts with others served a dual function both of protecting him from fears of being rejected and also recreating those rejections with his feeling in control. I could see also that it was part of his masturbation fantasy to feel himself to be the one who has ownership of the phallus. Therefore, I directed my interpretations toward his loneliness and isolation, and tried to recognise his desperate clinging on to the image of phallic power to console himself for having none in the real world. I linked this to the abuse and rejection he had undergone at the hands of his own family. The rest of the staff seemed to find the discussion useful because Robert had induced profound feelings of hopelessness. After some weeks the staff group registered a change, in that he seemed more sad and depressed about his life. He began to make demands that he do more about getting work and so forth. Eventually he moved to semi-independent living, a move that was thought impossible only some months earlier.

This sequence of events shows the interconnectedness of the treatment that was fortunately possible for this young man in the context of his placement. The complexity of individual work combined with that of a therapeutic community is discussed in more detail in Chapter 4; here the significance of the combined treatment is that the therapist was thus freed from the oppressive sexualisation by the patient that would otherwise have effectively barred any progress on his emotional difficulties.

David (see above) initially presented himself as 'keen to get better', to do 'whatever it takes to change'. For a series of sessions a seductive and increasingly erotic quality developed, especially in non-verbal communications. He would stand just a little too close to me, parts of his body were revealed, at first apparently by accident, then increasingly by intent. When I commented that he seemed to expect me to be interested in him sexually, he became coyly indignant, saying, 'Oo, you have got a dirty mind!'. Comments that seemed to reduce his excitement were those that responded to his need for closeness which was represented in this distorted and inappropriate way.

Both Robert and David had histories of extensive sexual abuse since earliest childhood and each showed the pervasive quality of sexualisation in their way of relating. Although highlighted in the therapeutic setting, this was also typical in their general interactions with others, though concealed from people less well known to them. While these sexual signals are learned responses from abusive relationship with adults from their past, they are also invitations to new abusive interactions. They are sometimes gestures of submission, or of more active seduction, or indeed of threat. They are largely automatic and unconsciously driven, but full of emotional significance for the young person. It is important that the therapist address them openly and quickly rather than let them go unacknowledged, because the young person will experience this subliminally as a welcoming acceptance. This may heighten anxiety and further propel re-enactments rather than change. Instead, the patient in therapy needs to become aware of the safety of the setting and will communicate more of his internal world rather than play out his defensive ways of coping with the victim/abuser pattern.

Lanyado *et al.* (1995) discuss the strain on the adult working with these kinds of difficulties. They point out how important it is not to be drawn into the perverse world: 'the perverse core...of the therapist must not respond to seductive overtures' (p.235). And I would add that it is equally important that there is nothing that could be perceived by the young person as being seduced by the perverse world of abuse. This is difficult enough for a therapist sitting in a chair with a verbally communicative patient giving the therapist time to think, but even more so if an adolescent or child is having to communicate by action techniques such as play, drama or artwork which require an immediate response. As pointed out above in the discussion on boundaries, it is essential to have clear limits to what is acceptable in the therapeutic situation.

RE-ENACTMENT OF TRAUMA

Grudgingly coming to therapy because of a requirement from the court after sexually assaulting his sisters, Peter (18) talked continually about events and people in his extended family that may have had some significance for him, but he was extremely intolerant of any discussion of these stories. I had to fend off intense drowsiness, and had the overwhelming impression of a two-dimensional world, without depth, where people had no feelings or thoughts, events had no meaning and nothing could be learned, or even thought about. My comments were so ignored I felt reduced to a piece of furniture. He was enraged when I challenged his stream of stories as being like an endless soap opera that had nothing to do with the reason why he was there. I linked his fury with what I knew about his violent and terrifying father. On one occasion, as he sat simmering in resentment, I remarked that anything I now said would be felt by him as an attack. He told me then that he had a picture in his mind of bashing me over the head with a chair, so as to prevent me doing it to him first. I said that this must come from a fear I would be like the father who had actually bashed him over the head, and that he needed to know that he could be safe from me. Over a period of months he felt less persecuted by my words and gradually could engage in dialogue. Later on we could reconstruct a strategy of being absolutely still in order to ward off his father's attacks. The surreptitious nature of his sexual assaults on his sisters could also be understood better in this context.

After about a year in therapy David (see above) would engage in wild bouts of physical activity, throwing himself around the room and sometimes hurting himself on the furniture. On one such occasion he threw himself on the couch and forced his head up against the wall. He was face down and thumped his body repeatedly into the corner. His arms were held tightly behind him, with his bottom raised. His muffled voice cried out, 'Get off! Leave me alone! Just let me go! Please, please, you're hurting me. Let me go!' and so on until his energy had gone or until something changed in his re-enactment to stop the violence that was being done to him.

The two instances, from different phases of adolescent development, show the different ways in which trauma may be brought into the therapeutic arena. They require quite different techniques of handling by the therapist. What they have in common is the adolescent tendency to re-enact, to recreate the situation from the past rather than communicate about that experience. Tonnesmann (1980) has shown how in adolescence there is a process of recapitulation of childhood experience that was not integrated in earlier childhood, and how this can be drawn into the psychotherapeutic process. The therapist's stance is very important here: interpretations in response to the encounters with abuse described above could be that the patient wishes the abuse to continue, either with the patient identified with the abuser, or in order to gain masochistic gratification, or both. Such interpretations would have to be resisted by the patient, and most likely therapist and patient would be caught up in a back-and-forth argument that could be experienced by both as abusive. (These scenarios cannot always be avoided; see some of the detailed case histories in later chapters.) The goal of psychodynamic work is the creation of a space for thinking, something that depends on at least the possibility of a non-abusive relationship. It follows then that an interpretation that is experienced by a patient as abusive should not be made, irrespective of the therapist's belief that he or she is right. As Alvarez (1995) maintained, the patient's desperate paranoid elements need to be contained by the therapist as someone external to himself; interpretations that produce 'premature re-introjection could only increase his desire to hurt any baby as long as it is not himself' (p.180). Even though the treatment may be under a degree of compulsion, the therapeutic task in psychoanalytic psychotherapy remains the finding of symbolic forms in order to communicate and thereby modify the experience of trauma.

THE EMERGENCE OF CREATIVITY

Creativity is the hallmark of a treatment that is under way. Both perversion and creativity can be see as alternative ways of dealing with loss (Kohon 1999, p.96). The achievement of a young person in treatment as they find their way towards creative expression is in having tolerated some of the pain of their former abuse, and abusing.

> David's irritation with me for being 'old and boring, just sitting in your chair' led to his determination that I should 'do some work for your money!' I was to be the actor in his theatre. One of his dramas required me to play a child murderer named Ramsbottom (he was not apparently conscious of the double meaning), entering a child's room in the dark. David played the child who disappeared through a crack in the bed, much to the rage of his attacker. However, the child became an 'undercover cop' and returned to apprehend the criminal and bring him to justice. Each stage in the story had to be rehearsed again and again, so that it was 'just right' and also, it seemed, in order to relish certain moments, especially that of seeing the child murderer (the abuser played by me) put to violent death by electrocution.

A space for creativity is the unique contribution of psychoanalytic psychotherapy because of the non-directive stance of the therapist. Whereas behavioural changes may best be achieved through cognitive behavioural therapy, good management and appropriate placement, there is still a need for an internal transformation of abusive patterns of emotion, cognition and repeated relationships. For David to make the inner change of being no longer a victim to his father's abuse of him (which included becoming an abuser himself), he needed to reveal the abuse, an opportunity that unfortunately was not provided by the adult world. He could show, at this point in his therapy and in a way that was compelling for the therapist, how his childhood was murdered by his father. For him not to continue to inflict that experience on others, a solution, in the form of justice, was found. The creative and spontaneous drive toward this may not be given space in a pre-ordained treatment programme. His drama used the same elements that were evident in earlier phases of David's treatment, the repetitious re-enactments of abuse on the couch, described above, but to very different end.

There is much less interpretation by the therapist when creativity makes its appearance, though he or she may be having to 'work harder', as David put it. The therapy now has its own momentum, and probably the most important thing at this stage is that the therapist should do nothing that might inhibit the process. It would for example, have been undermining to David's play if I had pointed out the connotations of the name 'Ramsbottom', which are obvious enough, but for a young person trying to build a concept of a non-abusive world, should perhaps remain unconscious. Equally, the deception of the 'undercover cop', or the delight in seeing the death throes of the abuser, all contain aggressive and hostile expressions that could be highlighted by the therapist. But, as Alvarez (1995) has shown, we should not be surprised that the abuse still plays a part in the healthiest of symbolisations.

CONCLUSION

Young people who have abused often fall through the net and fail to get treatment of any kind; the family may be unavailable for the family work that would otherwise be indicated, the referred adolescent himself may not fit in to a structured programme because of complicating emotional and psychological problems, and there may be behavioural difficulties that make him unplaceable. There are also many factors that have meant that these young people never get near psychoanalytic psychotherapy. Professional systems are very nervous about the unpredictability of the course of this kind of treatment, there is uncertainty about theoretical basis, a difficulty in monitoring the conduct of therapists, and problems of evidence about the outcome of psychotherapy as a distinct entity. However, the strength of this particular approach, as I have tried to show, is its adaptability to the needs of the whole person, not just the abuser in him. Also, as I hope will be evident in subsequent chapters, there is a flexibility to psychoanalytic psychotherapy that can produce the sort of combined treatment that these young people, with their multiple emotional difficulties, so often need.

CHAPTER 4

Regression, Trauma and False Self, in the Treatment of an Adolescent Abused/Abuser

Short-term treatment may be of assistance in producing symptomatic improvement both in those traumatised by abuse and those given to abusing behaviour, but as Sinason (1996) points out, long-term treatment is necessary to produce internal change. Frequently there will be a spontaneous regression when there is an open-ended therapeutic space available. In these cases the patient might appear to be getting worse rather than better, functioning less well, becoming depressed, even hopeless about their life. This negativity may not extend to a refusal of therapy, even though sessions may be filled with hopelessness. The sessions may become the most important time of the week for the young person, and the therapist, perhaps alarmingly to some, will seem to be a most important person to the adolescent. The understanding and containment of states of regression between psychotherapy sessions is therefore indispensable. Increased dependence on the therapist causes anxiety in workers, including the therapist, because it would seem to militate against the development of responsibility in the young person.

It is proposed here that regression sometimes needs to take place, for the patient to 'reconstruct' their traumatic experience (Bentovim 1996b, p.310). As a means of gaining access to early levels and phases of development it can be very effective. It may be ultimately related to that capacity

Winnicott (1959) described as bringing about 'self-cure'. Even though some people like these abused/abusers may seem to have had little or nothing good in their environment, nevertheless the process of treatment may reach to something else, some kind of experience that '...represents the individual's hope that...the environment which failed originally may be relived...this time succeeding instead of failing' (Winnicott 1959, p.128).

As emphasised earlier, any therapeutic exploration of the inner world of an abused/abuser must take place under the correct conditions of containment, nurture, and also the availability of other forms of treatment. Psychoanalytic psychotherapy in cases like these can be effective only in the context of other provisions (Woods 1997; Griffin *et al.* 1997; Vizard and Usiskin 1999). The psychotherapy itself therefore has a dependence on this facilitating environment and this is also a reflection of the infant/mother dependence evoked by the regressed patient. The regression which might otherwise be frightening for the patient is therefore made possible in safe conditions.

The young person, whose psychoanalytic psychotherapy is described here in detail, was throughout this period, a resident in a therapeutic community, which was run on psychodynamic principles. Thus, the individual work was supported both in spirit and in practical ways, such as the reliable provision of escort to and from sessions and the regular passing of information. Without this important aspect of the setting, the psychotherapy could not have taken place.

Concern has recently developed about intrusions into the privacy of psychoanalytic psychotherapy. The attacks on absolute confidentiality in psychotherapy in the United States have been seen as destructive of psychoanalytic psychotherapy itself (Bollas and Sandelson 1995). The position taken here, however, is that young people who are in danger of acting out sexually abusive impulses need the protection of a network of adults, which should include the psychotherapist. This is consistent with the approach advocated by Adshead and Mezey (1993) of working in collaboration with the patient. Secrecy is a necessary precondition of sexual abuse and it would be alarming to the patient in treatment if he were permitted to abuse the privacy of psychotherapy. A distinction is made with the patient between thoughts, feelings and fantasies which can remain within the therapeutic relationship, as against impulses or desires that have the intention of affecting others, and therefore go outside the therapy session itself. An

equivalent is the case where a young person has a suicide plan, or becomes
so ill that he or she needs to be admitted into hospital. These situations
require an extension of the setting to include other professional workers.
Young people such as the one whose treatment is described here have
accepted limits to confidentiality as much as for their own benefit as for any
possible victim. In keeping with this spirit of co-operation the patient gave
permission for the present discussion of his treatment to be published, with
the proviso that his actual identity is suitably disguised.

'Andrew R', aged 12, was removed from his family, along with his sister,
one year younger, after disclosures of sexual abuse by both parents and their
friends, against both children. There had already been evidence of physical
abuse and neglect, and much missed education. Among the disclosures of
abuse it was alleged that the children were themselves made to have sexual
intercourse for the entertainment of paedophile rings. In the foster
placement Andrew was found to be continuing sexual activities with his
sister, Christine. They were separated, but in his children's home he targeted
other girls. Moved from that children's home to a specialised foster family,
his behaviour continued to cause concern, with aggressive behaviour
focused particularly on the foster mother, touching her breasts, threatening
violence and masturbating openly. He would leer at children and openly
admit his sexual fascination with them. Ordinary management interventions, whether by foster parent or by social worker, produced the same
result; having agreed with the adult and acknowledged that he should
change his behaviour, it seemed that another set of standards was interposed
when opportunity presented itself. As Sperling (1959) has shown in her
account of the development of deviant sexuality, Andrew's personality, and
in particular his superego, was distorted and corrupted by the
internalisation of parental attitudes.

Assessed at the age of 18, it was clear that Andrew had a longstanding
sexual orientation towards young children of both sexes. This seemed to
bear features of the 'fixed' type of paedophilia described by Groth (1978).
Underlying this problem, there were also symptoms of Post-Traumatic
Stress Disorder. It seemed that he was so damaged by his experiences of
abuse that he persistently re-experienced traumatic events through
recurrent and distressingly intrusive recollection of these events, and these,
it seemed, led on to masturbatory fantasies about younger children. His
poor impulse control, lack of ego development and poor ability to sublimate

his desires could be described as an undifferentiated conduct disorder, and this was an important factor in his anti-social behaviour. Since there was such a high risk of continuing sexual assaults against younger children, a combined approach to treatment was recommended: first of all, a structured programme of cognitive behavioural group therapy, focused particularly on sexually abusive behaviour, as described in Hawkes *et al.* (1996), followed by open-ended individual psychotherapy.

During the course of the group-work programme it had become clear that Andrew should leave his current foster home since there was no immediate sign of change in his sexual preoccupation with children, and the foster parents were at the limit of their tolerance. He was very upset about this and reluctant to transfer to the residential community where he was to be placed. But he made his protest passively. His participation in the group-work programme for offending behaviour was superficial, even though in an infantile and indiscriminate way he became attached to all the people involved. The group leaders reported that at the end of the year his sexual orientation to children remained unchanged.

BEGINNINGS

When I first met him Andrew seemed quite unprepossessing. He looked awkward, tall, thin, and angular, with a cast in one eye, but most off-putting was a manner which could only be described as 'creepy'. He would sit curled up in a chair and unfold himself like a snake. Emerging from a self-absorbed state of misery, he would leer, smile or laugh inappropriately, apparently at his own private joke. It occurred to me in the early sessions that this suggestive leer was not only a symptom, but also a weapon, a way of making people feel uncomfortable about his sexual thoughts and intentions. However, he said that he needed help, and talked about some of the people he was missing. Thus, he was expressing an attachment that had grown during the course of treatment, something that augured well for continuing therapy.

Andrew conveyed an acute physical and emotional discomfort. He seemed unable to be in one place. He struggled with his inability to think of anything to say to me. He twisted himself around in his chair, and clutched his head in his hands. He seemed persecuted by noises outside the door, flinching violently at the slightest sound. Then he would listen out anxiously for the next sound. He admitted that he wanted to run out of the room but said that he had nowhere to go. I found that focusing attention on what might be so frightening increased his fear. He responded more positively to comments about a need to feel safe from intrusions; but these were marginal changes in his mood and very soon he would become oppressed again by his inner states. I could not be sure whether it was dissociation or depression. One of his frequent appeals to me was that the session was too short; looking at me desperately, he said that he wanted to be able to say something, but that as soon as he found he could, it was time to go. Because he had a long journey from his placement and would ideally have come more than once a week, he was offered longer sessions than usual, lasting one and a quarter hours.

Gradually, it seemed possible for Andrew to find ways to communicate. His first pictures were blobs of black, which were then destroyed. Making a mark on the page in the midst of a rather dissociated silence was the best that he could manage, but had to be quickly erased. Yes, he agreed, there was something in him that needed to be thrown away:

'I should be thrown away.'

This was said with some satisfaction and I sensed that though such statements intimated self-harm, he was also in a concealed fashion communicating aggression and resentment. He tried to explain:

'I feel like doing myself in, because I still have the thoughts. It's not because you have got rid of them, I think you are a really good therapist, really brilliant, it's me, I am no good.'

He would make such statements as these and then withdraw into a state where it was more difficult for me to reach him. After a while he would suddenly express a wish to go to the toilet. This often occurred toward the end of the session. If I linked his behaviour to thoughts and feelings he might have about me, he would look amazed, saying 'You do say the strangest things', and then lapse into silence. Supervision helped me see the sexualised nature of some of this interaction, and to understand why our communication regularly drifted off into the realms of his fantasy. He seemed to be yearning for a contact with me that he felt was impossible.

The developing therapeutic relationship revealed something of the attachment relationships that Andrew acquired from his family. It seemed he had turned passive into active, as a way of adapting and coping with the experiences of being a victim, through choosing to be one. Partly through his own sexual arousal, the victim can develop a sense of responsibility for the abuse (Bentovim 1995, p.296). The heaviness in Andrew's sessions conveyed much more than the common adolescent reluctance to be in a room with an adult; there was a sense of resignation and inarticulate need for help. Through defining himself as an abuser Andrew was also paradoxically constructing a reality to perpetuate himself in the role of victim. This particular dynamic seemed a major stumbling block in the quest to find a part of him that was not an abused/abuser; in retrospect it can be seen that his questioning became a productive way of distinguishing between true and false self.

Andrew seemed unable to be in the room, although he did not seek to get out or express a real intention to be elsewhere; as he said again, 'there is nowhere to run to'. It seemed he knew that he was unable to be anywhere. He seemed alone in the room, in that he was unable to relate to me. He was persecuted by an internal abuser of some kind, but could not afford to relate this to me. His placating, appeasing and idealisation of me could be seen as a denial of his fear that I might abuse him, but interpretations along these lines seemed to exacerbate his pain. Rather, it seemed for him that there was no-one else there, even though he knew that he needed someone. In 'The Capacity to be Alone', Winnicott (1958b) described the therapeutic value of finding an 'id impulse' that will give a personal experience, instead of a meaningless existence. Andrew's inability to sublimate his impulses, and therefore the lack of play, was fixing him, so it seemed, in the role of traumatised victim. It would be this state, if unchanged, that would drive him to find brief moments of self-realisation through the only means available to him, by abusing another child. Thus, his traumatised experience had to be worked with in order to render him less likely to abuse again.

PICTURES FROM THE INNER WORLD

The first picture that was allowed to survive comes from two months into the therapy. Andrew depicted different parts of London in their significance for his life. He was travelling from one side to the other for his therapy session. In a third quarter (for the whole was constructed in a mandala-like pattern) he placed the foster family where he had been living up until a few months before this point. In the centre of the pattern he wrote the word

'Mania'. 'That is rudeness,' he informed me. This picture was an important step forward in our communication since each part enabled him to refer to different areas of his experience. I noticed that the roads going from one quarter to another seemed to pass across each other without any sign of a bridge. My comment on this brought no immediate response, but he seemed much more lively when I remarked on the complexity and the length of the journey, all the way across London to his therapy session and how he had to go through quite a difficult stage of 'Mania' and 'rudeness' in order to be with me. In this way, Andrew was teaching me perhaps about the most appropriate responses that would draw attention to his needs and to his achievements, rather than to the obstacle of 'rude' or forbidden subjects.

Further pictures came gradually. They cannot be reproduced here for reasons of confidentiality, since they all use, in different ways, the elements of his name. At first I wondered if the picture of London was an isolated oasis in the desert of our silence; however, I was hearing that Andrew was more engaged with people in the therapeutic community and less isolated. Sometimes there had been conflicts with other young people. One of these led to Andrew absconding. He walked a distance of some 15 miles away from the placement in the direction of his former foster home. He turned himself in at a police station in the early hours of the morning. He told staff that he had not looked for a child to abuse. In the following session, he sat in silence staring balefully out of the window, until I mentioned that I had heard of these recent events. As he talked about his anger with another resident, there seemed to me something positive, in that he was able to express feelings other than the dissociated depression that I had been witnessing. I commented on this. His acknowledgement of this change conveyed a rather coy sense that I had caught him out. Cautiously he said that he would worry that if such arguments were to occur between us here.

'You would kick me out wouldn't you?'

This interaction seemed to free something within him and he moved to the paper and coloured pencils to produce a picture that seemed to give him great delight. There was a coffin with his name (and 'the dragon') written on the side. By the coffin stood a man making a triumphant gesture and with the words in a speech bubble, 'At last he is dead.'

As he drew this Andrew laughed and quickly went on to draw a thought bubble from the coffin, in which were the words, 'One of these days I'm going to kill someone.' He clarified for me that the dragon was not really dead.

The man standing by the coffin looked suspiciously like myself and I remarked on this, but he said no, and wrote in much bigger letters than everything else, 'This is Dad saying it.'

What is the transference relationship here? It would seem obvious that the man he calls 'Dad' also represents the therapist. However, if Andrew really experienced me as his father, he would not be able to be in the room alone with me at all. There is the coffin which conceals a not-dead Andrew and it could be that this was the only place where Andrew could feel safe, but the containment represented by the coffin only occurred to me later. Instead, I commented that it seemed very important that I should not be like the father who wishes to abuse or kill. The abused child is therefore Andrew himself, whom he has now located, albeit in a coffin, and perhaps this is why he seemed less of a danger to others when he absconded. There is a therapist-father who is abusive, just as he would probably see anyone that way, but more important, there is now a longed-for therapist-father in Andrew's mind who is not abusive, and who could help him think, play, live.

There were changes reported from the residential unit. It seemed to residential staff that Andrew expressed his sexual interest in children only at certain points where there were tasks or challenges that he wished to avoid. It seemed to them that he was seeking to create anxiety in workers, so that they were deflected in their work with him over sometimes quite ordinary things that he might find difficult. They came to doubt that there was now a genuine sexual interest in children, or that he would really be at risk of assaulting a child. These perceptions did fit in with some of my own observations that Andrew was indeed capable of deceiving an adult and give a view of himself as damaged and helpless, like the 'secondary handicap' described by Sinason (1986). However, in our discussions it was realised that there was a paradox in his management; any threats of abusiveness had be treated as if real, otherwise Andrew might be forced to more extreme measures to obtain the kind of attention he craved. Communicating and bearing this lack of certainty is an important aspect of the therapist's role in relation to the network of carers. What is unhelpful for all concerned is when the uncertainty is expressed through an air of mystification by a therapist who does not communicate with the other workers.

Winnicott's conceptualisation of the 'False Self' describes how a trau-matised real self can be protected by false-self functioning. Symptom formation masks the true self because historically this is how the emerging self found that it could exist without being overwhelmed by the environ-ment. The neglectful environment would have replaced or ignored creative gestures. If there are no other avenues of expression, then suicide might be the only option to protect the true self (Winnicott 1960a, p.143). The picture of the coffin perhaps demonstrates the need for the death of an old (false) self in order for something else to emerge. The marathon walk Andrew undertook in order to find something good was a heroic and creative gesture to demonstrate how desperately he needed at this point to separate himself from the internal persecutors which he had projected on to others in the therapeutic community. As something of this process was shared with his carers, their watchfulness over Andrew was not so much relaxed, as if he was less of a concern to them, but changed in its quality; he could be seen not so much as a person who was dangerous, but someone who might still be vulnerable.

THE DRAGON PICTURES

During the fifth and sixth months of therapy there appeared a series of pictures cleverly combining the letters of his own name in graffiti style to appear as a dragon breathing fire, with sharp claws, scaly spikes and a spear-like tale. (Interestingly, the vernacular in Greek for child molester is 'Drakos' meaning dragon, the equivalent perhaps in English of beast or monster.) A great deal of concentration went into these pictures which were colourful and striking in their appearance. They were a great contrast to Andrew's general style of personal presentation which was, up until this time, vacant, awkward, and unrelated.

'The dragon has power. It wants to be free!'

We talked about the contrast between this and his own self that he felt was 'crap'. When he was not producing pictures he seemed absent. If I commented upon this contrast, then Andrew would resort again to his idea-lisation of me.

'You mustn't think that I hate coming here, or am bored. You're the only one who cares about me. You're probably the best therapist in the world.'

Nevertheless, these obsequious expressions caused me some revulsion. I became aware of a particular problem that was happening after going to the waiting room to meet Andrew and bringing him back through the corridors of a large multi-department clinic to our treatment room. It was a long journey, because, given Andrew's history, he could not be allowed to wait where there might be children. He always seemed rather pathetically glad to see me and began giving me his news as we walked along. He seemed unable to hear me asking that he wait until we were in the room. Even when he was not excitedly chattering at me, I was embarrassed whenever we encountered other members of staff along the corridors. I realised that I did not wish to be associated with him. I began to wish that I could find some way of getting him to the therapy room without being seen in his company. My sense of shame walking along with him I realised, after a time, was my reluctance to admit how much I might actually hate being with him. It was not easy for me to admit this to my supervisor. I felt encouraged then to explore with Andrew his ideas about what others might see in him. He said, 'You must hate me, because of what I have done.' My stock response, 'I might hate what you have done...', was insufficient because of his invest-ment in being despised, and because of how I could actually feel repelled by him.

'Hate in the Counter-Transference' by Winnicott was helpful for me to understand these conflicting feelings. 'If we are to treat these patients [i.e. borderline], we have to have reached down to these things in ourselves (Winnicott 1947, p.196). I realised that Andrew was introducing me to aspects of the personality and emotions that I did not wish to recognise in myself at all. Winnicott encourages therapists to be able to 'hate the patient objectively' and yet to continue working with them. The dragon pictures showed me that there was another side to Andrew than the beaten-down and abused victim that he presented. It was the power, and even beauty in that power, as it were, of the child murderer, which on paper at least, in his pictures, could be contemplated. If I could allow myself to hate, then I could also accept some aspects of Andrew, just as he could begin to differentiate those hateful those aspects of himself. Thus, they could be integrated in the whole person, instead of being denied, split off or projected.

A witch appeared, hidden at first in the scales low down on the dragon's back. I had to pay careful attention as Andrew drew in the hidden face. He explained that this was the dragon's mother, a witch.

'She digs her heels into him – to drive him mad and make him go and kill children.'

The next picture showed the witch on top of the dragon.

'He has no real power of his own. She rides him.'

But Andrew seemed to run out of steam, as he stopped drawing and slumped in his chair. I said that I thought perhaps as he feels there is a witch mother inside him driving him and taking his power, so he feels defeated by this. He spoke then about his mother's abuse of him, his anger and how much he hated her for it. He clenched his fist and looked at me straight in the eye (unusually).

'I could smash you across the room – no, no, of course I would not. It's all right really.'

After a pause, he twisted his face and said with great effort,

'I want to get a beautiful child and abuse her. Then I would kill her and…then kill myself.'

I said that I thought he felt this now because he had realised how the beautiful child in him had been abused and killed by his parents and now that had to be done to someone else. He became tearful, put his head in his hands and lay across the table. After a few minutes silence, I realised that he was sleeping. He woke after 10 or 15 minutes and seemed to acknowledge that we had spoken about something important. He asked how long it was till the end of the session and I spoke about the thoughts he had described to me. Perhaps he then had slept, I said, in order to show how he could feel safe with someone and so did not need to cause harm to others in order to get my attention and concern.

Fonagy and Target (1998) have shown how the child develops a sense of self through perceptions of itself through the mind of another. If significant others have failed to recognise the child's inner experience or their real emotions, the child has no representation of himself, other than something, as in Andrew's case, to be abused or neglected. This dehumanising effect of abuse is powerfully described in the work of Pelzer (1995). In contrast Fonagy and Target (1998) describe the stage of dependence where the child needs the physical presence of the other for at least the possibility of a therapeutic experience, ultimately to repair the damage to the sense of self. This perhaps explains why Andrew seemed so dependent on me even where there seemed to be so little being done in the sessions. For him to bear his inner world, he needed the guiding presence of the other, not only as an object of transference, but as embodying those ego functions needed for integration.

'WHEN HE IS GOOD'

A series of pictures followed over the next few months of therapy, which still incorporated elements of the dragon, the claws, spiky tail, and tongue like an arrow but seemed more like grotesque self-portraits. The 'alien one', or abuser, he acknowledged as part of himself, or a self that he could be. One of these pictures had stitching around the neck of the 'alien one' which showed, he said, how the head had been taken off and then sown back on by social workers and psychotherapists. The ring around the neck was the means by which social workers and 'shrinks' could keep control of him.

The alien one came to be differentiated, through a series of drawings, from another self that 'wanted to be good', and was not being controlled by others. However, the two faces, usually graphically depicted on opposite sides of the page, were often confused and melded with each other. I remarked that it seemed to me that elements of the abuser were present in both.

'Yes, they're both hidden in there.'

A session occurred at a time when storm clouds had been gathering outside. The windows to the therapy room were large and I could not help but be distracted by the overcast skies. Andrew looked very carefully at me and asked if I was feeling sad.

'You look sad', he said. 'There is something bothering you.'

As it happened I was preoccupied by another matter unrelated to Andrew; I agreed that there was something, but it was not to do with him. He accepted this without question, came and put his chair next to mine where we could both look out of the window.

'Let's watch the storm together.'

And, as if on cue, the storm began. We had a very good view of the forked lightning. It was like being a spectator in a firework show and it struck me then how Andrew had created for himself the experience of a child being accompanied to something of that kind, an experience unlikely to have been provided in reality; but it was made possible perhaps by his perception of a feeling in me that was not a projection from him. He had thereby in effect created me as a separate person with their own feelings, which were real, not any more his projection.

There was more freedom of communication at this time. He spoke to me of his interest in football. He referred to his favourite team as 'Man United', and though this is of course the usual abbreviation for Manchester United, I commented that this discussion on football was also perhaps about him becoming a *man, united* in himself. He laughed, looked at me sideways,
'You should be a chameleon.'
'Do you mean comedian?'
He laughed and said, 'No! You are a chameleon, you change. You change yourself, you change the things I say.'
And he burst into laughing at his own joke.

However, at other times the depression seemed to dominate him just as severely as before. Particularly, this occurred around break times. He would say that his holiday was 'shit', bitterly bemoaning that I would be having a 'great time' with my family, glad to be away from all my patients.

His growing attachment to the therapy and the therapist also of course revived some old problems. The closeness that was developing between us became sexualised. He would copy my movements, my sitting position and my words, giggling triumphantly when there was any sign that I was disconcerted by this. When I said that it seemed that he almost wanted to be me, he agreed readily, 'Yes I am being you now.'
Omnipotently he could deny separation, and thereby try to dispel anxiety about closeness. He denied that there was any break between sessions. Leaving the room he would check all around it.
'It will be exactly the same when I come back.'
He pretended on his return not to have been away at all. At each of these statements that repudiated reality and claimed that we were one, he would

leer at me and linger in his look toward me in a manner that made me feel most uncomfortable.

THE BURNING BUILDING

A picture was produced nine months after the beginning of therapy, which was the last for a time. This was a crude and dark picture of a house using the same graffiti style of the dragon (his name) covered in black smoke. Out of the building scuttled a spider, a small black hairy thing, indeterminate in shape. The page had been divided in two and on the opposite side, he wrote,

'This is me when I am upset and angry and really want some one to help me and myself.'

It emerged during our discussion that he had been thinking a great deal about his sister. He had really been missing her. Grieving for her loss he had felt unable to talk about these feelings because I, or others, he said might think only of his sexual interest in her. As he spoke about this he added a speech bubble coming out of the spider's mouth with the words

'HELP ME.'

He sat weeping and seemed more hopeless than distressed. I found myself trying to see something positive in the burning building and the escaping spider, that this could mean change from an old self and an integration with some part of him that really needed help, but it seemed that all I had in front of me was the traumatised child who was incapable of making sense of his situation, and I too felt helpless.

I think that I was seeing his regression to a state of dependence in which there was a hope that the early experience of an abusive environent would be changed (Winnicott 1959, p.128). Elsewhere, writing on Counter-Transference, Winnicott (1960b) points out the effects of this on the therapist. The primitive needs of the patient are forced on to the attention of the therapist, and so the countertransference can give a 'precise statement of the original deprivation' (pp.162–3). I felt a complex mixture of disappointment and revulsion as well as helplessness at Andrew's state of mind. I could see how he had been rejected by the parents and abused, and how in the countertransference I too rejected him as if he was the dirty scuttling little spider. 'The borderline patient breaks through the analyst's professional attitude and forces a direct relationship of a primitive kind' (Winnicott

1960b, p.164). It came to my mind to say, 'you really did love your sister, didn't you?' He looked up at me and stopped sobbing to say, 'Yes I wanted to marry her, but I can't. I miss her.' Then he seemed stronger and somewhat able to accept that what he had just said was the truth.

CHRISTINE

Andrew's sister was a preoccupation over the next few months. Partly this was provoked by the sporadic news he was receiving about problems in her placement; her delinquent boyfriend, her absconding, then being caught by the police for stealing, being thrown out of the foster placement, finding a new placement, getting another boyfriend and becoming pregnant. It was as if he had no life of his own. Andrew seemed to alternate between his pre-occupation and his misery about Christine, and a bizarre idealisation of me. On one occasion I had heard from the residential workers about an incident over the weekend when he had been looking at children in a suggestive way. In the session, he wept over his grief for Christine. After I talked about his behaviour with the children as an attempt to compensate for his pain over Christine, he slept for 20 minutes or so. When he woke he seemed tremen-dously relieved and after a while broke into a gentle song, 'you make me happy, you make me sad, you make me suffer, you make me glad'. Being fixed with his eyes during this song, I asked if he felt that I was responsible for all these feelings about what was happening to him.

'Yes, you do it all. – Oh, I meant to ask you about the tube station on the way here. Saint John's Wood, is that named after you? Is it your place? Is that where you live?' He grinned and partly he knew that this was a joke, but he was also conveying something of his continuing idealisation of me, that I was a kind of Saint or Saviour, a way of him getting a life of his own.

Andrew reported a dream; he was being accused of touching a girl in the street. The girl disappeared and he was chased by a group of men, caught and stabbed in the arm. He said that he had woken feeling sad that he had not been killed, because, 'then it would all be over'. His associations to the dream were that of his sister and his hatred of residential staff. I mentioned that the imminent break could be making him feel that it was all over here. (I would now think of this as a poor interpretation, ignoring the desire to be caught shown in the dream.) He lapsed into a state of dissociated depres-sion. There was a change in me however. Where before I had felt defeated by the distance between us, I began to see his self-pity. Who was being stabbed? I asked myself. When he was being a helpless heap before me, was not I also being attacked? I began to feel less tolerant of his apparent helplessness. I put it to him on one occasion that it was as if he was still being victimised by his parents. For the first time it seemed he was able to come up with a determined response, 'No, they bloody well won't do that again!' Anger toward residential workers became a stage of transition to an awareness of anger toward his parents, just as he was becoming more assertive with me. Standing up to the abuser became a possibility. He could still wallow at times in his depression, submitting as it were to the 'alien' in him, but there was also an Andrew who had some backbone and could show determination that he, and others, should not be abused.

A PROSPECT OF FREEDOM

The release of Terry Waite from captivity as a hostage in Lebanon was in the news at this time and, in his rather concrete fashion, Andrew informed me at the beginning of one session that he thought he had seen the man himself on his way to see me. He spoke about what he knew of Terry Waite's experiences of being abused and I remarked that he himself was no stranger to that sort of thing. He looked at me in bemused fashion and asked,

'Have you?'

But he went on immediately, giving me no chance to answer, 'You couldn't. If you'd abused a child you'd never get a job like this, would you?' I saw that he had condensed victim and abuser. I commented that the prison for him then was being an abuser. During a long silence he seemed to be thinking about this.

'Have you ever had a beard?'

This made me think again of Terry Waite and then he asked, 'Did people forget about Terry Waite during all that time?' I said that Andrew too needed someone to remember about him, and that he felt himself sometimes to be in prison. He lapsed into silence. During this silence I could not help but recall my own reactions to Brian Keenan's description of the relationship that developed between himself and one of his jailers, Said (Keenan 1993). I had been powerfully affected by the claustrophobic intensity of Keenan's account, just as now I had a glimpse of a sado-masochistic dependence in Andrew. At this point it seemed possible for me to think about that more objectively, rather than some months before having felt so oppressed by sessions that contained only his dependence. After a few minutes he asked,

'Where does space end? How far do you go till you reach the bottom?'

'Do you mean how long till the next session?'

'Two years, it feels like.'

'And when there is such a long gap and you might feel forgotten about by me, then thinking about bottoms, seems like all you have left.'

'I'm not so angry with you about being away, it's those social workers who tell me nothing about my sister.'

Hearing Andrew's hatred and anger, some of it justifiable, some of it irrational, made me feel that I was now in the presence of a real person. The certainty that his life should have been different seemed in my eyes to give him strength. Suicide, and its equivalent, the abuse of children, seemed now less of a danger.

After two years of therapy a theme emerged in a new way, though it had been around in the background. A wish to be female, hinted at but then seeming to gather in momentum, was interwoven with feelings about a change in Andrew's placement. There was to be another move from the residential community to a provision less supervised, more semi-independent. This external change seemed to expose a deep confusion about his gender identity. The need to establish something more firm in him about what kind of male he could be became a major task for the therapy.

Women could be desired by men, as Andrew perceived it, in a non-abusive way, unlike children, especially himself as a boy. Forbidden desires for his sister, for children, his need to be loved, seemed to be fused in one unconscious fantasy that if he were a female then he could really be loved. By repudiating maleness he thought, could avoid responsibility for abusive acts. Living more independently brought up all sorts of fears for him. Separation from his placement, although exciting, was also terrifying. He imagined he would be lost forever, and would be forced to abuse a child as the only way to be looked after. There was some insight, at least in the session, that this was about the lost and abused child within himself. At times, however, he would feel panicked about the move. He could not decide whether to be angry with the social services authority, the staff at the residential home or with me. He revealed that he had molested a child some years before, which had gone unreported. A lot of time and energy was then expended by social workers in examining the nature of this disclosure, the conclusion of which was that no action needed to be taken. It was a confused story that he gave, concerning a child in a children's home about whom there had been concerns, though no definite indication of abuse. The suspicions by residential staff that Andrew could arouse such anxieties and concerns to masquerade other difficulties he was facing, seemed, to them at least, well founded at this point, but taking responsibility for past abuse was also evidence of an important internal shift. It was part, so it seemed to me, of finding a new identity of himself as a male who was not an abuser.

The privacy of the therapy session gave Andrew the opportunity to think through the complexity of his feelings now that he was to move on from the community. His tears at previous separations were real, but seemed almost too much for him to bear. It was easy for him to talk about his hatred of the social workers, but the attack on therapy was more concealed. He would lapse into despairing silences and so at times I felt hopeless again about our work together. There was some cruelty shown to me in his games. For instance, he would come into the session, insist that he was tired because of being up late, or because of hay fever medication, and go off to sleep, either on the couch or in the chair. Having made attempts to keep him engaged, I would give up since I was talking to an apparently sleeping person. Then I would begin to drift off into my own thoughts only to be startled by his wide-awake eyes staring at me, and him laughing triumphantly that he had caught me sleeping! This happened more than once and so I said that his sleeping was a way to test me. Then (after supervision) I understood that the game was more than the wish simply to get one over on me and that he needed to know that he could rely on me. Clearly, I should watch over him as he slept. Although outwardly now a young man of 21, he was emotionally at a stage where he still had a right to a vigilant and reliable adult. It should not be surprising that such interactions retain elements of the original abuse. Another game consisted of going to the toilet, which happened to be next door to the therapy room, knocking on the wall and coming back in to ask me whether I had heard him, and to ask why couldn't I tap messages back and forth.

'Why can't we pass messages here in the room?' I asked.

'It's too sad to talk about.'

'But it makes you sad anyway, even if you hide away in the toilet.'

'It's about my sister.'

He had heard that she had had her baby and could think only of car accidents and horror films. Links to his own childhood experiences and his sister's in the family produced not the sorts of dissociation and fragmentation that I had been used to before, but a hope that his sister could look after this baby better than had been the rule in his family.

Christine was persuaded to give up her baby for adoption. At a meeting with Andrew, which he later described to me, she explained to him that she just could not look after a child. He was led to think, could this have been his baby? Could he himself have been that baby, sent to live in a different family? But the fact of the adoption, resonating as it did with all his placements, and with his transference relationship with me, and the necessity for these transitions, was eventually a healing process. This sense of reality, painful as it was, was in the end helpful to Andrew.

In the ensuing two years of therapy he made steady progress, gaining some educational qualifications, moving into semi-independent accommodation, finding work (looking after injured animals!), but perhaps the most extraordinary development was the gradual burgeoning of a relationship with a young woman. As someone with learning difficulties she was being looked after by the local authority, but had parents and professionals who naturally needed to know if she was safe with him. Once again his therapy had to be placed in the context of the system of social care. The fact that he was in treatment seemed to facilitate the network of carers in their roles, and reduce the anxiety about his potential dangerousness. In this way the social workers and others could also accept some privacy for his wishes and anxieties about a sexual relationship. I too was reassured that he was not being left to drift in the community. Between the two aspects, which reflected his inner and outer needs, the conditions were created for a satisfactory sexual relationship, an outcome that I think no-one, certainly not I, would have thought possible at the beginning of this five-year treatment.

DISCUSSION

The process of this psychotherapy shows an increasing differentiation between elements in the complex defensive structure that led Andrew to maintain his potential as an abuser. Whilst an overview of the treatment seems to show a movement toward a non-abusive personality, the minutiae are intricately bound up with abuse and its derivatives. The games, for instance, that emerged towards the end of this account retain elements of abuse, secrecy and perversion. However, they are also indications of a more healthy personality than was evident in the collapsed posture of Andrew's early presence. To reach this stage the splits between false and true self, between 'good' and 'bad', with all the contradictions and ambiguities needed to be worked through in a painstaking manner.

The transference/countertransference interplay is crucial to this process. Therapists giving recent accounts of their work with severely traumatised young people give accounts which are strikingly similar: Evans (1997) talks of the tremendous difficulty in staying with the annihilating mental states conveyed by his patient. Just as Evans was forced to accept his hatred toward the patient (a shameful thing for a child psychotherapist perhaps), this was also an essential stage in my work with Andrew. The importance of working with uncomfortable feelings such as shame in adolescent psychotherapy is acknowledged by Anastasopoulos (1998). Incompatible images of the self may be uncovered as a result of working through these previously unacceptable feelings. Identity then becomes an available area for change (p.107). Working with my own feelings of wishing to disown Andrew as we walked through the corridor may perhaps have helped him eventually to be more able to tolerate shame at what he had done, and be less bound up with self-disgust at what he was. By accepting his reality he was then in a better position to change. In the process he became more able to express feelings of anger, and in this way the regression to fixed states of self-pity was modified by Andrew's access to his own aggression. The aggression behind regression needs delicate management, however, because it needs to be fostered, not inhibited by premature interpretation (Alvarez 1995, p.181).

If the traumatised self had been protected by identification with an omnipotent and destructive self, then narcissism is a key factor. Andrew's wish to possess me in idealised form, and then to protect me from his destructiveness, was palpable, but this left him with an empty triumph, in effect, over his own life. The narcissistic injury needed to come to the fore. Campbell and Hale (1991) have shown how narcissism is bound up in suicidal depression. They start from Freud's (1915) formulation in 'Mourning and Melancholia', that the ego can kill itself only if it can treat itself as an object. Thus, the state of self-regard may represent the ego's original reaction to someone else in the external world. The authors go on to show how the body is treated as an external object and is identified with the lost, loved and hated person. This can also be linked to core complex theory (Glasser 1964) which shows how the regressive longing to merge with a primitive omnipotent caretaker can give rise to anxieties of annihilation which may be brought to a head by a suicide attempt: the equivalent in Andrew's case was the abuse of a child. Andrew's destructiveness toward both himself and towards the therapy had to be converted to an acceptable aggressive impulse toward suitable external objects. As described above, these were first the residential staff, then the therapist and only then could hostility be directed towards the parents. By these stages, therefore, the interlocking roles of abused/abuser could be sufficiently loosened in order to allow space for the acceptance in Andrew's mind of a non-abusive relationship that could include parts of himself previously denied and kept hidden. His more infantile dependent needs then became bearable. The parent–infant togetherness in the storm cloud session above showed I think a stage on the way of this process. Defensively perhaps, he needed to be the parent to me in that interaction, but what was demonstrated in his eventual progress was an acceptance of a non-abusive parent in the other.

Sinason (1996) has described the transformational encounters that can reverse the malignant movement from abused to abuser. These moments seem to have been possible at times in Andrew's treatment. Traumatic experiences can be deconstructed in long-term psychotherapy (Bentovim 1996b, p.306) and this seems to have been a natural process in Andrew's case. At times this necessitated the recreation of seemingly negative and unproductive phases. There are of course still unanswered questions about the lasting effects of treatment and how much long-term improvement to expect. At the very least the provision of therapy may have supported this young man in not reoffending during the period of treatment; but the therapy may also have produced a better possibility of change, where little existed before. It is established after all, that positive parenting, or its substitute, mitigates the worst effects of abuse (Bentovim 1996a, p.113) and this may finally be the value of commitment to a long-term therapeutic relationship.

CONCLUSION: THE CONTEXT OF INDIVIDUAL PSYCHOTHERAPY

Finkelhor (1984) defined four factors that could explain abusive behaviour, and these can be very briefly summarised as follows: first, there must be an emotional congruence in the abuser to the abused/abuser relationship; second, a sexual arousal towards children; third, a blockage of emotional development; and finally, disinhibition of normal impulse controls.

These four factors can be addressed by particular modes of treatment. First, the relationship of power and control, arising often from identification with the aggressor (Freud A. 1936, pp.109–21), and the need to overcome the shame at having been abused, is a pattern of relationships that can be most readily addressed and remedied by a psychodynamically informed placement, whether it be a residential community or specialised foster home. These settings can provide the experience of relationships in a culture of honesty, and open communication.

Second, many of the specifics of sexual arousal toward children can well be addressed by cognitive behavioural therapy. The development of masturbatory fantasies, the cognitive distortions to include children in these fantasies and, above all, the evasion of responsibility can be examined and modified in the cognitive behavioural framework. However, these aspects can also be brought into the field of attention of psychoanalytic psychotherapy, which can provide an essential place for working through (Freud 1914).

Finkelhor's third factor, blockage of emotional development, is more clearly the province of psychodynamic psychotherapy. In the above account themes of self-development and maturation appear in the spontaneous unfolding of a therapeutic transference relationship. The identifications that take place in the mind of the abuser can be revealed and played out in symbolic form. The therapist learns to respond from the abuser or rejecting parent in himself or herself, but in modified form and, with insight into the countertransference, guides the young person to change.

The fourth factor, the disinhibition of normal impulse controls, or 'conduct disorder', is another aspect of the young person that has to be contained in an appropriate placement. In these extracts from Andrew's treatment I have tried to show how from a different perspective the psychodynamic psychotherapy can inform and strengthen the necessary provision of the placement.

CODA

I asked Andrew what he thought about the things I had told him I had written about the therapy.

After a pause, he said cautiously: 'I am pleased with the therapy I have had. I think I'm OK now, as I told my social worker last week, I'm safe now. I don't have thoughts about...you know, having sex with children...I just want to improve my life, do some exams, get a job, go to a sports club, these things are more important than thinking about poor children. And I feel happy with this not being on my mind. I have got more important things to think about like money at the moment needs sorting out, but I've got an appointment with the benefits person next week, and I hope to hear some good news.'

'Can you see a situation that could possibly arise when you would be less safe?'

'No, definitely not, I think I've really learned and changed, it's a long time since I really thought of children in that way.'

(*Pause*)

'My social worker is going to get in touch with my sister, as I asked and I hope to see her, though I don't know if she wants to see me, maybe she just wants to get on with her life. But I know that if she doesn't want to see me, then it's not just because of me, it's that she doesn't want to be reminded of the past...I would like her to know that I'm safe now.'

'Could you say something about what the therapy was like?'

'It was hard talking to you at first, when we were in the small room before. It was a bit boring compared to the group, and there were no biscuits or drinks! (*he laughs*). I used to sleep, but I don't do that now, I can't remember what we talked about, I suppose it must have been to do with the abuse. Sometimes I think I couldn't be bothered to talk or maybe it was too hard to talk and so I used to get very tired. Sometimes I remember that I felt like hurting myself, but not all the time. I don't want to remember the past, it's all over and done with, finished and gone! But we had a few laughs as well, and I liked playing noughts and crosses, and hangman, even though you said after a while that you didn't like those games that much. I do remember my drawings and they showed my feelings, they showed my feelings instead of me getting angry.'

(*Pause*)

'How do you think that worked?'

'It was my name, wasn't it? My name made into a devil and that showed how I felt there was evil in me, that I was evil, a devil, or, yes, that was it, a dragon. And at the time that was how I was feeling, like hurting myself. But I know now that this would get me nowhere, just create more trouble for myself.'

(*Pause*)

'Was there anything about the therapy that you did not like?'

'Sometimes you said things that made me angry, and made me want to hurt someone, or break something…but I've forgotten what those things were now. I suppose if you said something about the past and kept on about it, that would make me angry. If you kept on about my abusing and if you did not believe that I have stopped wanting to do it, then it would feel like you were accusing me, but it has been easier to talk about my feelings, I've learned that it can make me feel so much better if I talk. For one thing, I don't get so tired, I do a bit, but mainly I feel relaxed and I get on with you fine now.'

'What about the times when you weren't getting on with me?'

'You were probably talking about things I did not want to talk about and I would get peed off with you. I felt sometimes that you were pressurising me and that's when I would get tired and go to sleep.'

'Is there anything you would say to someone who is in the situation you were before you started therapy and maybe they are not sure if they really want to do it?'

'I would say to that person, you need a lot of help, to keep your life from being a misery, because if you carry on sexually abusing children, then you will end up in jail. If you don't talk out your feelings then people will get hurt, and they will hurt you as well. It's no good covering it up even if you say that you won't do it again, you always will, if you don't get the help. You might get a thrill, but you are ruining a child's life, and some people enjoy that, but I get no thrill out of it. I know my responsibility and what is no good for me. I've only been able to learn that through talking. Being beaten up in prison would not have helped me. You have to talk, and keep on talking. That's the answer, not to do it, but to talk about it. Maybe you don't believe you'll get there, but you do in the end.'

CHAPTER 5

The Interweaving of Individual Treatment and Staff Group Dynamics

From Re-enactments to Creativity in Residential Treatment

THE ENACTMENT

Christine, a residential worker well known to Micky asked him to accompany her through the dining area and remain under supervision during meal time, which was a normal expectation. Angrily shouting abuse at her, Micky picked up a dinner knife and waved it in front of her face. There were several members of staff in the vicinity whose attention was drawn. Nobody moved and after a short while Micky put down the knife. After a meeting with young people and staff, Micky was informed that the police would be informed and charges might be brought against him for this threatening behaviour.

INTRODUCTION: THE SETTING

A model of residential treatment, as opposed to custodial care, should espouse the principle of open communication. The structure of such an organisation is complex and multifaceted. I am describing here just one aspect, the context of the individual treatment in the residential setting. For a full description of the philosophy and treatment programmes of this type of therapeutic community see Kennedy *et al.* (1986), Baker and Gibson (1995). Although therapeutic communities may vary enormously, the principle of open communication is one that militates most effectively against the closed 'internalising conversations' that underlie abusive systems (Bentovim 1995, p.51).

In order to follow this principle, staff of each discipline, whether it be teaching, residential, cognitive behavioural therapy, psychotherapy, or psychiatry, should aim to be consistently open and honest with young people, including passing on information resulting from any liaison with social services departments (the referrers), and family contact. For a young person to come into residential treatment he needs to accept that this is a very different context for him than merely being 'accommodated' in residential care. This means that, at least to an extent, he begins to accept responsibility for his abusive actions. Rather than emphasising control, whether by punishment or inducement, the therapeutic environment should provide opportunities for self-expression, through group work, individual therapy, and education at an intensive level; these will support the slowly developing capacity for self-restraint by choice in a young person. Feedback from other young people about each others' interactions should be encouraged and is a powerful source of therapeutic change. Openness of communication needs to be fundamental, with no secrets about the work between staff members.

This kind of culture combines some elements of traditional, psychodynamically based milieu therapy (Dockar-Drysdale 1968) but with the addition of family therapy, cognitive-behavioural work and individual psychotherapy.

Sexualised and abusive behaviour is expected to crop up in the day-to-day life of the therapeutic community and must be immediately challenged. Responsibility for his actions is expected of each young person and he is expected to work toward a safe (i.e. non-abusive) way of relating. There should be no physical coercion in a therapeutic placement, and a young person could leave at any time, although of course this would not be encouraged. Instead, a high degree of supervision by staff is necessary, apart from bed times, of course, and 'taking space' in their own bedrooms, bathroom or toilet. This supervision can be reduced in stages as the young person earns a measure of trust. Regular reviews of the young person's progress should take place with him being present and invited to contribute.

INDIVIDUAL THERAPY IN THE CONTEXT OF A THERAPEUTIC COMMUNITY

An open system of communication would seem at first sight to militate against the provision of psychodynamic therapy, dependent as it usually is on a separate relationship in which a transferential dimension can be used to deconstruct the sado-masochistic interactions that underlie abuse. If the therapist is in constant communication with other staff, how, it may be asked, can a young person differentiate between a therapist and any other worker?

The therapist offers a set time for that young person to express their thoughts and feelings, to an extent more freely than with other staff. Within limits outlined by the therapist, a relationship develops, and, because of the focus of the discussions, this tends to arouse some of the emotions connected with the young person's experiences of abuse and abusing. Transferential elements arise in this relationship, just as there are intense transference reactions to other staff and to the organisation as a whole. In the one-to-one session there is an additional possibility for interpretations to be made which are intended to help the adolescent withdraw their projections and to start thinking and communicating instead of acting. There is a tension between this contact and the work undertaken with other staff. If successful, the process represents a development of links between the young person's inner and outer life.

It is made clear to a young person that his therapist does communicate with other staff as and when needed. The therapist participates in general discussion about his patient's progress, usually with the young person present. Specific information that indicates a threat to anyone's safety will be taken outside the session. In theory this would seem to leave little room for a psychotherapy patient to freely associate about the reasons why they are in such treatment, but in practice a therapeutic rapport usually does develop in which a degree of privacy can be achieved. It sometimes happens that a young person chooses to tell their therapist something that they have not felt able to tell others who need to know. Generally some discussion will result in the young person agreeing that others do need to know that information. It is as if the therapist is a suitable person with whom to 'rehearse' a new (and sometimes painful) degree of honesty. Privacy and trust is offered to facilitate this process, not to provide a cloak of total confidentiality which can so easily for this group of patients be perverted into the secrecy of abuse.

Thus, the enclosed and isolated inner world of the abused/abuser may be transformed into a world of intersubjectivity.

For an 'offender-patient' this process has a particular significance: integrating inner and outer connects the abuser with the victim in him. The split between the traumatised victim-self who cannot bear any consciousness of the abuser-self is gradually brought into the light of day. It is as though a paternal element (the palpable authority in the organisation represented in the decision-making functions of residential staff and teachers) can include something more maternal (close attention to the infantile self and some permission to regress to infantile needs). The healing of a split parental couple can have profound importance in the psyche of someone who has been abused by a father figure, with whom he then identifies, and been neglected by a mother-figure whom he has gone on to objectify, and externalise, as a victim. (An outpatient service for offender patients also may represent this integration of maternal and paternal transference in the form of a link for the psychotherapy with social work, though the process is much slower than in a residential placement.)

A psychodynamic therapist could easily find such a situation difficult – even impossible, since the usual focus of attention, the therapeutic relationship between therapist and patient threatens to become muddled and confused by the therapist's contact with other staff; but such a modification of psychotherapy is appropriate to deal with the kind of psychopathology that leads to severe and habitual abusing. Boundaries have already been broken in a profound way for these young people, the internal parents have already been so destructive, that there is no basis for the traditional confidential structure between therapist and patient. A working alliance between therapist and patient is normally an adult agreement that will not be perverted into a kind of secrecy designed to perpetuate abuse; but these are conditions that do not apply to patients who have enacted sexual abuse. The impossibility of containing their abusive impulses unaided requires the additional support of a total therapeutic setting in which psychotherapy might take place. As is pointed out repeatedly in the literature (e.g. Carlson 1990, p.249), it is essential not be deflected by a victimisation that may be used to excuse, deny or protect, but to engage first and foremost the perpetrator-self. The pseudo-victim has a powerful false-self function of protecting the real victim-self. This has always presented a difficulty for non-directive psychotherapy, but in a combined treatment the psychodynamic therapist is allowed greater leeway to address the real victim, because the real perpetrator is there, inescapably, in the residential setting.

CASE ILLUSTRATION

Though Micky, aged 14, had made the minimum admission of responsibility to gain entrance to the therapeutic community, he quickly established a position of denial, both as victim and perpetrator, and tested the limits of his acceptability. With a history of rejection, abused by family members, and then by child care workers, before becoming himself an abuser, Micky knew that he needed a safe place to live. Less conscious and less acceptable to him was the need for a therapeutic experience that could lead to change. After some months of fierce resistance in the placement, he was gradually becoming more open to a more real acceptance of responsibility for his abuse of others. This account is intended to show how the individual therapy interacted with the work that needed to be done by residential and teaching staff in order first to contain and then begin to transform his abusive behaviour.

Personal history

Micky's life had been one of abuse and neglect. His violent father disappeared early on. From the age of about five he was sexually abused, with oral and anal penetration, by an older brother and then by cousins. He was accommodated by the local authority from the age of seven. He was then extensively sexually abused whilst 'in care'. His family has never acknowledged the reality of the intrafamilial abuse, his mother saying it was 'just boys messing about'. The local authority similarly let the abuse by its employees pass by. By the age of 13 he was demonstrating a pattern of sexually abusive behaviour towards younger boys including anal and oral intercourse. These acts involved a certain amount of coercion through manipulation and blackmail, but not violence. He would try to get his victims to perform the same sexual acts upon him. His verbal aggression and threats of violence had been a major problem for the children's homes that had attempted to look after him. Educationally Micky was severely delayed in his development, having been excluded from numerous schools for disruptive and aggressive behaviour. Psychometric testing revealed that he had good intelligence despite his very poor attainment. He was small and under-weight, and seemed to compensate for his shame and low self-esteem by loudly demanding attention and making as much of a nuisance of himself as possible.

Early sessions

Denial of the abusive quality of his sexual behaviour and fantasies was the major feature of my first few months' contact with Micky. This argument between us ran alongside his interaction with me. He seemed to want an emotional contact, indeed he asked for the psychotherapy sessions, which were optional, and yet immediately had to push away the personal contact involved. This pattern of demand, and pre-emptive rejection, driven by the fear of rejection is indicative of borderline pathology (Bateman 1998). For Micky the profound emotional damage to his internal world and relation-ships had to be played out in the arena of sexuality.

Whilst he insisted that he wished to remain in the unit, he also main-tained that this should not interfere with his set ideas. He knew he had nowhere else to go, but it was some time before the need for a home, in a physical sense, was experienced as an emotional need as well. A series of idealisations helped maintain his defence. He idealised his brother, main-taining that he had really been loved by his brother and not been abused. This enabled him to minimise his own actions. 'I enjoyed what I did.' he said, 'and so did the people I did it with! They only complained because they were stupid! Victims!' he said contemptuously. 'There's nothing wrong with sex at any age,' he insisted. 'You're being prejudiced against gays! It's natural pleasure, look at the rock stars, they have a wonderful time. Yes, I know they died, but they had a great time first!' He idealised certain pop stars who were said to have been promiscuous, bisexual, some of whom had died of AIDS or otherwise committed suicide. He would make drawings of himself as a rock star, but these were crude and messy pictures that he hated and always destroyed. His anger at this seemed to make him louder and more bullying in his efforts to convince me that he could be and was (in his fantasy) a successful rock star. When I commented on the picture of this fantasy self which was clearly not working since it had to be destroyed by him, he tore up more paper and made a mess of the therapy room. 'I talk to them!' he proclaimed loudly and provocatively, regaling me with tales of pop stars famous for their wild behaviour. I wondered was he talking to me boastfully as if I would be excited by all this? Was I the idealised brother for him with whom he was identified and could gratify with stories of abuse? When I spoke of the mess inside himself that he was showing me, and the need for someone to see him as a star so that he might feel better about himself, he became noisy and verbally abusive. As I talked then of the amount of help he really needed, he would hang his head in mock sorrow and talk of suicide. If I took these threats at all seriously, he would jeer at me for being stupid for having believed him. Everything I said was ignored or drowned out by his noise. He was like a much younger child restlessly moving around the room, opening the door, or at the window shouting and attracting the attention of other people. The drawing materials and the hastily scribbled pictures were destroyed, and especially if I showed an interest he would make a point of destroying them.

Pictures from the internal world

I copied one of Micky's earliest pictures because, although it was tossed off and disparaged as 'rubbish', it seemed to express something of his state of mind under attack, and also something about the beginnings of structure and a creative possibility of finding a form for chaotic experience.

Figure 5.1

After scribbling in the middle of the page, he scratched in the arrows aggressively, saying, 'they get him here, and here!' I commented that he sometimes felt attacked on all sides, as in this picture, but he quickly tore up the drawing. In making my own copy later I was hanging on to that brief recognition of the vulnerability in him that was concealed beneath the layers of bullying, jeering, denial and so forth. Months later he was fascinated to find that I had done this and was delighted to see how this picture developed into the rest of the series represented here. At the time however, the struggle seemed unrelenting.

Stoller (1979) refers to the particular moment of erotic excitement as a 'microdot': '…a tangled, compacted mass of scripts made up of impulses, desires, defences, falsifications, memories…a piece of theatre whose story seems genuine because of the truth of the body's sensations' (p.165). The need to create this coded form of expression to sexual fantasy arises, according to Stoller, from humiliation. The sense of humiliation was already well known to me, in a direct way, from the frustration of my efforts to make contact with him. Decoding the content of Micky's sexual fantasies was made possible by his continuing production of unsophisticated pictures.

I began to realise that he was flaunting himself and almost falling on me physically as he darted about the room. It was not easy for me to keep my therapeutic stance. I felt I should not allow too much space for an eroticised transference to take hold. He was watching my reactions carefully. Sneeringly he would say, 'I like being buggered, I like sucking men's dicks. Men have been shagging me since I was 4!'

I said, 'You are trying to disgust me I think…so that I should know what it feels like to be as helpless as that 4-year-old'

Or, at other times I would ask, 'Do you really think I want that?'

'I wouldn't mind,' he said challengingly, 'I'd be happy with that!'

Nevertheless, I continued to address the denial, deliberately avoiding the provocation of his sexual taunts. Instead I said that I believed he was *not* really that happy with what had happened to him, that it *was* abuse, not fun. He retorted, 'How do you know, you weren't there!' I said, 'Well, this in the room is not fun, this shouting and threatening is abusive.' He stormed out of the room and shouted at me from the hall, disturbing others and embarrassing me. The only option seemed to be for me to bring in a senior member of residential staff, one who is normally on call for anyone in a difficult situation. This was helpful since it gave Micky the opportunity to return to the room, and state his complaints against me. With another person present, the intensity of the one-to-one contact was reduced to manageable propor- tions. He protested that I was saying he was nothing but an abuser. 'He keeps on accusing my family!' But without getting drawn into taking sides in the conflict, my colleague very skilfully absorbed the anger expressed, and quietly put back to Micky the rational points that I was trying to make.

Later on the same staff member drew my attention to Micky's sexualised manner with me. Though vaguely aware of this, I had found it difficult to recognise it fully. This development allowed me some freedom from a claus- trophobic sense I had of being trapped in Micky's abusive world. It assisted me in putting back to Micky some comments on the anxiety that he was avoiding with his barrage of noise and bullying manner. I found a way to say that he needed to be sure that nothing sexual or abusive would happen here. I referred to his experiences with workers in previous establishments. How difficult it must be, I said, for him to be able to trust adults when in the past they had betrayed him. A gradual calming down seemed to date from this point. Moments of lucidity began to extend and become periods of dialogue. There were of course recurrent flare-ups of noisy resistance, but the continuation of drawings provided points of contact and a sense of purpose to the sessions.

During this period I had been feeling under too much pressure just managing the sessions to be able to think much about the meaning of his communications. The sequence of events described above was a significant stage in recovering my therapeutic stance, with the support of my colleague who, not in the role of a psychotherapist, could provide some distance for him from his alarming impulses. As I too regained some calm so he began to make use of the attention I could now direct toward him. He began to make connections with his real feelings about the kind of family life he had expe- rienced. He began to talk about the neglect and abuse that he had suffered and to tell me the stories behind these experiences. The excitement disap- peared. He drew a bird's-eye view of the school grounds where the older boy had taken him along the path surrounded by trees and, in the centre, the spot where he had been assaulted. (It is interesting to note the similarity here with Andrew's first picture, mentioned above (Chapter 4), where he also needed to locate himself physically as a first step in a therapeutic process.)

Figure 5.2

Some anger was evident as he scribbled in dark brown over the place where abuse took place.

'And you try to scrub out the pain that is still there,' I said.

He simply murmured his assent.

The picture is also somewhat evocative of a dirty anus, but this observation I kept to myself until a later date when our working relationship was better established. At this point he was locating the abuse, as it were in his mind; it was the beginning of telling the story, a more real version this time, of fear, pain and powerlessness.

Nonetheless, while he was opening up some of these issues in his sessions, and in his cognitive behavioural therapy, residential and teaching staff frequently found his behaviour extremely difficult to manage. It was reported that he was often unsettled after a therapy session. In staff meetings there was the opportunity, therefore, to link our struggle as professional carers with Micky's own difficulty in managing his feelings. It was not necessary for me to give the details of Micky's sessions in order to convey something of the work that was happening. The psychotherapy could in some ways then be seen as an effective support of the residential work because there were parallel themes in his contact with other professionals.

(Sadly, it is not always like this; I have heard all too often from residential and other workers elsewhere who feel undermined by the completely separate and confidential type of psychotherapy. It is not surprising, therefore, in those circumstances, that there is little faith in psychological treatment. Then psychotherapists complain of lack of support for their work.)

Abuse in focus

With better containment in his placement he was also able to benefit from the education available in the unit. Positive feedback from staff was on the increase. Often he seemed compelled to spoil these achievements. From the detail of the sessions it was possible to understand why this might be so; with the diminution of his attacks on me, he was more open in the therapy sessions to the traumatic pain that remained within him. Whereas before his traumatic and unbearable pain would have to be forced into another, he was now able to experience something of his own pain. Neither the pain nor the sadism could simply disappear. It came out in verbal attacks on female members of staff. Whilst he regularly lapsed into abusive behaviour toward those women, his rage against them was also expressed strongly in further pictures, which meant that it was possible to bring it into my particular therapeutic arena.

The teacher (Fig 5.3) has been sliced up and put back together so that she 'looks like a real person, but the blood's dripping out!' He took great relish in this. I said that I thought this was also himself feeling chopped into bits even though he might look like a real person. His responses to these links being made became more depressive and inward looking. I wondered aloud if they were his tears leaking out. There were silent periods in the sessions. At times he would be scratching at his skin with pins or his own fingernails. Ripped up pieces of paper were stuck and stapled together. I spoke about the torn-up Micky who was trying to get himself together here. But he would resort to the pictures of sadism as some relief from the attacks now consciously against himself.

Figure 5.3

Figure 5.4

As the pictures were executed there would be venomous remarks about that woman or about women in general.

'I hate their bodies! Their fat tits are disgusting! And that, there!'

He scratched in a vagina and scribbled over the whole thing in red, (Fig 5.4). While he was doing this I noticed that he was touching his own body. I said that I thought he might be talking about his own body too. He said that boys should fancy him because he is better than a woman, laughing lasciviously.

'And do you think that I would fancy you because of that?' I asked.

'No,' he said ruefully.

I said that I thought there was something a woman has that he does not.

He said, 'I've got an arse! All I want is to be the one with tits!'

'Would you then feel that people loved you?' I asked.

Silence

'The woman in the picture seems to be crying,' I said, after a while. He put his head on the desk. I said that I thought he was perhaps sad now that he had missed out on something good from his mum and that this had made him hate women and want to get his own back on all of them.

He said, 'I want to change! But, but the trouble is I *like* sex with boys, and I can't stop thinking about wanting to do it again.'

'And would it be someone here in the unit that you would abuse?' I asked.

'Yes. I keep thinking of Gary.'

I told him that this would have to be shared with residential staff now, because this was a problem that went outside of our sessions. Subsequently I heard that he was able to talk about these feelings about other young people in group meetings. This included the content of some of his sadistic fantasies, drinking blood for example, and he derived a great deal of support from the shared knowledge that he would have to remain under close supervision, and not be left alone with another young person.

It seemed that the object of his sexualised aggression veered between adult women and younger, more vulnerable, boys. It was boys that he had abused, and there were continuing erotic and sadistic thoughts toward them. Feelings toward women were more complex. There was perhaps a deeper hatred, though it was also sexualised. There was clearly his envy of the female body, expressed as angry contempt. He could divert from this hatred, it seemed, by resorting to arousal at the thought of boys. The oscillation between these violent alternatives was itself causing him some distress. He would complain that I was driving him mad, but at times could accept that it was the thoughts he had that were unbearable.

The above sequence shows the complex interplay of these themes and the development of the relationship with the therapist. It seemed that Micky was expressing an increased tolerance of his internal world through the medium of the transference-laden relationship. He would be infuriated if I was late or changed an appointment time. There were many pictures of mutilated women that were destroyed and I felt that he was also trying to rid himself of these thoughts, as if into me. It seemed that I was intended to be the one to be alarmed or horrified. Although he frequently threatened to stop his sessions with me, he never seriously demanded this with other staff, which would have been the process to negotiate an ending, as he well knew.

He confessed a plan to hang himself. Initially demanding that this should be a secret, he eventually accepted the need for other staff to be informed, and did so himself. Again, the principle of openness of communication meant that steps could be taken to ensure the personal safety of this young person. Much discussion took place around his suicidal fantasies, and about the murderous side of him that endangered himself. Some relief came when the fragmented parts of himself could be linked in terms of himself as victim and himself as perpetrator. Bringing the two together, as happened at one point in this picture of himself and his brother, seemed to produce an illumination.

Figure 5.5

In this session some discussion of feelings about his brother produced insight as he reflected on what his brother really had done to him and what he must have felt toward Micky. He conveyed a realisation that he had to relinquish the dream that his brother really loved him. There was an unusual moment of calm just then, and it was possible to hear some classical piano music just audible in the distance. For once Micky allowed himself to take a breath and listen to something outside himself. Surprised, he said,

'Hey, that's quite nice!'

But such moments of acceptance and relief were rare. He would often arrive for sessions in a rage, anticipating, it seemed, the horrible feelings he was going to confront. One picture from this time shows himself behind bars.

Figure 5.6

I said that I thought it showed the prison in his head.

'Yes – prison! I'm in prison here!' he shouted. But he knew that it was something within him, as he said, 'because of everything that has happened to me!' He acknowledged that he was feeling worse, and it was shortly after this that I heard that there had been a series of rows and that he had threatened a staff member with a dinner knife. The police were called, statements were taken, and Micky was charged.

From the staff meeting

Micky had recently been a particular source of anxiety; when not miserable and withdrawn, he could be most provocative, loud and abusive in his language. He had targeted certain female members of residential and teaching staff, asking them where they lived and cleverly collecting information on their family life. He had threatened one worker that he would abduct and kill her children after he left, and that there was nothing she could do about it. She was terrified. He was known as someone whose placement often seemed about to break down, though he would also be quite careful to stay just within the rules in terms of his behaviour. The incident with the knife was unusual.

There now follows a description of some of the processing that went on between members of staff of different disciplines, in the regular staff meeting.

> Christine was asked how she felt after the threat of assault by Micky. She seemed calm and said she had not really felt too frightened. She had felt that most likely Micky would not use the knife, and that the threat had taken place in an area where there were others nearby. Nevertheless, she was a bit shaken up by it. There were expressions from the others that it was good at least that Micky had to face up to some consequences. After all, he had been increasingly threatening and abusive in his interactions lately. Someone said, 'He has been getting away with murder!' And someone else added, 'It's all very well to keep trying to understand, but you get to a point with Micky when he is just rubbishing everything we offer, and no amount of therapy is going to make any difference!' The group fell silent and I began to wonder about my own role with Micky, and my role in this staff group meeting. Once again I was asking myself, 'Should an individual therapist be here? Is the individual therapy for a young person being compromised? Were the issues for this group clouded by perceptions of what I carried as a therapist of the young people?'

Recently I had been finding it difficult to contribute in these group sessions. There had been no overt criticism of me, but a lot of each other. Staff members had been expressing the strains they were under, and there had been a tendency to attack each other, finding fault, and so it felt to me, nit-picking over the details of procedural rules. These rules were, of course, important means of trying to establish control over the young people's behaviour, and of handing on a sense of responsibility, but they had taken on a different significance. It seemed that an abuser had to be found, and that if someone slipped up, he or she would be seen as the perpetrator. This also applied to different professional groups. Little reference had been made, until now, to 'therapy', though teachers were often criticised and blamed for acting out by young people. Meantime there were hints of resentment about their own status. (Even in the best therapeutic communities there seems to be a tendency for residential workers to feel that they are perceived as less important than other more specialist staff, in other words to undervalue themselves.)

> 'We just fetch and carry... all the important work seems to go on in the therapy sessions,' sentiments that were often repeated. I had previously expressed the view that 'therapy' was going on for the young people all the time, perhaps especially when they are being fetched and carried. In a way the therapist also was being carried since it would clearly be impossible, say, for me to work with these young people if they were not being looked after in a place like this. But try as I might to convey this, the idea was not being taken up. I felt that I too was affected by the siege mentality that was around. I said that perhaps the emotional strain affected everyone. Someone then said he felt as though he was putting on armour and going into battle when he set off for work each day. He laughed and said that he quite enjoyed this but it was clear that the others did not. I felt there was a reluctance to look at any differences between staff group members. It seemed impossible for staff, including myself in this context, to think about the traumatic experiences that the young people were presenting to us. After a silence, I said that bringing in the police had produced a great deal of relief, and perhaps it felt that this form of control was a lot better than all the so-called therapy, which just seemed to make things worse. Someone said, 'change seems so slow to take place' and somewhat sarcastically 'but of course we're just residential workers, we're not therapists'. I said that I thought people could be aware of how essential their role was and the complaint was perhaps that I had not been enough of a policeman in order to provide control for Micky. A group member then said, 'Well, it was a good thing he did that because the other young people are certainly impressed with our way of putting a stop to it.' Someone else said they were glad

that he did rather a minor thing, not serious enough to be chucked out, 'After all we don't want to lose him, do we?' There was general agreement to this and I commented that this was very different to the way people had been feeling at times before when Micky could almost succeed in making people reject him. 'Going through all that must be a form of therapy, isn't it?' I asked, and there was a sudden reduction of tension as every one smiled at each other.

In Micky's next session he was initially very defensive and hostile, 'Who does she thinks she is, she's just trying to get me thrown out, she hates me, I wish I had stuck her with the knife, it would have served her right, the bitch! He then quickly and angrily drew a picture of all the staff,
'They're dead, stabbed to death, all of them!'
I was struck by the way he showed everyone in separate boxes. It was as though he was aware of the fragmentation that was experienced in the staff group. He talked about his sense of being victimised by the event.
'I didn't mean it. They should have known that I wasn't going to stab anyone! It's not fair!'

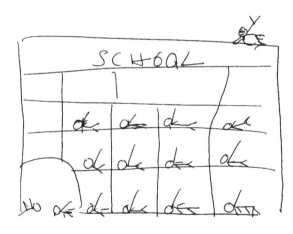

Figure 5.7

However, Micky could see that waving a knife in someone's face was actually a threat, and his indignation gave way to despair.
'I'm a monster, a bastard, I should be locked up…'

He slumped on the table. I said that he had *not* stabbed her because deep down perhaps he does want something good from her and from being here. After a thoughtful pause he turned the picture over and it seemed that he realised he had gone too far. He talked about the choices he had. He drew a picture of where he felt himself to be 'at a crossroads'.

'I know I could leave but where can I go? No one would have me, they all think I'm a monster. At least if I stay here I can take that path and be free, be myself.' He became tearful and silent and after a while asked me if I thought he could get better. Sadly he said, 'Sometimes I behave like a monster because people think that's what I am. I don't know what else to be.'

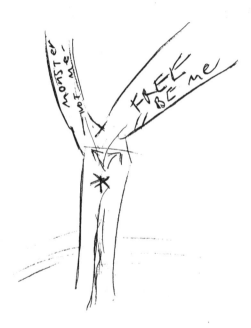

Figure 5.8

He buried his head, and said, 'You don't know what it's like, thinking all the time about horrible things. I can't be away from here, I think about Gary all the time. I want to get his blood. I want to eat him, suck him, drink his blood, does it mean I'm mad? Will I have to be locked up all my life? You'll carry on with me, won't you? I'll just keep on talking with you. I'll work on my problems, you'll see.'

He then spoke about going home for a visit and his worries about what would happen if he met his brother. I asked him to tell me how he was working on this with residential staff. This he could do, in a constructive frame of mind, and think about important practical details of the visit. Toward the end of the session, almost absent-mindedly he produced another picture.

Figure 5.9

'This is us two talking, sitting on our chairs,' he said. 'Oh dear, my drawing's no good!'

'And what is that above the two of us?' I asked.

'That's our minds, yours and mine, yours trying to figure out mine, and mine trying to figure out yours.'

I stop the narrative here, not at the end of treatment, but in a sense, at the beginning, for it was from here that there was a much more adult working alliance. Shortly after this point his supervision was relaxed, and though there were, naturally, a few hitches, when it came time to leave it was generally felt that he was much less of a risk to himself and others. Perhaps one of the most optimistic signs at leaving was that he asked how he could get help to sort out the 'sexual problem' he now recognised was his. Having had a degree of freedom during a transitional period of semi-independence, he realised that he was terrified of a relationship, sexual or otherwise, with anyone. He had not been cured, but he knew to ask how to get more therapy for himself. It seems at this point that Micky at least could know of a way forward, away from the corrosive effects of years of abuse.

DISCUSSION

What are the therapeutic factors at work in a treatment such as this? At the point of the staff group described above my relationship with that group seemed completely stuck. Micky had the ability to make people feel helpless, and traumatised, as evidenced for example by the woman who feared for the safety of her own children. We can see how this flows directly from Micky's difficulty in dealing with his own traumatic experiences in any way other than by forcing them onto somebody else. Finding himself in treatment the perpetrator looks for a victim in the worker, whether that be residential staff, teacher, or therapist. As a cumulative process the staff group find that they are losing the emotional capability of holding their own feelings of being under attack. The anxiety and fear is handed around, as it were, within the group. In the illustration I tried to show a point at which the trauma that he was defending against had the most impact on us all, and a point at which, for a time, it seemed impossible to think. Sometimes only in retrospect does it seem possible to have a theoretical discussion.

A view about the functioning of groups affected by trauma has been advanced by Hopper (1997). Developing Bion's theory of basic assumptions that inhibit the functioning of work groups, Hopper has proposed a fourth basic assumption, that of 'incohesion', when thought and work have to be avoided because awareness is associated with too much pain. Hopper goes on to elaborate concepts of aggregation and massification as being two forms of defensive functioning as means of warding off the 'incohesion' that itself becomes a threat to survival. In states of 'aggregation' according to Hopper there is 'a high degree of role differentiation, cross pressures, specificity...' but, 'no basis for shared hierarchies, and...differences become a source of invidious comparison' (Hopper 1997, p.455). The aggregate is barely a group; power is not supported by authority, and administration is seen as manipulative. I felt unable to function in the group at the time described above, believing myself handicapped by my role; if only I were the same as the others, I thought, then I would be able to contribute. I was beginning to worry that I was seen as responsible for the difficulties engendered by the staff's struggles to work with the young people. If aggregation describes a state where individuals become singletons, that is to say, that each feels isolated in an emotional sense and unconnected with the others, there is often, according to Hopper, a move toward massification as an attempt to merge with a perfect group. The incident of Micky's threat with the knife produced, so it seemed to me, a change in this direction. The group became united, no longer fragmented, with members out of contact with one another. There was a 'fantasy of perfection', as Hopper (1997, p.455) describes it, where at last the persecuting object can be dealt with effectively and the traumatic threat to survival can be eliminated. This is still a defence against a state of incohesion, but the fact of change produces a possibility of insight and development. As it happened, the recognition of this transition enabled the members to move onto an appreciation of the young person's right to as much help as possible, rather than punishment, and then to draw closer to an appreciation of their own work.

How does this group phenomenon relate to the intrapsychic processes for the individual? The repeated patterns that underlie apparently senseless acts of violence stem from childhood experiences of abuse and deprivation. These create a fragile sense of self and lead to aggression in order to protect a self that is felt to be under attack. In these children's early experience attack has come without warning, so the child learns that it is safer to be expecting it at all times. As he has been an object of abuse in someone else's mind, so the child builds an identification of himself on that basis. Attacks on the other, and on the thinking capacity of the other, can be understood as attempts to escape from the intolerable thought of oneself in someone else's mind (Fonagy 1999). This perspective also shows how the incapacity to conceive of an object at a mental or psychological level causes him to seek identifications via the body. 'The bodily self becomes a refuge from intolerable feelings of fear and pain at being abused' (Fonagy 1999, p.11). All this is given a very direct confirmation in Micky's pictures. I believe that by the stage of the final drawings reproduced above Micky is at a threshold of change whereby he is beginning to conceive of objects as having a psychological reality. Having worked through some painful and confusing bodily experiences, there is the beginning of a differentiation of mind.

Is an emotional impact on the worker inevitable in this work? Is it necessary for change to take place? Bateman (1998) describes the impact on the therapist of processes like these. Since the narcissistic defences conspire to produce a desperately needed though illusory feeling of safety *because* no change is possible, any change has to be catastrophic. Drawing on the work of H. Rosenfeld, Bateman shows how the 'thin-skinned' narcissist rejects objects in order to pre-empt rejection, thereby destroying contact, In contrast to the 'thick-skinned' who withdraws and so prevents contact. Movement between the two types of rejection can result from therapeutic work but also may produce catastrophic enactments of traumatic experiences and the acting out of sado-masochistic fantasy. In these states, Bateman (1998) suggests, interpretation alone is ineffective; instead the analyst (for which we might also read staff group), should demonstrate a 'shared sense of reality. It is likely that…narcissistic and borderline patients need an analyst [or *staff group*] who becomes entangled with their terror, who becomes embroiled in subjectivity and objectivity, and yet is able to survive' (p.23) (my parenthesis added).

Tolerating a negative series of transferences is the key to any worker's ability to survive. Whereas residential workers rely on a peer group to share and process the hostile projections, a psychotherapist is, to a degree, more isolated. Initially idealising me, as if I were perhaps the brother, then feeling exploited, and abused by me, as he really experienced the brother, I then became for Micky the mother who failed to protect, and finally, perhaps, I was needed as a father who is hated because of the rules and limits to gratification. All this while a glimmer of hope was kept alive, even if only in the therapist's mind, that I could be the sort of parent who could represent a sense of purpose and wholeness in himself. As Fonagy and Target (1996, p.231) put it, 'The analyst's mind acts as a scaffolding designed to enhance the development of representation in the child's psychic reality.'

THE CREATION OF NARRATIVE

As enactments give way gradually to creative expression, the content is decoded, as in Stoller's metaphor of the microdot, and a *narrative* takes shape. The creation of a narrative structure with which to make sense of otherwise disconnected experience is being recognised as one of the most significant therapeutic achievements (Keenan 1998; Fonagy and Target 1998, p.4). Despite his struggles against the process Micky was making progress toward a conception of himself as a thinking person in relation to another, responsible for himself at points when a coherent narrative was being constructed. Toward the end of his time in treatment I asked him if he had any objection to my writing up the work with him for publication, with his identity suitably disguised of course. After some initial anxiety that this might mean that he was the 'weirdest' of my patients, he said, 'Yes, you can tell my story.'

He asked to look over his pictures from the previous year and a half and relocated, with great surprise, the various reference points in the journey of self-understanding that had been made. He seemed especially astonished at the different feelings he had had about me.

CONCLUSION

Emotional and psychological trauma can cause actual brain dysfunction and damage, as has been well established (Van der Kolk, 1987). Memory is particularly affected (Laub and Auerhahn 1993). The traumatised child is speechless, and manages to erase feelings associated with unbearable memory. Employed as a self-protective device, this cutting-off also forfeits the creative possibility of coherent narrative. In a therapeutic context, however, the microdot becomes the beginning of narrative. Through this process a person is able to recover, not necessarily the memories themselves, but the true feelings associated with the experiences, and eventually perhaps the true meaning of the experience. It is clear that in Micky's case the memories were dissociated, to the extent that appropriate affect was lost to consciousness. Painful feelings of being overwhelmed and the humiliation of being forced into compliance were covered over with triumphant feelings of being powerful and special. These conscious attributes were maintained in the face of reality, while the unconscious meaning of abuse persisted in the form of his repetition of abusive behaviour. These abusive patterns were in themselves also microdots that contained his own abusive past and the distortions of his own experience.

The integration of residential treatment with psychotherapy depends on a staff group's willingness and ability to act in a concerted way as a collective therapeutic team, whilst there is differentiation of roles. One of the main obstacles to this is professional rivalry, which arises from a number of sources, including the different tasks, and the different anxieties of each discipline. Personal issues may also be expressed in professional conflicts, so personal therapy is recommended and supported for all staff working with these young people. The role of the policeman bears a different kind of authority to that of the therapist; offender-patients however need both. Integrating psychotherapy with residential work produces conflict and tension between the disciplines. The staff group needs to be sufficiently structured and also free enough in its communication to hold those conflicts. Only then will the young abused/abuser receive the combination of containment and understanding that he needs.

CHAPTER 6

Group Therapy for Adolescents Who Have Abused

PART I: TOWARDS A GROUP-ANALYTIC MODEL

Dreaded scenes in adolescent therapy groups

1. The group was discussing the week's news for each of the boys. Will was happy that his father was due to visit this coming weekend (omitting to mention that there had been many disappointments at previous such arrangements). Ali said proudly that he had avenged his girlfriend's rape by beating up the assailant and putting him in hospital. Peter expressed his scepticism about this by making faces, which annoyed Ali. The therapists were both aware of Ali's tendency to fantasise. The senior, male, therapist commented that this was perhaps how Ali, like all the boys in this group, very much needed to see himself as someone who protects girls, not as the rapist himself. The female co-therapist added that such a feeling of being powerful was also perhaps in order not to feel left alone by fathers who do not turn up when they are supposed to. However, the therapists were having to speak louder to be heard, since Peter continued his grimaces, and jeering noises, in response to which Ali started making threats of violence. Peter, who was much less able verbally, was waving his fists and grunting at Ali, who stood, shouting that he would hit Peter. The therapists had to act quickly, each intervening with one of the protagonists in order to prevent a fight.

2. It is David's turn to say how he feels his victim may have felt. 'Dunno,' he says dismissively, and looks out of the window. The others smirk, but look evasive. The two (male) therapists catch each others eye, and share their sense of weary exasperation. The senior therapist says, 'Well, maybe we have to go back to the session where you told us the words that she said, do you remember, where she said, 'Stop' and you carried on, because I think you said, you thought she didn't really mean it. We looked at that, and we discovered that it was because you had the idea that all girls really want sex but they feel they have to say no, even though they don't really mean no, right?' Again the faintest of triumphant irony from David, as he says, 'Right'. The other group members look bored, impatient. It seems to the junior therapist that they want something to happen. He says to David, 'You know you are wasting everyone's time here.'

'No, I'm not, it's not my time anyway, it's your time.' The senior therapist finally finds his notes from the earlier session, but as he begins to read out he senses the dissatisfaction and tension in the room and puts them aside saying, 'Look, it's up to you, I know you don't want to be here – and perhaps' (looking around the room) 'no-one does, but if you do not take part properly then we will have to let your social workers know that you are not doing the work, OK?'

These examples will be seen to derive from different models of groupwork, though they also show the universal difficulties in work with young people who feel under compulsion. Neither the cognitive behavioural method nor the psychodynamic approach can avoid encountering the resistance of the young people to the task. Furthermore, since the therapist becomes identified in the young people's mind with the necessity to confront the painful, and sometimes traumatic, events that caused them to be there, it is not surprising that such a group will endeavour by all possible means to arouse feelings of helplessness and hopelessness in the therapists. But these incidents (drawn directly from the writers' experience) though not unusual, should not be typical of any group's functioning. It is to be hoped there will be periods of more constructive work, otherwise the group would hardly be viable. In this context they represent some of the most intense expressions of the difficulty that group members will have had with authority in the social world, now brought directly into a transference relationship with the therapists.

In both instances the therapists are faced with awkward choices: too direct a confrontation with Ali in Group 1 about his confabulation will be felt as a humiliation and will reinforce his refusal to accept the experiences he has had of being helpless. The freedom of expression allowed by a psychodynamic approach is inevitably going to lead to communications of a less desirable kind. Resorting too quickly, or too slowly, to the assertion of adult authority, to keep order in the room, will undermine the group's potential for self-regulation and autonomy. In the structure of Group 2 the therapists have more means at their disposal to challenge the denials and evasions of the young people, but they encounter a more passive form of resistance. One major difference between the two models is the relative permeability of the boundary of communication of information from the group session. In the psychodynamic model there is more emphasis on the relationships in the room, as they develop through the sessions. Interpretations of unconscious content in that framework may, or may not, make sense to the adolescent. Or they may simply be ignored. The danger here is that a young person may be enabled to deny external reality. The psychodynamic ideal of spontaneous production can lead to unrestrained acting-out in the session and intolerable stress levels for therapists. The cognitive behavioural method model places more emphasis on reporting to other professionals but, by deferring to outside realities and agencies, they may detract from their own authority within the group, and lose the impact on the young person of his experience in the group.

With such difficulties in both models it might well be asked, why put these young people together in a group at all? Surely, with their history of sexually abusing, when together with others with similar inclinations, they may do no more than cynically support each other's perverse gratifications, and associated defences. The only way for adults to have sufficient leverage against this tendency would be to instigate such authoritarian control as to prevent any genuine and spontaneous expression by the young people, something on which not only psychodynamic but all therapeutic work depends. What if anything, it will be asked, can these young people learn from each other?

A rationale for groupwork with young people

Since Kolvin's (1981) major project in Newcastle schools, there has been evidence concerning the effectiveness of group work for behaviourally disturbed young people (Wood 2001). Group work would seem, in general, to be an appropriate provision for adolescents who are (or who should be) at the developmental stage of separating from their family and finding an identity as an adult personality, usually alongside people of their own age. This will be both an internal process of psychological transformation, going hand in hand with changes in social relationships. In the case of young abusers, however, it is most likely that their family of origin will have been disrupted in varying degrees of severity, and their social development is most unlikely to be adequate. Nevertheless a young person such as this, like any other will be impelled primarily by the physiological changes of puberty and will have a need to find an adult identity somehow or other, if he is not to continue typically in isolation and in terror that others may find out his shameful sexual secrets.

S.H. Foulkes, the founding father of Group Analysis had a great belief in the normative powers of the group. Seeing symptoms as failed attempts at communication, he held what might be seen as an idealistic view that 'disruptive forces are consumed in the integration of the group as a whole' (Foulkes 1964, p.90). This may be contrasted with the Winnicottian view in which the adolescent needs to (symbolically) destroy the internal parents (Winnicott 1971, p.145). This a potentially disruptive process and tends to threaten a viable relationship with social reality. The peer group would normally be a means by which the adolescent is able to reject the values, or at least the power, of the parents in his mind and to establish a sense of identity including that of his sexuality. It is primarily through the peer group that a person has to negotiate some form of (appropriate) sexual relationship in the world. Personal values, a sense of direction in life, are all developed and tested in relation to the peer group. A gang mentality is the obverse of this and can reach malignant proportions. In this case the group forms, not only a culture, but also a refuge from the adult world, a way for individuals to disown responsibility and unleash their destructive fantasies. The paedophile ring is one kind of gang and it is necessary for group therapists to be aware of the tendency of an adolescent group to form delinquent anti-authoritarian allegiances among each other, which may be quite dangerous.

How can therapists turn these powerful forces to therapeutic advantage? Slavson (1943, p.232) described how a child forms an attachment to the group and thereby internalises a more coherent superego, thus allowing transference issues of authority to be worked through. Foulkesian theory has long held fast to the notion of the group as having inherent socialising value, as for example can be seen in Del Balzo and Judge (1998). From a different theoretical orientation Reid (1999) concentrates on the development of self-expression in the group context and she describes a process of the group's evolution into a socially coherence; the need to be socially integrated had been in effect a suppressed characteristic in disruptive or conduct-disordered children. The underlying need for socialisation reaches expression and fulfilment, says Reid, in the therapeutic group. Following Kolvin's pioneering work, Canham and Emanuel are representative of many child psychotherapists who are taking psychological treatment into schools by this means. 'The presence of others with similar and different problems allows for an exploration in each other of aspects of themselves that have hitherto been denied' (Canham and Emanuel 2000, p.283).

Despite all these ventures, many psychoanalytic therapists seem to be put off groupwork, perhaps because of the, sometimes, florid expressions of anxiety and hostility from young people, who are gathered together for a reason that they do not properly understand. William Golding's (1954) *The Lord of the Flies* comes to mind as a portrayal of the barbarism into which a group can descend without limits or controls. Elsewhere I have tried to show how the group analytic mode is suitable for the establishment of an adult authority that young people can perceive as rational and evokes respect rather than fear or resentment (Woods 1993; 1996). Leadership in this context offers an attachment of a particular kind, one that is intensely desired and needed, especially by young males, who may have never had an effective father-figure. The playing-out of negative transferential elements in the context of the group, far from being a deterrent, may be one of the most important therapeutic factors in group therapy. The fatal outcome of the *Lord of the Flies*, can be seen perhaps as not so much about the innate destructiveness of human beings, but as more about the failure of adult authority to channel the energies and meet the needs of the young. In her discussion of bullying and violence Waddell (2002) points out the 'predisposing factors' to gang violence and, in relation to that particular novel by William Golding, the fact that the dominant subgroup of boys had already

been conditioned by an authoritarian education system. To paraphrase
Winnicott's (1952) statement that there is no such thing as a baby, without a
nursing couple (p.99), one might say that there is no such thing as an adolescent group, without an adult authority to define it. The absence of rational
adult authority is experienced as an act of sadism by some groups who then
identify as it were with the aggressor, in order to form their own power base.

To move from the microcosm of the therapeutic group to the wider
society, it can be seen that the sado-masochistic perversion of relationship
behind sexual abuse has important meanings for the wider social context
over and above the intrapsychic. The predisposition to abuse cannot be seen
as a quirk of nature that happens arbitrarily to some unfortunate individuals;
these pathological developments are clearly the result of malign social influences, primarily mediated through the parents and through their failures to
provide adequate emotional environment but also through their relationship to a wider social reality. The failure of some parents can be seen as necessarily resulting from their fractured relationship to the rest of society.

Acts of sexual abuse can therefore be seen as attacks on the fabric of
society just as much as they are crimes against particular persons. In this perspective it could be said that the abuser needs a profound social re-education
to enable him to see that the satisfaction of his desires cannot be stolen, as it
were. They may indeed be unrealisable, but there needs to be some hope
that experiences of pleasure, including that of love, might be found
somewhere in the world, without the use of coercion.

Group theorists such as Dalal (1998), and Stacey (2001) have been
developing a group-analytic view of interpersonal behaviour as less of a
manifestation of intra-psychic functioning than of mind as social at its core:
'…the mind that is usually called intrapsychic is a property of the group'
(Foulkes 1974; quoted in Dalal 1999, p.55). Dalal goes on to demonstrate
convincingly how power is a ubiquitous and inescapable influence on communication. The idea of a social unconscious, first put forward by Erich
Fromm (Hopper 2001, p.187) also begs the question as to the significance
of the perpetrator to the rest of society. His life experience has taught him to
take, if he is not to be taken from, even though in so doing he becomes a
scapegoat in society. A truly therapeutic group should enable him to find a
different role. Group work therefore may replicate the social world in
miniature, and perhaps more usefully than in the one-to-one therapeutic
structure.

Secrecy and 'the negative imbalance of power' have been identified as two crucial factors that perpetuate abuse (Baker and Gibson 1995). Group therapy militates against both; a young person has the opportunity in the group of sharing his hitherto private world. This may be resisted, of course, and very painfully so, but the relief he feels when finally the shameful secrets are unburdened to sympathetic others is very evident. As the therapists know that this is possible, so they can encourage self-disclosure and offer emotional support when needed. Bearing this in mind will also counteract the hostility coming from the group, which, in the form of negative projections, may make therapists feel that they are persecuting group members. Of course, the adult is to some extent in a position of power, but this is mitigated in a group where members can find their own power, feel supported by others and are less dependent on the adult. In the relatively open and public arena of groupwork the therapists are seen to be more accountable than in the one-to-one situation. As Naglieri (1996) makes clear, the issue of rules and boundaries is under constant scrutiny in an adolescent group, and acting-out often results from the apparently arbitrary and perhaps inconsistent actions of adults. The negotiation of the power relations in a group is of crucial importance in the adolescent's recovery of faith in a non-abusive world.

Which theoretical model?

As noted by Fonagy and Roth (1996, p.10), 'the growth of group therapy transcends theoretical models.' Most therapists, it is pointed out by these two research-oriented authors, practice in a 'pluralist' fashion and '…psychodynamic interventions are probably impossible without a substantial and supportive experiential component' (pp.10–11). CBT groupwork has long been the standard treatment for adult offenders and belief in its effectiveness has held for a long time (Becker 1990; Becker and Kaplan 1988). However, since there is no reliable evidence that could come from large-scale independent research (Print and O'Callaghan 1999, p.144), it follows that caution should be retained about espousing any one theoretical model. As I have tried to show in earlier chapters, it is necessary, though not sufficient, for treatment programmes to focus on offending behaviour. The developmental stage of young people and their emotional needs are equally important (Ryan 1998).

Working within an Attachment Theory framework Friedrich (1995) brings in the affective component in work with boys who have been sexually abused. When group safety has been established, and the members of a group can begin to understand the perspective of others, then, Friedrich proposes, the abuser/victim dynamic can be interrupted, exposed and dismantled. He gives detailed instances of work on boundary issues, such as standing too close, interrupting each other, and provides exercises on the interaction between group members. Although he is not dealing here with young people who have abused, the important links between abuse and abusing make his findings very useful for group therapists who want to address the needs of the whole person, not just the history of abusive behaviour.

Sermabakian (1994) and her colleagues report on the development of a group treatment for adolescent sex offenders. Based on Bandura's concept of 'reciprocal determinism', which refers to a triad of person, behaviour and environment (Sermabakian and Martinez 1994, p.969), the group element is part of a comprehensive programme including family, individual and systemic work. The group programme lasts a year, and covers these topics; after taking full responsibility for a detailed admission of offences, the group members must explore their sexual arousal patterns, following which they work on the cognitive distortions that enabled them to commit the offences. Finally the group moves on to victim empathy work. Discussion sessions and structured exercises are used throughout, together with anatomical dolls to help them to be explicit about what they have done; they would also read poems and letters from victims of child abuse, and write 'apology letters' to their victims, though they may never be sent. The theory places value on the person as a self-regulating organism and the development of the capacity of 'humanisation' to counteract injurious behaviour: 'It is difficult for an individual to behave cruelly toward people when they are characterised in ways that personalise and humanise them' (Bandura 1986), quoted in Sermabakian (1994). This is an extremely valuable programme; however, it does depend on a good deal of ability in a well-functioning young person. It assumes that a perpetrator has the capacity to personalise and is able to give up those cognitive distortions that allow him to abuse. The many young abusers who are affected by their own deprivation and/or learning disability and have a personality that seems fragmented, that knows only compliance or subversion, may pass through such a programme untouched. It may not be only bad practice that has produced the false 'apology letters' that this author has seen; there may be a limitation in the applicability of the theoretical model.

The unique feature of group therapy is the presence of the peer group; given that the adolescent finds his place in relation to others at this stage, the group should become an agent for change, to develop an identity not based on the abuse of power. Scheidlinger (1972, p.375) describes the purpose of group therapy as a support for the ego in its struggle with internal and external reality. The adolescent's interaction with the adult world represented by the therapist in a one-to-one meeting changes enormously when it is mediated by the group. Most adolescents, even those untainted by such anti-social behaviour as sexual abuse, are capable of splitting off unwelcome aspects of their identity as and when needed. However the more 'normal' adolescent, that is to say, most young people, will by and large be able to integrate different aspects of himself in the course of development. How is it possible to withstand the impact of the anti-social influences emanating from the combined life histories of a group of young abusers? This brings us back to the question of what actually happens in a treatment group.

Given that it is unrealistic to expect that a number of impulse-driven young people will sit in a circle and discuss their problems in a self-directed way, with occasional reflective comments from the adult(s), what then are the appropriate activities and structures to be made available? The first principle, as in medicine, is to do no harm. Translated to this particular setting, the first priority is to make the group safe. Psychoanalytic psychotherapists with children naturally acknowledge play as valid and necessary for communication, the equivalent of the free association of the adult analytic treatment. In this regard each response of group members is an implicit interpretation of the previous communication. But to what purpose? Clearly safety is not enough. The crucial issue of the abusive behaviour could easily be lost if the group members have no interest in examining it. There are many structured programmes of group work of what might be called a 'psycho-educational' type. These can be tailored to a particular group who will be more or less available for different forms of expressive work – for example, art, drama and music therapy. Good examples of these are: Thomason (2001), and the various publications of Safer Society, for example Kahn (1990) and Cunningham and MacFarlane (1991).

Such programmes, however, may not be suited to the particular characteristics and needs of a given group of youngsters; instead the exercises need
to be adapted or they may provide ideas to spark off thoughts to move in
different directions. They are certainly useful as supports in order to prevent
the dreaded scene of therapist helplessness. The Greater Manchester
Abusers Project (G-MAP) has evolved a groupwork programme that is
based on cognitive behavioural therapy (Print and O'Callaghan 1999).
Again, the group treatment is but part of a comprehensive therapeutic
package, including family intervention, detailed child protection-oriented
case management and individual work. The 'groupwork curriculum', like
that of Sermabakian and Martinez divides into blocks of work on, first,
accepting responsibility, second, the cycles of abuse, and third, relapse prevention. These broad themes are broken down into further subheadings,
and further details are available from G-MAP in Cheshire. Cautionary
remarks are made – for instance, that therapists cannot expect each theme to
be covered and 'completed' before moving on to the next element. Excellent
as it is, the programme put forward by these authors does not allow much
room for the young people to express their own concerns that might be
crucially relevant to their offending behaviour, but not on the programme
that week, if at all.

The strengths of the cognitive behavioural approach are in its consistency, its openness to monitoring, its predictability. Maybe it is not
necessary to know about motivation and the unconscious, as CBT therapists
maintain (Becker 1990). However, it *is* surely important to know about
resistances to treatment, and especially to be able to evaluate the significance of the therapeutic relationship as a vehicle for change. Milton (2001),
herself a psychoanalyst, presents a balanced appraisal of the relative merits
and difficulties of CBT and psychodynamic treatment. She raises the possibility of combined treatment, which is especially useful for the patient population under discussion here because this provides a link between the
abuser and the victim in the same person. Milton quotes research that
suggests that it is the more 'dynamic' elements in cognitive treatments that
seem to be most relevant to outcome. 'This was in contrast to more typically
cognitive procedures;' 'the control of negative affect through the use of
intellect and rationality;' and 'encouragement, support and reassurance from
therapists…were not predictive of positive outcome' (Milton 2001, p.43).

The group-analytic perspective

A group-analytic model can provide a basis for an integrated approach which avoids the non-directiveness of a purely psychodynamic approach, draws upon a range of techniques from many sources according to the needs of the group members, and binds them together in a comprehensive view of group functioning, a combination of activities and interpretation. An instance of such an effective synthesis is described by Henry *et al.* (1997), who illustrate psychodynamic group work that consists on the one hand of an unstructured discussion format, and interpretation of unconscious content, but also includes, as the authors point out '...subtle but essential forms of structure...' (p.375). These involved a good deal of attention by the therapists to questions of physical and psychological boundaries. The creation of such structure and boundaries, far from being anathema to the group-analytic way of thinking, is natural to the good functioning of any group where diversity is valued. Just as differences between members produces therapeutic learning about the 'other', so contributions from 'other' forms of therapy should in principle enrich the group experience. This integrated view provides the flexibility to use creative forms of thera-peutic work as and when needed, for example the model of Group-Analytic Drama outlined by Willis (1988).

Foulkes' Principle: Communication as the therapeutic process

When Foulkes brought his patients together, he encouraged them to com-municate as freely as possible, an equivalent to Freud's free association method. Foulkes observed that the group's associations were made on the basis of intuitive or unconscious understanding of each other. They had the value of interpretation of unconscious material. Communication became central to Foulkes' theory; he regarded symptoms as failed attempts at com-munication (he used the term 'autistic' in a loose, but evocative sense) (Foulkes and Anthony 1957, p.246). Like Freud he regarded symptoms as compromise solutions to internal conflict, the meaning of which could be traced back to origins which were kept out of consciousness, i.e. out of com-munication. The young person who has abused usually finds his own actions unspeakable, to himself and as well with others. As group members open up about themselves they begin to develop an understanding of one another, which leads to the possibility of change in their understanding of themselves. Foulkes called this 'ego training in action' (Foulkes 1964, p.82) and here there is a difference with Freud in that this view of therapeutic change does not necessarily require insight. In fact, Foulkes proposed that insight follows change, rather than vice versa. In other words, communication with others, in a social sphere, promotes internal connections and different aspects of the self are brought into touch with one another.

Open communication has special significance with this patient group because the secrecy and cognitive distortions around abuse depend on blocked communication. Those obstacles can be remedied by re-establishing vital connections between people and between parts of themselves. Denial, in varying degrees, is of course common among perpetrators, whether it be calculated concealment of the truth, or a withdrawal into a shut-down world of resentment, losing contact with others, the endpoint of which is imprisonment. In these cases the individual shuts off awareness of what he has done and is aware only of what has been done to him. As we saw with Bentovim's model in Chapter 2, it is important for the confirmed abuser to prevent communication between members of the trauma-organised family as much as it is to prevent any of them communicating with the outside world. To reverse this pattern a young person needs to be open not only with others but to ensure that traumatised and needy parts of himself remain in touch with other aspects that organise his relationship with others. For these reasons we can see that the development of deeper and more meaningful communication can be seen as an antidote, if not a cure, for abuse.

But is communication enough? The spectre of the abuse of therapy is never far away: does one group member's understanding of another's vulnerability simply produce a more sophisticated abuser? The therapist too may want to avoid unpleasant realities and we may not want to know too much about what is on the mind of someone who may have committed many sexual assaults. If we suspect from our contact with a young person that he holds a belief which will eventually be revealed, that it is perfectly all right for young children to be inveigled or otherwise forced into sexual activity with an older and more powerful person, then we may have to overcome a resistance in ourselves to confront this. The extent to which he will be able to question his own beliefs is also a matter for selection, just as there is a judgement about the capacity of the group to tolerate questioning of their own secret beliefs, as opposed to their tendency to collude with a perversion of the treatment. As is often the case, this is more than a technical issue; it touches on the theoretical question of whether we believe that change can occur through an insight-oriented psychodynamic intervention, or through a form of social control albeit based on psychological understanding of abuse/abusing pattern.

The aim of group-analytic treatment is, therefore, to produce as much communication as possible, about areas of experience previously inaccessible, due either to traumatic reactions against past events, or to more current feelings of shame and fear. Work toward such new communications may not produce behavioural improvement, at least in the short term, and so, just as in individual work, it must go hand in hand with constant attention to management, which in turn depends on communication with other responsible adults.

To illustrate some of these points this is a sequence from a therapy group in a residential unit:

> Michael, a younger boy has complained that he feels bullied by Jerry, and James, two of the older ones; Jerry says, 'We were only teasing, what's the matter with you, can't you take a joke?' he sneers contemptuously.
>
> The therapist asks the group, 'But does the person being teased think it's a joke?' Derek says, 'Well, I think it's abusive because Jerry and James put down people smaller than themselves.' Jerry and James start to protest but the therapist says, 'But look, this is perhaps a bit like sexual abuse, isn't it?'
>
> Jerry says, 'No, that's stupid. Anyway, it's not such a bad thing to have sex with children, it don't hurt them. I just pretended it was wrong to get in here, it's more cushy than secure unit. But as long as you don't hurt a child, in fact I liked it when my cousin first showed me.'
>
> Therapist: 'And how old were you?'
>
> 'I dunno, five or six.'
>
> Derek says, 'Well there you are, you don't know, how could you know? Maybe you learned to like it. I learned to say I liked it, even to myself, when really I didn't. But I wish it never happened and you would too if you thought about it.'

Some technical questions

The setting

Practitioners will find that a fairly tight control is required for such a group as this; the first steps consist in establishing the setting in terms of structure, of time, place, etc., and expectations of behaviour, commitment to attend for a given period, the reason why they are there (which is explicitly to correct their sexually abusive behaviour) and ground rules (of which there is really only one: no harm is allowed to anyone). It is essential to have escorts provided, preferably by the social services department who will have responsibility for this young person. The risks entailed if these young people get together outside their sessions, are unacceptable. The achievement of reliable attendance requires constant negotiation particularly as young people grow older, since it so often happens that they are handed on to other social services teams or organisations without information or planning.

As discussed already an important feature of treatment is the need for therapists to have more exchange of information with other professionals than would normally be the case for someone in therapy. The group may need to made aware, particularly at the early stages of treatment, that this arises from the purpose of the treatment. Group members may not like this but generally they accept its necessity. Information relating to offences, old or new, must be communicated between adults, although respect can also be agreed for relative privacy of what goes on in the session. Communication with outside agencies may involve the therapists directly, though is best conducted by colleagues who remain in contact with the professional network.

The group therapist also needs to be concerned with administrative matters such as the attendance of group members. Incidents at the boundary of the group can be seen to have enormous impact on young people (Behr 1988, p.120). It is easy to feel defeated by the inconsistency of agencies who have referred and have undertaken to support group attendance. Sometimes it seems extraordinarily difficult for professionals who may well be concerned about an adolescent in trouble to actually get him to regular weekly appointments without mishap. Cancellations due to all sorts of reasons – escorts not available, unwell, forgot, got lost, mixed up, etc., etc., – are common and have to be worked with in the group as well with other agencies. If his attendance at the group becomes irregular, often through no fault of his own, the young person becomes disillusioned, negativistic, and it begins to seem that the disappointment over the therapy is going to produce precisely the opposite of the intended effect. Although the group therapist may not have direct responsibility for these arrangements, treatment should not be undertaken if the network does not seem to have sufficient will or capacity to support it. Vulnerable young people can easily feel that once again the adult world cares little, and this then leads to a justification for delinquent, or even abusive, acts. When it works, the group session can become a connecting point for a young person who at last can express some of his pain and anger, finally to people who will listen.

Paying attention in this way to the setting leads naturally to all participants holding in mind a dual perspective, or perhaps better to say figure and ground, that a 'young abuser' is also a 'child in need'. Both the abuse and the abusing can only be understood in relation to one another. When joining, the group members are asked to say what it was they had done to get them into treatment. Young males seem to have more difficulty talking about the abuse against them, and it is perhaps best to leave this aspect of the problem to emerge in its own time during the course of the therapy. This contrasts with reports from adult offender groups, where it seems that such victimisation can be employed, more often than not, in order to avoid responsibility for what the group member has done. This is not to say that young people do not try to avoid talking about their offences; being not yet adults they need from time to time to be reminded why they are there.

It is important for therapists to clarify to the group that they are interested in the rest of the young people's lives, and will make space in the group session for reflection on relationships with family, or other carers, education, and work prospects, but never to the exclusion of the offences, the implications of which should regularly be brought into discussion. This boundary setting, and continual reinforcement, is to do with social control, and perhaps at some points group members have little emotional engagement with each other, but they do have a choice whether to accept their treatment on the basis of adult authority, or to leave the group. At the outset the group might seem to have little intrinsic value to the young person; he may be relieved that he is there rather than locked up, or he may also be resentful and feel forced to attend. This treatment may well have felt like 'an offer that cannot be refused'. However, experience seems to show that for the majority at least, the group gradually acquires an importance to them and it is through this development that the therapy begins to offer some hope of change. We can expect that each will project on to the others the unwelcome aspects of himself, whether that be victim, or perpetrator. As group members begin to see each other they may not like what they see, and as they begin to see themselves as they are seen, they may not like what is being seen. Referring back to the initial agreements about the setting of the group will help weather those storms.

The therapeutic team

It is a truism that therapy for a young person cannot take place in isolation but attention is seldom paid to the therapist's need for a cohesive group of professionals; this will include those who attend the sessions for young people, colleagues in touch with staff from social services, education, family, fostering and residential placements, senior colleagues who can offer consultation or supervision. This larger group will also include other staff of the unit where the treatment is taking place, since the group meeting will inevitably be having some impact on other people's work. The terms of agreement about the common sense of purpose, and a toleration of differences is crucial to the fate of the project.

It also needs to be remembered that child protection issues are very likely to come up during treatment and that therapists bear as much of a responsibility as social workers to take the action of at least communicating their concerns when a child is at risk of harm. Splits between professionals who have statutory responsibility, as opposed to those who are carrying out the therapy, will destroy the benefits that should come to the young people from this treatment. Planning the groupwork programme should include clear lines of communication with colleagues outside the treatment team.

Supervision, or consultation, that is to say, a non-line management, and reflective discussion about the work in hand, is important for therapists to process the projections that are drawn out on all sides in psychodynamic treatment. This is particularly so in the case of work with these young people who are both perpetrators and yet still so close to being victims; the rapid switch between the two can be bewildering in its intensity and complexity. Typically each therapist will identify with one aspect of this duality and become opposed to the other. In group work there is the additional risk factor that if therapists lose track of what they are doing, and the group goes off the rails, the results can quickly be disastrous. Supervision by someone already experienced in this work may be hard to find, but should be provided by an analytic therapist who starts out from a position of offering support of a psychodynamic kind, acknowledging that there are no preordained methods, and that the therapists are probably doing the best they can and need help in thinking their way through to keeping to their complex task. 'Analysing' the therapists motivations and defences will not be helpful, but as each co-therapist will have different responses to the group, and different ideas about how the group should be conducted, it is their working relationship that need to be explored. The therapeutic team as a whole will need help in tolerating the emotional stress of the work. A finely tuned balance needs to be achieved between action and thought. Therapists may not know what to do in a given situation, nor indeed may their supervisor, but each should instead be able to recall to mind the values that bind the team, in order to reorientate the work. These principles will include the containment of the young people, and the continuation of the task, to explore the offending behaviour in the context of the young person's own trauma. If an overall aim is the self-regulation described by Friedrich (1995) then this will be found to be achievable in the group context, especially if the therapists find their own self regulation via the therapeutic team of which they are members.

The therapist's role
Foulkes (1975) emphasised the responsibility of the therapist for administering the group environment. He placed more therapeutic significance on this than upon transference interpretations (Foulkes 1975, pp.99–157). With adolescents it is often the physical aspects of the setting that become highlighted as they test limits with challenging behaviour. Despite appearances to the contrary, this is often about the need for young people to feel secure enough to express their vulnerability. It is important for the therapist(s) therefore to ensure that the setting is safe, and seen to be safe. Putting feet on the table might seem a trivial matter, and for the therapist to be repeatedly commenting on members leaning back in their chair might seem tiresome, but it is also true that, if a boy can accept a limit to those impulses (and express his irritation in an appropriate way), then he might be more amenable to curbing his impulse to punch a fellow group member in the face (and yet speak about his anger). There need to be clear rules about conduct for the young people, and about the consequences of ignoring

them. Excluding someone from the group goes against the grain for most psychotherapists, but time out in the waiting room (with of course the escort), or failing that, a referral back to the social work agency who brought him to treatment, may be the most helpful thing for him. Clear agreements should be made between the therapists about limits of acceptable behaviour. It will be seen that arrangements for the waiting area are important as this can become the venue either for delinquent acting-out or preferably some appropriate socialisation.

Apart from these 'management' functions, psychodynamic as they may be in their implications, what else should the therapists be doing? Surely they should be making interpretations, and helping group members to achieve what in the classical Freudian formulation is the aim of psychodynamic treatment, that of making conscious what was before unconscious. In Foulkes' view the main duty of the group conductor is somewhat different, to make interventions only insofar as they would facilitate the process of communication. Transference interpretations especially should be made only when these appear necessary to unblock communication (Foulkes 1975, p.112). The overall aim here is to model open communication and to have available some deeper understanding that will derive from the psychoanalytic basis of the therapist's understanding, for example that hatred and anger may be met by addressing emotional pain, or that shame rather than deviance may be preventing a young person from speaking out. The therapist should definitely avoid presenting an image of someone who is remote and unresponsive, emerging from silence only to make 'deep' interpretations of unconscious content that will appear to these young people obscure, meaningless or at worst, completely mad. The opposite extreme, that of an educational model, is one on which the therapist only feeds in the 'right' attitudes and explain the theory of abusive behaviour even to the extent of using the jargon of 'cognitive distortion', 'victim empathy', etc. Somewhere between these two ends of the spectrum is an optimal level of responsiveness by the therapist to spontaneous expression of the boys' thoughts and feeling, but in the context of a structure and clear expectations of the group.

A young person who has abused is very likely, to perceive adults as either severe punishers, or corrupt and covert abusers themselves, or indeed a complex combination of these contradictory characteristics. Such negative transferences are crucial to the relative effectiveness of the group and need to be worked with. Exactly how these factors can be utilised to therapeutic advantage will depend on the individual style of the therapist, but no therapist can afford to ignore their importance. Excessive attention to expressions of hostility and over-interpreting negative transference will produce increased resistance and eventual disintegration of the group. A therapist may more usefully make comments that reflect the ambivalence of the young person who knows he needs help, but at the same time wishes to protect himself from the pain that receiving help inevitably entails. Difficult as it may be to see anything positive in the acts of sexual abuse, it is worth recalling Winnicott's (1958a) concept of the Anti-Social Tendency. Winnicott found something more in the adolescent's attacks on his environment than simply the release of destructive intention. He thought that there was an unconscious hope of achieving the emotional gratification that had been previously denied, that there was a desire to have something that could be translated by an understanding adult into the need for human contact and meaningful interaction (Winnicott 1958a, p.314). There is a danger in the pressurised atmosphere of the group that the therapist might become too much identified with a force for social control. The group therapist needs to find ways of catching hold of the healthy aspects of a young abuser's personality. To give an idea of this combination of confrontation and understanding here is a brief sequence from a group session:

> Gary is complaining again about his 'girlfriend' 'dumping' him. (By this the therapists understood that a girl he had seen at college was paying him no attention.) 'She can't do that! It's totally out of order...she is not going to...if she thinks she can do that...'. He glances at the therapists as if concealing (but also conveying) his aggressive thoughts.) JS (the female therapist) said, 'It's very upsetting when you can't get what you want isn't it?'
>
> 'Yes,' said Gary, 'I feel like doing something...'.
>
> Ali, another boy who had assaulted pubertal girls, said leeringly, 'Yeah, go on...give her one! She deserves it!' But Will protested, 'No, you shouldn't, why don't you just move on...if you do something nasty you will only get into trouble...'.
>
> 'I don't care,' said Gary. He looks at the therapist, and says, indignantly, 'You don't understand, no-one dumps me!'
>
> JW (the male therapist) said, 'Yes, you have to be a real man to take it, otherwise what are you? If you assault a girl, what are you?'

Will said 'You are an abuser, if you do that.'

'Is that what you are, Gary?', continued the male therapist. 'You keep telling us you are not.'

'I'm not, I'm not…oh, alright…I won't do anything, I just won't talk to her any more, it's her loss!'

Foulkes (1975, pp.157–8) encouraged the group conductor above all to be true to himself, in other words perhaps, to be open as much as possible to the use of countertransference. However, the personal reactions that an adult has to a young person who has sexually abused may be problematic. This will continue to be important at various stages. Whilst it may not be too difficult to maintain a professional stance early on, saying in effect 'I may reject what you have done, but you as a person I can value', this will take us only so far. Once again, it must be recalled that it is impossible for a therapist to be neutral on questions of child abuse. A narrow path has to be trodden, however, because the therapist who is too ready to present the official, or superego view, is going to inhibit the expression of psychological truth by the group members. This is less of a pressure in 'one to one' therapy where the therapist can be more private with their own feelings. The male therapist above felt anxious and also critical of Gary. Fortunately this was contained and modified by both his co-therapist and group members. A skill that is gradually acquired in the practice of group therapy is to model openness to the group members, by presenting the therapist's own feelings in a useful way, that group members can accept.

Co-therapy
There is a general preference for co-therapy in groupwork of this kind. One set of considerations is pragmatic, that is, the sharing of tasks of assessment, liaison and dynamic administration, such as managing the group if one adult has to leave the room for whatever reason, or if a therapist is away. But pre- and post-group discussion between therapists becomes an essential means of thinking about the group, processing feelings that are stirred up, and planning for progress in the therapy (Barratt and Segal 1996, p.27). Given that so much goes on in a group, one person is bound to notice things missed by the other. Male and female co-workers seem to 'hear' different things. There are also going to be personality differences in the therapists, and so differing views will develop of what has happened and what should

be happening in the group. This can possibly lead to splits between the therapists. Given also the level of rivalry and conflict between group members, there may also be a polarisation of feelings between the therapists. Westman (1996) describes how co-therapists may come close to being split, but need to work on their differences, in order to resolve complex transference issues in the group. By splitting the transference, or dividing ambivalent feelings about the therapists, a group member can find his hostility, and fears directed to one, whilst the other seems to be 'the good one'. Differences in the personalities of the therapists can lead to complementary roles, as long as they do not become rigid and exclusive of the other. In this way the co-therapy couple can model a process of co-operation and resolution of conflict. This could become a kind of 're-parenting' process for those whose parents could not negotiate a tolerable relationship with one another. Westman (1996) goes on to show how co-therapists can work together, on their own differences, in the context of a shared philosophy and sense of purpose. Naturally the joint supervision should be directed toward this goal. (See below for an illustration of this.)

Gender differences can be very usefully explored with a mixed pair of therapists; the male might well be expected by these boys to have the dominant role, although their experience will most likely have been that of an absent father and a mother who has had to manage the best she can. Often the father is to be feared not only for his aggression against the child, but as much for his threatened departure. The fear of father is perhaps more to do with abandonment than the classical notion of castration anxiety. There is thus a wariness of him which does not usually apply to the female co-therapist who tends to evoke feelings associated with the mother, who is needed and relied upon, though also hated, partly because of her failure to produce the wished-for father who could, it is hoped, provide the much needed model of secure masculinity. Contempt for women is often to be found as an important factor in sexually abusive patterns. Women may also be despised because of their special value for father; in attacking the woman a boy who is insecure about his masculinity is attempting often to repudiate fears of homosexual wishes. The hostility to mother (often disguised) is of course multi-determined, fuelled also by resentment for the failures of mothering in the boy's early life.

At the beginning of a session two boys were sniggering at sexual jokes that clearly conveyed aggression toward women. JW notices that his colleague JS looks uncomfortable. JW says, 'I don't like what you are saying here.'

'It's only a joke!' protest the boys somewhat contemptuously.

'Well, I don't think it's funny and you should think where such jokes will lead you.'

They carry on muttering to each other, giggling and glancing at the rest of the group, who are trying to discuss someone's serious matter. Eventually JS says sharply, 'This is not acceptable! This is a group and you are here to take part and if you are going to carry on like this you can leave now!' She stands and opens the door. The two boys apologise and say they will join in the group discussion, which they do.

The use of the female therapist's anger here was crucial in this effective intervention. Whereas the male therapist tried to put his foot down, the fact that it was a female seemed to have more meaning for the young people who were compelled to recognise her right to respect. She reminded them that they had a choice to remain, or not, which led to their own restraint. She in effect undid an important component of their abusive impulses, a pattern in which they can feel bullied and therefore justified in their attacks. Behind these manifestations there is a vast reservoir of hostility and pathogenic family influences that have to be contained and processed by the co-therapy couple who are tested sometimes to the utmost in their to ability to construct and maintain a good working relationship.

The group had been going through a difficult period, with the male therapist particularly feeling that that the group was becoming anti-therapeutic and that the adults authority was being undermined by a delinquent sub-culture, initiated by one member, Gary; but whereas JW felt that Gary was in the wrong place, and that he should leave the group, JS felt that not all avenues of work with him had yet been explored; she felt that Gary, like the others, needed to be able to express hostile feelings. If he were to be rejected from this group, this would in her view be anti-therapeutic. This particular issue evoked also a longstanding difference of opinion (usually contained), in which the two therapists debated the extent to which offence-focused, structured activities should be fostered, as against space provided in the group for the young people to express their feelings. Supervision did not for a time help resolve this conflict, with each therapist complaining of being frustrated and even bullied by the other. None of this had been openly expressed to the group, though in retrospect the group members may have been affected. In one group session at this time there were suddenly a lot of questions to JS:

'Have you got a pet?' asked Gary.

'No, she is too cruel,' Martin said.

Gary peered at her: 'I could make you cry!'

JW intervened: 'Maybe you can speak your thoughts without being abusive, Gary. Let's think why you should wish to make someone cry? And who is being too cruel…?'

But Gary chooses to shut down. Eventually he then spoke of a time when he had hurt a female teacher and made her cry. Perhaps, he said, this was unfair, and said he felt very sorry. JS spoke about his need to blame someone for the split-up of his parents. Later we shared the support felt by each other in being a couple of therapists together able to make sense of Gary's hostility.

Selection for group

Gary liked coming to his group sessions because he had been excluded from school and was doing nothing all day while his mum was out at work. Neither Education nor Social services could come up with alternative activities. However, it was also an opportunity for him to form an alliance based on delinquent interests with another boy in the group with whom he was making plans for burglary and other forms of stealing. On being confronted about this by the therapists, he maintained that it was nothing to do with the reason he was in the group, which was one sexual assault. Despite his initial acceptance of responsibility for his offences, he reduced any emotional engagement or willingness to explore what he had done. In and around group sessions he made many asides of 'sexist' and pseudo-macho remarks that were also evidence of rape fantasies. These proved impossible to discuss with him in the group. The therapists eventually sought alternative treatment for him.

This unhappy situation caused problems for the rest of the group as well as delaying appropriate treatment for Gary. It was a failure at the selection stage, because the therapists had themselves been doubtful about Gary's suitability, but were in a hurry to make up numbers and begin their group. The episode highlights several questions about the assessment of individuals for group work. The questions are complex in practice, because the decision is not only about the suitability of an individual but has to be based on the character and capacities of the particular group for which the assessment is being made. Some groups may be more able to tolerate and absorb attacks than others, and this is of course difficult to predict in the case of a new group.

A contributory factor in the case just described was the compulsory nature of the treatment. Group therapists in general are cautious about providing therapy where there is an element of compulsion (Jacobs *et al.* 1988, pp.287–8). Mandatory treatment is discussed elsewhere (Chapters 1, 2 and 7) in the context of individual work. In group therapy the problem is compounded, in that the group may make greater demands upon the ego strength of the young person, and may reinforce certain defences, and therefore increase resistance to treatment. With the justification that he is expected to submit to what he perceives as a corrupt authority, the recalcitrant youngster has the additional leverage, as was happening above, of taking the rest of the group with him.

Which young people then are more suitable for group therapy? Ginott (1961) a pioneer in child group therapy, wrote of 'social hunger' as an important indication for group treatment, and this remains a useful criterion, though our means of measuring it may be more of an art than a science; that is to say, the careful use of countertransference. Does the assessing therapist have a sense that this boy will open up with others, and feel some relief from the painful isolation that his situation will most likely have brought him? There is a certain amount of self-selection in this process because some young people will baulk at the idea of being part of a group and others will absolutely refuse, which must be respected. In other cases the clinician may have to make a decision that the adolescent needs something other than a place in a group. Clinical experience suggests that an adolescent with more severe psychopathology and/or additional problems is probably best worked with on a one-to-one basis (Print and O'Callaghan 1999; Vizard and Usiskin 1999).

Probably the most useful therapeutic criterion is the level at which a young person is able to be in touch with his own victimisation. This is what leads to responsibility, victim empathy and eventually to the kind of maturity that guards against the abuse of others. The more questionable case may need an extended individual assessment. Working with resistance depends greatly on the use of countertransference, and beyond a certain degree this is more manageable in one-to-one treatment. Balbernie (1994) undertook a review of the long-term effects of child sexual abuse and found much evidence for damage to the capacity to make relationships of a non-abusive kind. If the abused/abuser has to remain totally unaware of the effects of his own abuse, it is difficult for him to feel there is a possibility of hope, which was Yalom's basic requirement for the beginning group therapy (Yalom 1970, pp.6–7). Individual treatment may make it easier for the therapist to be the one who carries hope, at least for a time. Ultimately the effectiveness of any treatment will depend on the adolescent's strength to withstand his inner pain, rather than inflict it on others. He will need to be able to mourn the childhood he has lost, or perhaps never had, and to begin to make some kind of reparation for the harm he has done, and the two are intimately connected. The assessing therapist's responses will provide information as to whether the young person genuinely has this capacity. Is the response one of compassion for this boy's predicament, or does a hardened cynicism in the young person induce hopelessness in the therapist?

PART II: A TREATMENT GROUP

The groupwork presented here lasted three years. The group was conducted by the author and a female co-therapist (JS). The boys, aged between 15 and 17 when they were first referred, had all made sexual assaults on other children, though only two had been formally charged. All had themselves been sexually abused. All had had disrupted family lives, with the majority living with mother and siblings, one in foster care, and two in residential care. All had learning difficulties. There was an average racial and ethnic mix. A total of seven boys were seen in the group with only five completing the course; one boy early on asked for individual treatment, which was provided by another therapist, and another was asked to leave after a year, because he had reoffended and showed no willingness to talk about his problem in the group.

Introduction: Group development

In an early session Martin was causing concern to the therapists because he avoided contact with group members, complying only with the minimum requirements of therapy. His style of abusing consisted of targeting younger boys in his special school or residential unit, and making subtle and passive invitations to sexual activity, with no overt coercion. The therapists agreed that some role play exercises might be useful in 'bringing him out'. Six months later he was much more overt in his hostility to the therapists, calling them stupid, and so on. He said that the group was 'rubbish', but made no protest about attendance, which was a requirement of his boarding school. Six months later Martin was still reluctant to talk about his own problems, but when another member, Gary, was absent for a couple of weeks Martin said that he missed him and was worried about Gary, because 'he needs help with his sexual problem'.

The development of an individual member's self-awareness can be facilitated by the context of group development. The study of group development, for example by Agazarian (1994), shows how an ambivalent dependency on the leader gradually gives way to more autonomous functioning and the use of the leader as guide rather than oppressor. The therapist should aim to build confidence in the group, by regulating the amount of exposure that an individual feels able to tolerate. This means managing transference manifestations, since the group will tend to recreate the abusive father/neglectful mother environment and this cannot be entirely avoided. However, the pressure from the group to provoke therapists to be authoritarian can be utilised by presenting a more democratic form of leadership in which each individual's rights are respected. The creation of a group culture of inquiry, of allowing everyone their say, and a shared value of non-abusive interaction might be to some extent imposed by the adults, and artificially agreed upon at first, but gradually is taken on by group members. This process of working through takes place via the transference of members not only to those adults but to the group as well. Hostility is difficult for thera-

pists and for group members, but working with it produces change in all
sorts of directions.

Thus, the aim is to create conditions where concern for others becomes
more desirable than the abusive state of mind. At first this may need to be
modelled by the therapists:

> The boys at this point were trying their hand at making up their own
> plays. The plot proposed by Will, was as follows: 'Jim' is trying to get
> his parents' attention. The mum, played by the female therapist, was
> watching TV with her other children, all but one of the other group
> members. Jim (played by Will) wants to tell his mum that he has been
> thrown out of school for stealing and violence, but she does not hear.
> He goes to his room. The police (played by the male therapist and
> another group member) come to the door and demand to see him. Will
> hears them and escapes through a window. He darts dangerously over
> the rooftops and hides in the freezing cold until the police catch him,
> beat him and throw him into jail. It was left to the therapists to bring in
> other developments to the story, that the mother eventually goes to the
> police, that a lawyer was called and so on.

Before the group internalises this kind of development through narrative,
much work needs to be done on the relationships created in the group.

Early stages in a group for adolescent abusers with learning difficulties: 'Malignant mirroring'

> Gary started a discussion about a child in the news who had been
> abducted, and not yet been found (it was very much in the therapists'
> mind that Gary had attempted to abduct a child) and went on to
> mention the tabloid newspapers beginning to 'name and shame'
> people on the sex offenders register who might fall under suspicion.
> Simon was angry at this and said that it was very unfair, and that he had
> only just escaped being on the offenders register because of his age,
> and that he should not be in a group with 'child molesters'. 'They are
> the ones who should be on the register!' The therapist asked whether
> Simon thought that sexually assaulting a teenage girl was really less
> bad than assaulting a boy. 'Yes', said Simon, 'at least I'm not queer',
> referring to the fact that some of the boys had sexually assaulted other

boys. The male therapist was going to pursue this further (perhaps, we thought later, it was a product of Simon's own experiences of having been a little boy assaulted by an older male) when the group was taken over by Peter who was mimicking the others, but because of his speech difficulty was making no more than grunting sounds. Gary and Simon banded together in their threats to Peter who should shut up they said, 'because he's stupid!' Gary got up and made as if to punch him, and the female therapist said that Peter finds it difficult in this group because he perhaps gets anxious when others are angry. Gary sat down but the whole pattern repeated itself, so the therapists decided to bring in an exercise they had prepared called 'traffic lights'. This involved questions by the therapists as to whether a given situation, for example, going to a swimming pool, would get a 'green light', amber, or red from each group member, according to whether they thought it was OK, had some risk, or was too dangerous to do. (For similar exercises see publications by Safer Society, e.g. Kahn 1990; Cunningham and McFarlane 1991).

In the classic paper, 'Malignant Mirroring', Zinkin (1983) spoke about the unbearable experience sometimes of seeing one's own worst characteristics in someone else, an event akin to that described in the myth of the *Doppelgänger*, which is felt to be a harbinger of death. In these cases the other has to be destroyed before the feared annihilation takes place. These boys may not have met other abusers except of course when they were in the position of the victim. These complex feelings of victimisation are going to be aroused. As the young person takes on board the fact that he is one of these who have offended, he may be horrified by what he sees in himself. It is as well to remember the traumatic effect that the act of abuse sometimes has on the abuser himself, another twist in the interaction between victim and abuser in the same person. The task of the therapist at this point is to facilitate the move away from the malignant mirroring toward a more benign perception of the self through the eyes of the other. This is not always easy, especially if the group has an investment, more or less consciously, in destroying the whole treatment, which is exacerbated if young people are there under some degree of coercion. Group therapists need to actively and constantly discourage hostile projections between group members and explicitly encourage communications that contribute to the sharing of life experience. This is a sequence from a later stage in the group's life:

> The therapists brought in their knowledge that Martin, unsupervised momentarily in the toilet at his residential placement, had been touching the penis of a younger boy. He shrugged off the importance of this, saying it was not bad, because the other boy, though under age, had 'wanted to do it'. The therapists asked for opinions from the rest of the group. Ali said that Martin should go 'straight to prison!' This made Martin dig his heels in even more. However, Will said that Martin really should think about all this because if he goes on sexually abusing then he would be doing the same as what had been done to him. Will went on to tell for the first time in any detail how dirty and repulsive he felt he was for going along with sex with an older boy. He said that he wished he had never gone on to do it to younger boys, because he wished it had never happened to him. There was a thoughtful silence (a somewhat unusual event in the group) and though Martin did not respond it seemed an opportunity for him to think about what had been shown him by Will.

Imitation as a basis for group relating

Over several months we went through a phase of desperate copying, where certain group members who had more 'street credibility' would be slavishly imitated by the others in the most naïve terms, from similar stories of events in the week, down to style of speech and so on. If one claimed to have a mobile phone, then the others pretended likewise; they vied with each other in fantasies of girlfriends, brushes with the police, etc. So out of touch with reality did these seem that they were questioned by the therapists, but this often produced infantile tantrums that threatened to become violent. The need to imitate was also sometimes more constructively expressed in repetitive games such as ordering and re-ordering boxes of toys. At other times there were attempts at incorporating the attributes of the male therapist, for example, his bike or his way of speaking, perhaps as a means of obtaining his perceived power in the group, and especially his privileged position with the female co-therapist. However, as these patterns were taken up by the two therapists we also sensed how important it was that the boys in the group did not feel that their desires were ridiculed or crushed, but seen as their desperate need for connectedness, respect, and being valued.

The mirror theme changes perhaps because, as self-knowledge dawns, there is an increased awareness of vulnerability. Anxiety becomes at times more acute. In an adult group this would perhaps lead to greater dependence on the transference object of the therapist, and improved access to the group members' emotional lives, but such 'healthy' regression conflicts with an adolescent's need for separation and repudiation of adult authority. What is natural for a group of young people such as these, especially those with learning disability, is to use that very basic attribute of the human being's capacity to process experience, play. The desire to imitate is of course the basis of early forms of play and ultimately became very productive in this particular group's evolution as they invented games and dramas. The repetitive quality of play, just as much as its profound meaning, was first noted by Freud (1920, pp.14–15) in his observation of a child's play, throwing and pulling the cotton reel, the 'fort-da' game, which seemed, in Freud's view, linked to mother's absence and wished-for return. In terms of the psychic economy games are a way of reducing overstimulation whether that be pleasurable of painful. Repetition is much to do with mastery of potentially or actually traumatic experiences.

Creativity as a pathway to treatment

As the group learned to play together, their interaction and communication with each other became more valuable to them than adolescent status symbols, and for the therapists, more valuable than social control, and 'good behaviour'. For each group member this meant that being with people who understood became more important than the shoring-up of their defensive system. This shift became possible primarily by means of creativity. Play and fantasy are the precursors and also the ingredients of creativity. Here are some scenes from the creative period of this therapy group:

> The use of drama had originally been initiated by the therapists who wished early on to illustrate some therapeutic points such as the difference between aggression and appropriate assertiveness. Group members, who had always found it difficult to tolerate the anxiety of sitting in a circle and communicating with each other, had enjoyed

these little scenarios. They sought permission to make up their own plays. For several sessions, on and off, these represented adult work settings: for example, a delivery service, which had to organise parcels to go to families with presents for Christmas. The dynamics of these 'work groups' clearly represented issues of leadership within the 'real' group, and conveyed a sense of there being a place for everyone despite their apparent disability. The more able tended to compete for the position of 'the Manager' but, because it was 'only play', each could tolerate others having a role. However, there were also situations that reflected the boys' anxieties; people were sacked, for inefficiency, or theft, and this led on to many sessions where the preoccupations became those of crime and punishment. These could be linked in discussion after the play, to questions about abuse.

This group enacted many stories of 'cops and robbers', and the work done on the imagined crime and punishment was clearly a reworking of their painful experiences of offences both by and against them. The stories rarely concerned direct questions of child sexual abuse; rather they were about burglaries, street robberies, murders. Often a play was demanded by the group as a way of escaping the anxiety of sitting and discussing in the circle. The therapists had to struggle sometimes with boredom at the slow pace, or a sense of alienation at repetitive phases, but to have interpreted much of this play as disguises or defences against themes of child abuse would have been premature and counterproductive. This might sound contradictory to the main principle previously emphasised, of offence-focused work, but as Anne Alvarez indicates (see Chapter 10), there is a danger of interfering with the beginning process of symbolisation.

At a later stage, where a pizza restaurant was the location, the male co-therapist was asked to play a Health and Safety inspector who was to find the restaurant unclean and the management guilty of exploiting its workers (this despite having, as they said, the best cook in the world, the female co-therapist!). The manager then called a meeting and told his 'employees' that the restaurant was going to be shut down. The transference implications of this seemed clear since it was only shortly before that the group had been informed of its ending date, more than a year hence, but clearly evoking anxiety about the possible reasons for its being 'shut down'. Thus, the group was able to express anxieties about their dirtiness or abusiveness being the cause of the group's ending.

Links would be made in the post-play discussion, but often it seemed that it was the expression of these dynamics that was most important to the group rather than our interpretations.

In the ensuing months the two therapists were frequently allocated parts of parents who happened also to be criminals, drug dealers, robbers, who severely neglected their children. The young people of the group often took the roles of police officers, who brought the parental figures to trial or put them in prison. Throughout these times it seemed particularly important that the male and female co-therapist (whom the group imagined to be in a sexual relationship) should model a partnership of mutual respect and valuation including their differences.

Splitting the parents was a common theme, and could be expressed in ways that did not threaten the existence of the group. For example, the therapists in the role of parents would be put in separate cells, 'no talking allowed!' On one occasion, the 'script' (always improvised) called for a quarrel, and the delight of the group in hearing the therapists simulating a typical marital row meant that we had to repeat the scene several times.

This play clearly expressed, so it seemed to us, something more than the boys' despair at knowing they had parents who had significantly failed them, and never been brought to justice. It is interesting to note again the contrast with an adult group for perpetrators, where the anger and blame directed at the parents could easily be regarded as an evasion of responsibility. Expressing the need, however, that these parents be brought to account also meant for these young people that now those parents could no longer be regarded as being an excuse for the boys' own wrongdoing. As their view of parents became integrated, so they could accept badness and goodness in themselves rather than be split in their awareness of themselves and so remain in denial.

Discussion: The relative value of fantasy and creativity

Despite, or perhaps because of, these youngsters' very limited facility with intellectual or verbal skills, we found that this group had a powerful fantasy life. Perhaps when reality is so full of disappointment, alternative gratifications become more significant. Denial is of course partly dependent on fantasy. The typical cognitive distortions of the sex offender have an underlying fantasy component: 'it couldn't have been me, it wasn't me, it must have been someone else...that child wanted sex, he didn't really mean it when he said no...'. In less pernicious ways, however, fantasy and day-dreaming can soon be seen to occupy an important place in these young people's lives, lacking as they often are in social and educational stimulation. These are patchy and often pathetic attempts to restore a sense of a loved and loving object available to them. Here perhaps also are the beginnings of addictions to pornography, perversions, or in later life to prostitutes, accompanied by daydreaming and masturbation. These fantasies can be distinguished from true creativity because they mainly consist of the sheer indulging of sexualised aggression, and therefore function partly as a defence against change. The benign aspect of a world of daydreams was likened by Freud to a natural park preserve in which the original state of nature is preserved in pristine form (Freud 1911, p.222). Fantasy gives an opportunity to break from reality, and provide a refuge from trauma. When communicated in social play, and shared with others, the fantasy world has to undergo some modification. There are of course dangers here as when for example the gang mentality takes over and threatens to change reality by force, rather than modify the fantasy. As we know, individuals can do things in a group that would otherwise be impossible. Games are usually highly structured and may contain sometimes very violent impulses. Players can shake hands where only moments before they might have wanted to annihilate each other. When fantasy is translated into play and moves into the realm of communication, there is also much more opportunity for processing trauma and for finding a creative solution to previously indigestible experiences. Play is therefore more than a means of putting outside oneself the most disturbing thoughts and feelings, it is a means of finding competence and self-esteem, and it is a path toward the transformation of experiences that have been traumatic. The group gradually moved away from the repetition of pure wish fulfilment to a more complex expression of the residue of traumatic experience.

A psychoanalytic view of creativity is put forward by Hannah Segal (1991) who points to the wish to restore the loved object, to protect it against the effects of envious, greedy and sadistic attacks emanating from the same self that wishes to preserve something good. Whether destructive attacks on the good object have come from outside or within, the need is the same, and for adolescents who have expressed their sexuality in an abusive fashion, the need for a new identity is urgent. It is often said that sexual abuse is more about power than eroticism, and the task of this group becomes how to establish a non-abusive form of sexual identity. A lot of the imitative behaviour reported above resulted from the desperate search for an adequate male identity. Much of these young people's life-experiences have been actually persecutory; their own abuse and neglect, rejection by family, humiliation and bullying at the hands of the local community and/or school, as well as the vagaries of the social system, will tend to make the young abuser shut down and seal off his feelings about what has happened to him. This will lead him to nurture his resentment and envy of others, thus increasing the risk of his re-offending at a later stage. The task of the therapy group is to provide an opportunity for him to re-experience his connectedness with people, to see himself in a new mirror, as it were, to come to terms with his old identity as an abuser, and to meaningfully change this, not by denial and pretence, but by using what were destructive experiences for new learning at an emotional level.

CONCLUSION: TRAUMA REVIVED IN TOLERABLE DOSES

In Winnicott's (1968) article 'The Use of an Object' he describes how the object can be created as externally real by its survival of destructive attacks, thus placing the object outside the sphere of the individual's omnipotence. Garland (1982) extended the metaphor in an article which showed how the group is created as an externally real object that provides a new experience of freedom from neurotic and repetitive symptomatology. Elsewhere I have proposed that the therapist has to give up a certain omnipotence in order to trust the group to be the source of healing (Woods 1992). If the therapist has faith in the group's creative capacity, this will go a long way to withstanding the undermining that inevitably results from the members own demands that they avoid the psychic pain of the work. The therapeutic task of the group may well be sufficiently hated by group members to be destroyed in the internal world. If, however, the group is perceived still to be there in the external world, having survived the attacks, this experience can be internalised and so revive the group as a therapeutic object in the internal world. This is a process that has perhaps to take place first in the therapist's mind, in his or her conviction that the group will survive, in order to bring the rest along to a position where they can dare hope for a place in a non-abusive world. As a final illustration I give an instance of this particular group's powerful impact on the feelings of the therapist.

> The story had developed from week to week and now required a child abuser be brought to trial. This fictional character James was living with his father whilst mother was in hospital. No group member would volunteer for the part this week, and so JW undertook the role, whilst JS was asked to be an investigating social worker. The other group members took the parts of police officers, teachers, and family members, all of whom presented overwhelming evidence to overcome the denials of the accused. JW in his role of young abuser began to experience the despair of his situation and talked to his 'father' about suicidal feelings. Martin in the role of father tried to comfort 'James' (JW), but also determined that he would stop the boy from killing himself and get the mother back. The 'judge' (group member Will), accepted the guilty plea of the accused and listened to the social worker (JS), who was recommending that James get help. The judge then very seriously said to James (JW) that he had to work hard at his therapy otherwise he *would* be going to prison.

CHAPTER 7

Street Sex Offenders

A number of referrals to the Portman Clinic show a pattern of sexual offending behaviour rather different from that of the young abusers described elsewhere in this book, who will have committed their sexual assaults typically in the home. They may have started offending in the immediate family and moved on to target other children in the extended family or in the neighbourhood. Another type of offender goes for women previously unknown to the boy, carrying out the assault in the open street, in daylight and sometimes in the presence of passers-by. These attacks have consisted of grabbing or hitting the breasts, or buttocks of the women, displaying an erect penis and masturbating, pulling clothes or handbag, 'not that I wanted to steal but to spoil their day', as one boy put it. Eight of these boys were referred in the space of one year (quite independently of each other), all aged 15–17, and, it seems, quite early on in their career of offending. This is fortunate because there are indications of an escalating quality to their offences, which might well have progressed to more calculated and extensive attacks, including rape and more serious physical harm to their victims.

Although based on this very small, no doubt statistically insignificant, sample, the clinical impression is that these boys share a different profile from those who might have abused a younger sibling or cousin. As Bentovim and Williams (1998) established, most young abusers have in general been themselves the victims of abuse, physical or sexual, and may very likely have been exposed to the terrors of violence in the home. These

138

boys' actions can be understood as 'trauma-reactive', i.e. that the perpetrator is inflicting what was done to him on to another. Whereas these boys might have abused in a more extreme way, perhaps with forced penetration, the 'street offenders' make, at this early stage at least, very limited physical contact. The boys who have committed their assaults on the street do not seem to have had such damaging experiences as the other group; they come from apparently intact families, who seem shocked by what has happened and try their best to understand and offer support. Just as the parents seem mystified by what 'must have come over him', so too does the boy seem bemused by the reactions of his victim, or by passers-by who in some cases will have intervened. Although an unsuspecting young woman is regarded as a legitimate target, these boys express outrage at offences against children. So the question is posed: do these young men choose, or are they driven to offend in this particular way?

First of all, some thought should be given to the social context of men's assaults on women. The 'mythology' in culture that surrounds and permits the abuse of women has been the focus of attention in recent years: Moore and Rosenthal (1994, p.75) proposed a strategy to 'resocialise' young men, but later research by Doherty and Anderson (1998) suggests that little change has taken place. 'Why Men Hate Women' (Jukes 1994) offers an analysis of those social attitudes that create a background of power relations that enable men's dominance over women. When women try to resist this, says Jukes, men resort to violence in order to retain the sort of gender -related control that pervades human society. When women are not there to service men's needs, violence is used to bring the woman 'into line' (Jukes 1994, p.xiv). This seems a pessimistic view since, despite sexist attitudes and the alarmingly high incidence of assaults on women, these remain aberrations rather than the norm, and male aggression is more often directed against other males (Gilligan 1996).

Assaulting a woman on the street does not serve a young man's interest in any way. He may achieve a brief moment of excitement, if he grabs a woman's breast, or takes his penis out and masturbates in front of her, but this must soon be dashed by the unpleasant experience of seeing the woman's shock, distaste and rejection; and yet he goes on doing this. There is clearly some pathology that militates against this young offender's interests as much as against the victim's. He will often attempt to minimise the significance of his actions, saying that others do it, joke about it and so forth; but sexist attitudes, like the erotic imagery of advertising, are a constant, a background noise to some, and highlighted by others as justification for their sexualised aggression.

AGGRESSION AND MALE SEXUAL IDENTITY

Kohon (1999) refers to Freud's (1911b) 'On the Universal Debasement of Love'; following Freud, Kohon points out that obstacles seem to heighten libido, and that satisfaction seems to kill desire. Wandering alone in a world, as it were, of prohibition but no boundaries, this kind of offender is filled with desires that have no containment. Lacking in ego capacity to direct his energies, fuelled by resentment that others are better off, his desires turn to aggression. Perhaps his sexuality is not central to the offence, but is used in the service of aggression. By saying to himself, 'I'm powerful, I can do it' (like the advertising slogan used to entice all those who want to 'just do it') he overcomes fears and inhibitions of his own. This chimes in with the despair conveyed by these boys (if eventually they are able to use therapy), that just as their excitement is heightened, so it is destroyed.

In 'Motiveless Malignity', Alvarez (1995), draws upon the work of Meloy (1996). He distinguishes between types of aggression: the 'affectively provoked' and the 'predatory'. The one, an intense reaction to a perceived threat, is quite different from the calculated stalking of a victim who is unaware of the threat posed to them. Predatory aggression is the hallmark of the psychopath, whereas the borderline personality is more prone to outbursts of disorganised aggression, which though unpredictable is usually less dangerous, because it is not an ingrained part of the personality. Alvarez (see Chapter 10 in this volume) refers to a continuum of psychopathy as one in which at the less severe end there may be hope of treatability, before the child embraces the paranoid world of total identification with aggressor.

However, in these boys there is also something intimately bound up with their masculinity and a horror of being found wanting. 'I'll never get a girlfriend... I'm too short...too tall, I'm ugly, fat, too skinny, spotty, etc.... Everyone else has fun, why don't I? She would never go out with me... They don't care about me... I'll show them, I'll make them suffer, they should know what it's like, then they'll be sorry...', and so on. Thus, the sense of grievance can lead to compensatory fantasies of revenge and having the power to spoil other people's pleasure. 'They think they have everything, I'll terrorise them.' The aim is to turn the tables of humiliation and castration. The boy can feel that instead of having a worthless little penis he can suddenly and momentarily dominate someone, even as the woman turns away shocked, or runs off. Although sexual gratification is obviously not the main aim, something has happened to these boys' sexuality to turn it into a weapon.

The 'phallic stage' of the child aged three or four years old was originally conceived by Freud as a precursor of true genitality, and was later elaborated as a narcissistic phase (Edgcumbe and Burgner 1975) before the maturity of Oedipal object relations. Castration anxiety was fundamental for Freud in explaining the structure of psychosexual development, and therefore Mind. Phallic interests and preoccupations of the child at that stage of development determine not only sexual and personal identity, but the nature of internal object relations. Anxieties and fears of castration or phallic inadequacy will provide a spur toward the renunciation of incestuous ties to oedipal objects. In the classical view of Freud the threat of castration forces the little boy to relinquish omnipotent fantasies of doing away with father and possessing mother. Instead of these infantile goals, he internalises father's authority, which prepares the ground for the achievement of his own genital position, deferring gratification until the time when he will have the capacity to be a father himself. However Kohon (1999) takes us further back, to the work that needs to be done by the child in separating from mother. In Kohon's view the phallus, for both boys and girls, is a fantasy representing an omnipotent solution to the problem of dependency on mother, and this may be used as part of that separation process, but in a perverse direction. It may be that the urgency of the boy's need to establish himself as male, i.e. different from mother, may make him more susceptible to means that appear to short-circuit the emotional pain of separation and loss. Punch whacks Judy traditionally with his big stick, and immoral as adults may think it, children enjoy this because it both gratifies and satirises the absurdity of this particular primitive solution to a developmental difficulty. Usually of course Punch succumbs eventually to the control of the policeman. He also can eat the babies made into sausages, and perhaps this indicates the psychotic reaches that would eventually follow on from uncurtailed phallic violence.

The significance of dependency conflicts to the development of sexual perversion was mapped out by Glasser in his theory of the core complex (Glasser 1964.) The idea of the castration complex was insufficient for Glasser, who drew upon a wealth of clinical experience with perverse patients. He reconstructed a dynamic of object relations that will have developed in childhood and which operates as a powerful determinant of current relationships. As a first condition there is a longing for fusion or merging with the maternal object, a sense of at-oneness, but this gives rise to fears of annihilation of individuality. Thus, there is a flight from the object, but in the absence of a safe place as it were, this means in effect a narcissistic withdrawal. However, there are then attendant problems of isolation and fears of abandonment, so that attempts at controlling the object are made. Aggression is used not in order to remove or to destroy the object but to keep it at a safe distance. Thus, we see the calm control of the predator rather than intense reaction of someone under threat. Sadism and sexualisation are used in varying degrees to maintain an illusion of power and triumph and protect against fears of loss. Whereas phallic illusions and fantasies would be false attempts at solving the core conflict, Glasser pointed to the need for an effective and benign father-figure for perverse solutions to be avoided. However, the pattern of behaviour under discussion here does not seem to consist of a controlling sadistic relationship with the object, but instead a fleeting abusive encounter. Core complex issues may underlie the perverse pattern, but an ego deficiency would seem to be just as important a factor. Clearly there is lack of some internal father to provide a notion of safe boundaries for these young men.

In what way does the existence of a father restructure the internal world? Birksted-Breen (1996) has distinguished phallic power from what she calls 'penis-as-link'. The phallus, which may be a more or less concrete image of a never-ending potency, gives an illusion of wholeness, defends against fears of loss, or inadequacy, and also defends in her view against anxieties described by Klein as emanating from fantasies about the inside of mother's body. She sees the phallus as possessed by neither sex and as having little to do with the actual penis '...though the boy may believe his penis may give him possession of it' (p.650). Pathological derivatives of phallic fantasies may affect women just as much as men. A woman or girl may believe her whole body to be a phallus, which would bring with it of course many classic problems of femininity. The phallus is to be contrasted with Birksted-Breen's view of 'penis-as-link', which is seen as the connection between a parental couple that is allowed to exist in the child's awareness instead of being denied by a two-person relationship dominated by phallic power. The phallus she sees an instrument of Thanatos, which aims to destroy the link between internal parents. A perception of a penis-as-link, or even an awareness of its need, leads to a structuring of mind, an opening of mental space, a 'triangular space' as described in Britton's exploration of the Oedipus configuration (Britton 1998, quoted in Kohon 1999, p.15). This space is now defined by points of reference, mother, father, and the child, unlike the undefined, terrorising space of the offender.

Lack of mental space contributes to breakdown in adolescence. Fully established adult perversions have often been noted as defensive against a break with reality and fending off fears of psychotic illness, from Edward Glover (1936, pp.216–234) to Campbell (1994, p.321). What we see in adolescence is the incomplete structure of perverse or delinquent organisation and a degree of openness to more primitive anxieties. Whilst causing the young person a greater degree of discomfort, generally, than the adult, this augurs much better for treatment since psychic change is more likely. Laufer and Laufer (1984) described the processes of adolescent breakdown; a fragile sense of ownership of the new sexually mature body produces a weak ego that is unable to deal with the conflicting demands of inner and external reality. Unconscious masturbation fantasies, laden with infantile and pre-genital elements, break through and disrupt the adolescent's relation to external reality. The internal dangers are made manifest by acting out, with associated states of distress and crisis; this potential fragmentation of the personality can become therapeutically useful if, that is, it can be seen for what it is, a signal of an (unconscious) need for help. This is not an argument for going 'soft' on offenders, because the clash with the law is precisely where the father, symbolically, comes to have a role in the young person's mind. What is important, however, is that the effect of the law should not be to drive the young person into despair, a sense of being castrated, perhaps through being brutalised in prison, which will lead into further glorification of phallic power, and hence further crime. Instead, the young person needs to have an experience that will restore confidence in a social order that protects not only others but himself from violence, in other words, to find a good father.

There follows a description of two cases, which though similar in terms
of offences and family background, demonstrate contrasting states of mind
in a young offender who is being considered for therapy.

A: The case of 'Lee'

Aged 15, Lee had been caught by the police after complaints by
women that he had exposed himself whilst they were walking alone at
night all within a certain area. It seemed that he had followed them into
a dark passage, and drew their attention to his erect penis, which he was
masturbating in front of them. At the time of these offences he had
been in the care of the local authority for some months. Lee had given a
'no comment' interview in relation to the street offences, on the advice
of his solicitor. He was not charged, but given a warning by the police
after social workers stated that it was not in the best interests of the
young person to be labelled a 'sex offender'. However he was referred
for a 'risk assessment' because there were continuing concerns about
him. He was said to have been making inappropriate comments and
suggestions of a sexual nature to female members of staff, though I was
subsequently informed that this behaviour disappeared around the
time of the referral.

Lee had been in care because of family breakdown. His mother had been
unable to cope with his violent rages. He had been suspended from school
because of 'challenging' behaviour. The father had abandoned the family
some years before and the household had become chaotic, with older
siblings engaged in theft, drugs and promiscuity. Once in care he calmed
down and resumed education, but his carers were concerned that, apart from
his sexual preoccupations with members of staff, he seemed too quiet,
over-compliant.

I first met him accompanied by his social worker, and I had an
immediate impression of wariness and suppressed hostility. My attempts at
making contact produced little response. When I suggested that he might
like a private talk with me, he shrugged. On his own he seemed more vulnerable, and found it difficult to talk. I pointed out the difference between
this and a police interview, adding that it was up to him, whether to agree
that he had a problem and so get some help with it. He denied that there was
a problem: 'All that's over and done with,' he insisted. I asked him about 'all

that' and he declined to discuss the details of what he had done, despite my clarifying what the purpose of this meeting was. I explained that there was a limit to confidentiality, but that his offences had been dealt with. However, he was still most reticent and I said that I thought he was perhaps expecting punishment of some kind. Maybe he thought I was here to try and make him feel bad about what he had done?

'I want to put it all behind me, forget about it, and get on with my life,' he said.

'Yes,' I answered, 'it must have been upsetting to be accused and questioned like that.'

'They wanted to label me a sex offender!' (He seemed indignant and terrified at the same time.)

'That was frightening, and you still feel angry about it.'

There was a pause, after which I said, 'And perhaps you feel I'm still trying to label you in that way?'

'Yes, it's not fair.'

'I guess you feel about as abused as those women on the street?'

'I know I shouldn't have done it.'

Pause

'That's it, there's nothing else to say about it.'

'Nothing to understand about why you did it?'

'I don't know why I did it, I don't want to know, I don't want to think about it. I'm going into the Navy in two years, and I don't want anything like this to spoil my record.'

'You are worried that if you get help then it will count against you?'

'If I'm in the Navy, there won't be any women there, I'll be alright.'

'No women?'

'And I'm not queer, if that's what you're thinking!' (He sneered contemptuously.)

'So, you are saying, if you were around women, there would be a problem?'

'Don't twist my words, you're trying to trick me. You are putting words in my mouth!' (He seemed very upset.)

'I have the feeling that whatever I say will feel as though I am forcing something down your throat. Like an abuser with a child?'

'I don't need anything from you, I don't want to come back here.' (He seemed about to run from the room.)

'Of course you are not a child, and you are not being forced into anything here.'

'Well then can I go?'

'I would be glad if you would stay and maybe we could do some work with the problems you have had. It seems to me that some bad things have happened to you...' (But he interrupted, 'No, they haven't!')

'...and try to make sure no bad things happen in the future.'

'No, they won't, I will make sure of that!'

'But I understand that there have been some problems with women members of staff...'.

This brought a hail of denials and insistence that he had been victimised, lied about and so forth.

I tried various other tacks, his hoped for Navy career, his family, the father he might have wished for, but to no avail. He said some things on these subjects, but the more he began to open up the more suddenly persecuted he felt. He was particularly defensive on the subject of his family and I began to feel that he was concealing something, which I guessed might be to do with sexual abuse within the family, about which I asked as tactfully as I could, and then more directly, but to no avail. He was relieved when the interview finished and was extremely reluctant to agree to a further meeting. I heard later that he complained to his social worker that I had alleged he had sex with his sisters, and refused to return. He threatened to make a complaint, but was content to be released from any expectation to return. Since his worrying and abusive behaviour in the residential unit had disappeared, they had little reason to require him to return.

DISCUSSION

This unpropitious encounter may be seen as representing a number (albeit a small proportion) of referrals which offer little hope of helpful intervention from psychotherapy. It demonstrates the importance of a judicial and supervisory network around a young person who has sexually offended, which gives some clarity as to why they might need help. When this is lacking there is little or no means of knowing whether he has really learned from the consequences of his actions, or if he is just keeping his head down, nurturing his resentments, and his desires to abuse, and therefore would be at risk of re-offending when the opportunity presents itself.

However, there may also be some lessons to be drawn from this clinical encounter. Despite his conscious reluctance to convey any information, Lee communicated powerfully at a non-verbal level. Through his wariness and suspicion he conveyed a sense of fear and threat that was palpable in the room. He seemed frozen, and I felt, uncomfortably, that I was the source of his terror. It was as if I would intrude violently into his feelings. I felt myself, therefore, to be like an abuser if I probed too deeply, or even if I did nothing, by leaving him with the fear. By my very presence I seemed to be someone perhaps like the violent father who keeps control by terrorising and silencing the family. As things turned out I was made into an opposite of an abuser, rendered helpless and impotent by his refusal to accept my role. Thus, I became the rejected one, carrying the feelings of the rejected child, just as he had been once the helpless victim. My rational attempts to present myself as a benevolent father-figure, who might understand and contain his conflicts, and offer some help in growing up into a man who need not abuse, were met with contempt, as if I were instead the unwanted child he once felt himself to be.

What had been the purpose served by his sexually aggressive behaviour? His phallic exhibitionism can be seen as an attempt to compensate for feelings of inadequacy, that were incidentally also being concealed in the meeting with me. We can hypothesise that the development of his masculinity was distorted not only by the experience of the abusive/absent father but also by a closeness with disorganised mother and sisters that was perhaps threatening and overwhelming in its incestuous intensity. The attacks on women were therefore perhaps a means of defending himself against these fears by keeping women at bay. The object, any woman he targeted, was not simply rejected, since he would repudiate the idea of homosexuality, but kept under sadistic control. As his mother had clearly failed to protect him, she had become, unconsciously, the justifiable object of his rage. The assaults can perhaps also be seen in a slightly more positive light, as an attempted solution to the problem of where to put himself, whether to be in the role of abandoned child or abusive father (abused or abuser) in relation to a mother who is profoundly mistrusted and who therefore deserves to be attacked. Ironically the net result of his assaults was to bring himself back to the position of victim. I wondered if there might be some forlorn hope that these women against whom he had offended would, despite his treatment of them, care for him and value him. The pain represented by these realities, the absent/abusive father, the unwanted child, was inaccessible behind his defensive posture in the session. In assessments I might sometimes ask what the perpetrator thinks may have been in the mind of the victim, but I was not able to reach this point of communication with Lee.

As to the request to assess the 'level of risk' posed by Lee, there could be no certainty, except to say there was a potential for him to re-offend. Perhaps he had learned enough from the unpleasant experiences of being caught, embarrassed and humiliated, to be deterred from re-offending. In the contact with me, however, it seemed he was confirmed in his position of feeling a victim, and could thereby avoid responsibility. Thus, the way remains open for him to seek further outlets for his need to make someone else the victim, and to shore up his fragile self-esteem. His poor school performance and the perhaps unrealistic hopes that the Navy will provide a solution to his problems, do not inspire confidence in any ability to think, or to relate to others, rather than to act out perverse solutions to his emotional problems. His experiences with women and future relationships will be crucial in this regard. The sense of grievance will very easily be activated again and lead to sexualised aggression as a way of relieving his own emotional pain. Ultimately perhaps chance will decide whether he has sufficient good experiences not to touch on his vulnerability.

B: The case of 'Laurence'

This young man was referred for a pre-sentence assessment of suitability for treatment, having pleaded guilty to several counts of indecent assault. He was caught after complaints by women of having been molested in the street. Video evidence was available that showed him go up to women and grab their breasts and buttocks, the assault being very quick, and he would then run away. He came back to the vicinity of a shopping centre to commit these offences. It was also notable that each time he was increasingly aggressive to the women, who were progressively more frightened. On the last occasion instead of running away he pursued the woman who had run from him, wanting, he said, to apologise. This was not believed, either by the victim, or by the police.

Laurence was 16, in full-time education, and had aspirations for a professional career. His family background seemed outwardly at least perfectly respectable, though in treatment it has emerged that there are many tensions and resentments between Laurence and his father and older sister. His father is disabled and was so horrified by the charges, that he stopped speaking to Laurence, though his mother appears to have continued to offer her support. She has a responsible position in a helping profession. His previous position as treasured older boy has seemed particularly painful for him to recall. They are a religious family, well connected to their local community, and have made great efforts to keep Laurence's offences a secret because of the enormous disgrace.

Assessment for court

The question was asked, would this young man benefit from treatment? If not, the alternative would most likely be a custodial sentence. The difficulty with a piece of work like this arises from the potential for duplicity, since therapy would seem to be a softer option than jail. (However I have also been surprised to find more than one young person who has opted for a custodial sentence rather than undergo the pain of having to think about what they had done.) I saw Laurence for five appointments, met with the court social worker, a colleague saw his parents, and discussed the case with senior colleagues. I came to the conclusion that since he could be in touch with genuine feelings, had the motivation and capacity to change his ways, and had sufficient support to remain in the community, he could benefit from treatment, and that probably a jail sentence would increase his problem of sexualised violence. I found that he was able to do some work with me. He expressed a good deal of painful remorse that may have also arisen from fear of punishment. He was also in touch with real feelings of shame at having disgraced his otherwise respectable family. He was not hardened and habituated to crime. In Meloy's terms, the affective aggression had not yet converted into the predatory type. He could accept interpretations that the assaults were also attacks on his family. There was indeed a fear of imprisonment, but also a sense of having done harm, and not understanding why, and something of a wish to make amends. His family continued to be a stable part of his life. They attended appointments and, though they are in the background of the treatment, they remain a crucial part of this young man's life.

During the assessment Laurence attributed great power to me, and was respectful, to the point of submissiveness. The reality, of course, was that the court would make the decision but his perception was that, though I could be the castrating father, I also had perhaps a more 'maternal' power to intervene and spare him. His extreme deference covered, so it seemed to me, a deep sense of outrage at having been caught and some of his anger against women emerged in the assessment sessions: He did not like my comments about any of this, but within this ambivalence, he communicated much more about his complex internal world than could Lee. There was a powerful split in his attitudes to women, an idealisation of some and denigration of those seen as sexual. The attractive woman however was either 'pure' or 'sullied' – at opposite poles. As we discussed his victims, it emerged that they had certain characteristics: blonde, or fair-haired, attractive, and dressed in a way that suggested to him they were of the 'flirty type'. I put to him that this was about his difficulty in dealing with his own sexual impulses, i.e. that the object of his desire would inevitably be seen as a threat and would become the target of aggression. When I clarified that the difficulty was the terror of his own sexuality, he could think about this, to some extent.

Laurence was sentenced, as it were, to psychotherapy, and this raises questions about the setting for treatment, and perhaps whether a viable transference can exist in such circumstances. Compulsory treatment might seem fundamentally compromised, since it would seem difficult for a patient to be genuine and spontaneous in their communications, but this is one of those cases where it is essential. His acting-out behaviour required that he be held by a network of adult professionals who could agree on a space that may be private, but not secret. Following the assessment, where there was a clear understanding that I would be reporting, it might well have been better for him to work with a different therapist, but this would have meant a significant delay and he was asking to begin work as soon as possible. He expressed a wish to work with me because he said he felt understood, and safe. I raised the question of a new basis for confidentiality and was somewhat surprised when he said that he would be happy if I would pass on information only as it might relate to further offences. He did want privacy for some of his frightening thoughts and feelings but said that I could help him control himself if he thought that I would speak to his probation officer if he started to re-offend. Similarly, he seemed to have no problem about being required to attend, even though it was a long journey, about one-and-a-half hours on public transport each way.

As the assessment sessions led on to treatment we looked in more detail at his relationship with his girlfriend. He was immensely proud of her good qualities, but terrified of his sexual desire for her. This striking split between the 'good' female who has to be protected against the sullying effects of his own sexualised aggression, must, I thought, have to do with conflicting feelings about his mother, but as he would not be drawn out on that subject, I suspected that she had to remain 'good' and beyond thought. He would draw upon some aspects of the family's religion which tended to prohibit any 'impure thoughts', but in subsequent sessions these were translated into criticism and contempt for her. After one of his ranting rages over the phone he learned that she cut herself, which alarmed him, though I think that he was also unconsciously pleased. It was in an early session that some of the reasons for his aggression against her became clearer.

Session no. 4

'I'm feeling terrible, I can't work, my exams are coming up, I can't concentrate, why am I so nasty to Julie? I can't understand it, I can't control it, maybe I'm mental, I always feel so bad afterward, I rang her after midnight, and let her have it, I woke her up, swore, shouted, called her names, all the names I could think of, bitch, whore, why would I do that, when I don't really mean it, I feel so terrible about myself afterward, it's just that I lose control, why does this happen?' (He was ashamed, tearful.) 'Does it mean I'm sick?'

'I think you are very worried that you are destroying the relationship, or testing her to see how much she will put up with. Let's try and think why you would need to do that.'

'I get so upset, I even pretend to her that I've been unfaithful, touched other girls, I sent her emails about me and other girls, saying disgusting things. I know it's going to upset her, she does care about me, but…I can't stop myself…'.

'It really sounds like you're terrorising her, just in a different way from attacking women on the street, but whose terror is this? Are you perhaps asking me to stop you, to protect you from yourself?'

'I'm trying to stop it, I keep telling myself that I don't want to lose her, I can't bear the thought of losing her, I would be destroyed if I lost her, and that's why I get into a state after, I can't sleep after a night like that, the thoughts keep going around my head, why did I do that?' (Abruptly his mood shifted, and he became quite prim and proper.) 'I tell myself that she must really love me to put up with all of this, and you know, I love her...in her I have found true love, she is the one I want to marry, you know this, I really love her, and respect her, and yet how can I when I behave this way, and I don't understand why. Why would I do this to her, when I love her?... The thoughts keep going round my head, if only I could stop them, sometimes it's my worries about money, I owe my dad £700 for the phone bill from a couple of months back. I've been trying to pay it back, and trying to phone less, but it's hard to keep it under control...'.

'Like the sessions, perhaps, they get you a bit under control, and maybe feeling also a bit worse?'

'Well, God, I don't know what I would have been like if things had just gone on, if I'd gone to jail, I would have just lost my mind, maybe if I was never able to ring her, and think about her, well, it would have been crack up or do myself in. What sends me into this state? Why should I ring her so late?'

(There is more repetition which I interrupt.)

'It is as though you have done something to completely spoil things between you and her...'

(Eventually he admits that they 'tried making love'.)

'Yes, and this happens when I'm with her, like the last time we tried doing it, when we are you know, doing stuff, and I...you know, what do you call it?'

'Ejaculate?'

'Yes, before I even got it in...she must think I'm useless, but it was also her fault, she never helped me, and how could she look at me that way, like a whore, who does she think she is? I hated her at that moment...'.

'So, when you ejaculated before entering her, then that made you feel angry, perhaps because you felt so inadequate?'

'Then I can't stand her even touching me, I get so furious with her, I give her such shit, she seems hateful to me at the time, I can't describe it...'.

'Again, I wonder if this perhaps is the feeling of being inferior, that you can't go on, or your penis cannot remain erect...and when she wants more, it makes you furious with her.'

'Yes, that's it, when I'm you know, when its hard, then I feel OK, but when it's gone I feel as though I'm just...'.

'You felt as though you were shit?'

'Yes, it's terrible, does it mean I'm...what do you call it...impotent? Mad? Do I hate her really? Maybe I will never be able to do it?'

'I think the confusion is that you feel like shit when you've lost your power, and that's not so much to do with your feelings about her, but about yourself; it feels like it is her fault, and so you try to make her feel as bad as *you* do.'

'Is this ever going to go away?' (He seems desperate.)

I say, 'Yes, it is difficult going through all this. And I don't take the feelings away, do I?'

'I know it's supposed to be helpful, but, I do hate coming here, I know I have to. I'm not sure if I really want to say all this to anyone, its very...I need someone, there is no-one, my father, I feel so ashamed, if he knew. If he knew what was going on it would be the end. I have already been in so much trouble, there's my uncle I can talk to but I had to borrow a load of money to pay my father for that phone bill, and now I've got another only £200, but still...'. (There was more about the phone.)

I said, 'And I think you are also talking about the enormous debt you feel is being stored up here, and whether I will hold all this against you?' (But I notice he is not listening, looking at his watch.)

He says, '...and the other problem is I'm ready to kill someone... I went out after that, and walked around the streets... I rang her, no answer, put the phone down and came out of the call box, and there was some guy looked at me funny, and I felt like smashing his head, I just had to walk away, though I would not have minded if he hit me first, it would be a good excuse to beat the crap out of him...he is probably OK, can function, can do it with his girlfriend, I'll show him what it feels like to be a piece of shit! I won't be able to stop myself...'.

'So you are angry with a man who probably can have intercourse, and could be angry with me, and even feel like killing me, perhaps, especially when I am about to end the session?'

'Oh, no, no, it's not like that, it's just that I don't know how I can face her again, she must think I'm crap, I can't bear to see her, do you think I should see her?'

'Surely it depends on whether your anger will make things worse?'

'No, I don't feel angry any more, for some reason, it's gone away, maybe she can understand, maybe she will give me time...'.

'She might, but only if you give yourself time' (He is calmer, and smiles ruefully, but then looks nervously at his watch.)

I add, 'And sending you away with all these worries however, could be infuriating as well?' (He smiles again and it is time to go, he checks the next appointment time.)

DISCUSSION

In the light of this session, the history of offences take on a different meaning. Rather than instances of arbitrary aggression, they look more like failed attempts at an omnipotent solution to this young man's feelings of terrible inadequacy. He had been behaving as if the body of any woman on the street was available for him to touch, pull or grab, perhaps that he could refute a terrible sense of prohibition against such access to the woman. In this way he could evacuate feelings of humiliation and vulnerability into his victims, though these same feelings became available in sessions. Oedipally, it was as if the father and mother had nothing to do with each other: father had been castrated (not Laurence) as he attempts to maintain the fantasy that women (mother) are there only for him. The stage was perhaps set for this to some extent in the family, since father has been unemployed through his disability, in contrast to mother who spends long hours helping others. Both parents referred to the fact that Laurence seemed to mature very early and appeared to have little need of them when he was younger. Perhaps the only way for Laurence was to develop a false solution to feelings of emptiness and abandonment, an illusory independence which broke down under the stress of puberty. One hypothesis could be that he had bypassed the diffi-culty of rivalling a disabled father by fantasising that mother was there just for him. This might then bring its own terrors of engulfment by the female (which was then confirmed by his premature ejaculation). The psychologi-cal danger of this was the fear of an undifferentiation of his maleness, and he had already established a means of violently reasserting his power. Thus, he felt compelled both to attack the mother and defeat the father. He was in a vicious circle, driven to escape an intolerable state of mind by trying to return to infantile delusions, but in doing so exacerbating the destruction of the internal parents. Paradoxically, of course, his sexualised aggression brought him up against a powerful father in the shape of the law. His break with reality at the time of the offences (unawareness of video cameras, returning to the same place etc.) indicates that psychological breakdown may have been imminent, and that unconsciously he may have been seeking discovery, containment, and help.

He experiences humiliation from the premature ejaculation, but his desire takes a violent form, not directed toward the gaining or giving of sexual pleasure, but to shore up his inner terrors. Thus, the thought of her body, still in a state of excitement even though he has passed his climax, is felt to be intolerable because it is beyond his imagined phallic control. Her body, without a penis, creates fears of annihilation which force him to assault her verbally, and it would not be long, I conjecture, before he would assault her physically. More of this complex dynamic will emerge, perhaps specifically a horror of the female genital, and probably unconscious fantasies (of the kind described by Klein 1935, p.276) of the inside of mother's body filled with terrifying manifestations of his own aggression that she (the girlfriend in actuality) cannot sustain.

The process of exploring these terrors and defences, is enabled, first of all by a positive transference, in that I seem to him like someone who offers him a way out, i.e. that I am the possessor of the phallic omnipotence he so desires, especially in that I was able, so it seemed, to get him 'off' a prison sentence. However, there has been no sense of compliance or duplicity in the sessions, rather a concealed negative transference, evident at the moment of awareness in the session that I had become an intruder in the sexual scene he was describing. It seemed at this point of inclusion into the primal scene that I became the castrating father to him. Hence, he diverted his attention from me, looked at his watch and tried to escape. He is dominated here by a need for a boundary around his aggression as much as sexuality. Thus, he seemed to calm down when I acknowledged by implication his need for privacy despite having to let me into his fantasy world; and so his terror of me was less palpable than before. It seemed by the end of the session that there was a space for thinking. His rueful smile at the end of the session I felt was not so much a sign of having 'dumped' his anxiety and disowned it, but rather a recognition of its existence and perhaps also its absurdity. I felt there was an unspoken acceptance that he was going to have to go away and carry the responsibility of dealing with all of this that he had told me. His potential outrage against me was mitigated by his experience of contact in the session. Thus, his predominant fear of loss of control was lessened by the therapeutic relationship.

I felt by the end of that session that there was a space to think and I had become triangulated as it were, between him and his girlfriend, themselves perhaps standing now for the parental couple. Less terrified by his fears of castration, he could see her as a real person. If he could feel that I would leave him with that relationship, with his penis-as-link, rather than failed phallic omnipotence, then he would become more capable of thought. The way is more open to begin to work on deeper levels of terror at the inability to separate from fantasised fears of mother's body and to bring these terrors into an Oedipal constellation. Perhaps by then his creativity will have returned, and he will allow himself to think and to work, instead of fighting his terrors and fragmentation in forms of sexualised aggression. More simply, perhaps, it could be said that he was able to become more aware of her as a separate person with a real existence of her own, that he was no longer the absolute centre of the universe, and what a relief it was to him!

CONCLUSION

The two cases describe perpetrators of similar offences, though they were handled by the authorities in different ways. They also show contrasting pictures of psychopathology. They could be seen as representing each pole of the distinction between affective and psychopathic aggression, (Meloy 1995). Whereas Laurence was still in touch with his own terror, and castration fears, Lee had built a narcissistic, totally self-sufficient phallic world, using the Navy and his own ideas of rightness to protect him from psychic pain. Laurence's fear of breakdown was fast becoming intolerable and, if it were to continue, could easily harden, by the increasing violence of the offences, into a 'psychopathic' adult state where the predatory mode was gaining supremacy. Assaulting women might have become the only way he could feel potent. Lee however was able to 'lie low', as a predatory animal might do, and defend against dangers both external and internal, as he convinced himself of his invulnerability. An important criterion of treatability, therefore, is the degree of access the young person has to their own feelings, whether he is, in other words, not totally identified with the aggressor, and able to relate to another. However, psychotherapeutic treatment under compulsion is also indicated in these cases because of the security afforded by a network of professionals around the adolescent, which enables an emotional as well as behavioural containment to take place. Omnipotence may be projected onto the therapist, especially if the treatment is offered as an alternative to prison, but this can be worked with more readily than either the complete absence of the authority of father, or the emotional unavailability of a maternal object.

There is also a general feature of this type of offence that contrasts with the 'domestic', or intrafamilial abuser, who constitute the majority of those described in this book. These cases of street offenders, at least the ones seen in a NHS outpatient clinic, seem to come from a more-or-less intact family. They demonstrate once again the fundamental importance of a good attachment relationship. The seeking of victims outside the family might indicate something of an adolescent desire to separate from incestuous objects, but also to preserve something good. The perpetrator comes up against external reality, but still has his family as a basis for renegotiating a role within society. The destruction of the real family that usually accompanies intrafamilial abuse perhaps mirrors a more profound destruction of the internal family in the psyche of the incestuous abuser, and therefore offers less hope of recovery.

CHAPTER 8

Disturbances of Gender Identity Development in the Young Abused/Abuser

Disturbances in sexual functioning are well documented as a long-term effect of child sexual abuse (Sanderson 1991, pp.72–8), and some children experience profound effects on their gender identity (Trowell 1998). It seems also that in perhaps a very small number of cases the appearance of gender identity disorder is a complicating factor with patterns of abusing. Perhaps the most damaging scenario is that of the child who is actively sexually abused by his mother. Even where a boy is abused by males, it may be that a feminine identification is sought as a means of protecting the self against trauma. Where this might well lead to masochistic forms of homosexuality, in some it might form an impetus to sexual aggression.

Bentovim (1995, p.48) observed a tendency in abused boys to identify with the aggressor, in contrast to girls who tended to identify with the victim. We can understand this partly as a social phenomenon, the fact that in this society being male is equated with being powerful. During normal socialisation a boy accepts authority partly on the basis that one day he will be in the more fortunate position of feeling himself to be an adequate male. To achieve this, however, he will need, first, sufficient confidence that he is not going to be annihilated by those over him and, second, a capacity to accept the loss of his first object of desire, represented as the Oedipal, or pre-Oedipal mother. Neither of these conditions can be said realistically to apply to the young boy who is adapting to an abusive environment.

One aspect of the damage done to the victim of sexual abuse is the breaking of boundaries defining his or her gender identity, and this fragmentation may well become evident in early adolescence. I am going to present here two cases which represent some of these difficulties but which also contrast in certain important ways, particularly in terms of their treatability. The description of 'Sam', sexually abused by his mother, as well as by men, and who went on to abuse younger children, will focus on the specific problems of self-definition of his gender. Neither the treatment nor the placement had a successful outcome; nevertheless the attempt at work with this case reveals something about the perverse structures that can make sexual abusing an intractable character trait. The other case presents a more hopeful picture, despite the fact that the abuse against 'Rick' took place extensively from the earliest age. A major difference between the two is that Rick could preserve something like a good object in his mother even though she had failed to protect him for periods of time.

Core gender identity is a subjective state, a psychic structure that is fully established before the age of two years (Stoller 1964). The abused child at that early stage of development, and in the process of defining their being asks, as it were, 'What kind of male am I being used like this?… Does it make me into some kind of female?' The girl could also ask, 'What kind of female am I that I am being treated like this?' But the girl who has been abused seems unlikely to feel that her core gender identity has been attacked (Sanderson 1991, p.78). This is not of course to deny the many other ways in which the damage to that developing girl's personality can be severe. For some males it appears that this specific area is an important vulnerability, and one that may contribute to the underlying psychopathology that might perpetuate their abusive behaviour. It is as though they must attack another in order to preserve a fragile sense of identity.

Moore and Rosenthal (1993, p.95) described how men suppress their capacity their for intimacy. This may be traced to the need for boys to turn away from their primary love object, mother, as they attempt to identify with a male carer in order to develop a sense of masculine identity. It is not hard to see the danger if that significant male in the boy's environment is an abuser, and more confusing still if he has treated that boy as his own sexual object. Greenson (1968) introduced a notion of 'disidentification' from mother that is necessary for the development of a viable male gender identity. It is now a conventional view of boys' development that they need to reach a point of feeling free of their mother. If this is an unresolved process, it could lead to a 'monstrous' internal object projected onto women. Thus, it can be frequently observed among abused/abuser boys that their deepest hatred is reserved for mother and her substitutes rather than for the males who abused them. Fear, on the other hand, is reserved for the male who is more likely to represent the actual abuser.

Group therapy for men with a history of child sexual abuse produces issues similar to those of women – low self-esteem, shame, sexual dysfunction and relationship difficulties, but a very different atmosphere to the group (Hall and Sharpe 2000). Whereas women in such a therapy group will tend to be dealing with feelings of sadness, the men exhibit more anxiety, especially about being perceived as abusers; they alternate between jokey banter and anti-authoritarian aggression. Much less expression of emotion is evident as is a much higher degree of substance abuse and other forms of delinquency. (None of this will be very surprising to anyone familiar with males who have been abused.) Clearly their view of themselves is affected in a different way than for females. There seems to be a special fragility to the male gender identity in the abused/abuser that is defended in a number of ways, one of which may be to take the path of sexual aggression. Even for the man who has made a choice against abusing, there still seems to be a fear that his sexuality is, or might be abusive (Hall and Sharpe 2000).

The social significance of gender is intricately bound up with power differentials, especially in sexual abuse. As can be seen in so many cases, the attack on children represents unconscious hostility to mother. Sometimes the female child is the preferred choice of victim in order to bolster an illusion of heterosexuality and to fend off fears of homosexuality. However, in some cases the orientation to children expresses a pseudo-heterosexuality since the child may be perceived as equivalent to female, even if male, because that child is not an adult sexual object. It may be that the gender of the child is far less important than the common features of children (Wyre and Swift 1990). The smooth hairless skin of the child is felt as if it is the surface of the breast, uninterrupted by sexual difference as defined by secondary sexual characteristics. A crucial aspect of the paedophile object choice that bolsters the illusion of heterosexuality is the feeling of power over the victim. The young abused/abuser tends also to perceive adult male/female relationships as essentially the violent assertion of masculine power over a woman who would otherwise be feared as threatening. This view is bound by a primal-scene fantasy that may be amenable to analytic deconstruction. Homosexuality is frequently feared by young abused/ abusers and denied to themselves as an adult option because it represents submission to the (usually) male abuser and being made into some kind of (hated) female.

Gender studies may be helpful both in understanding the damage done to gender identity in abuse and also in modelling what can be offered to help repair that damage. Frosh (1994) reviewed how several theorists have in recent years shown that we can move away from a male/female polarity and instead conceive of a polarity consisting of fixed versus multiple gender identities. Butler (1990) introduced the notion of 'performative' gender identities to replace the concept of an essential masculinity or femininity. Our gender identity is seen here as infinitely variable and based as much on what we are not, as much as upon what we are. Benjamin (1966) defined the fundamental task of gender formation as that of mourning the sex that one cannot be. Gender identity itself might be understood as being based on a capacity for grief at the unfulfilled aspect of the self, and hence finding the capacity to seek it in the other. In normal or healthy development this pre-supposes contact between the sexes that can facilitate such a process and an internal world that will permit access to such experiences. Children with gender identity disorder have been found to show particular difficulties with mourning (Bleiberg *et al.* 1986). The abused/abuser, however, finds that differences between the sexes are reminders of deprivation instead of possibilities of pleasure, envy rather than desire, rage not love.

For the victim, the abuser is experienced as the other, and this can be felt as the other gender, thus affecting the child's perception of their own gender. However, the abuser, by the nature of physically intimate acts, particularly if the child is very young, may come to be felt by the child also as part of the self. The child may be treated as an apparently homosexual kind of object, or heterosexual (according to the abuser's preferences), but as we have seen above neither of these categories completely apply. In certain kinds of sexual abuse the child is both penetrated and used to penetrate the abuser. The child who is being abused is a device for the autoerotic or masturbatory activity of the abuser. This child is a sexual 'part object' for the abuser and so experiences himself as an erotic extension of the other. When the abuser is also the mother, the boy in this situation is not the kind of male offspring for his mother whom in normal development she knows must leave her. He will never leave her, unconsciously, because he will always conceive of himself as a part of her body. As Welldon (1988) has so fully shown, the abusive mother demonstrates her sexual perversion through her procreative powers.

In some cases of young abused/abusers, the divide between male and female is denied, elided into a sameness that triumphs over the pain of loss and inadequacy, and obliterates anxieties about further victimisation. Volkan and Greer (1964, pp.162–3) described the transsexual desire to be given a female body as a means of reinforcing the illusion of being forever fused with mother. This process it seems may also be driving some sex offenders, whether rapists, paedophiles, or perpetrators of other sexual crimes, where the psychological significance of the act may be much more obscure than behavioural or legal definitions. They have avoided the fundamental task of gender development, of accepting that one is only the one sex, and needs the other to fulfil wholeness. Instead they opt for a 'neo-sexuality' (McDougall 1986), the expression of an omnipotent fantasy of being able to possess the characteristics, and the potency of *both* sexes.

In later work McDougall (1995) explores bisexuality as the source of creativity, one expression of which may be in the form of a 'neosexuality'. Transsexualism however may also bring about the foreclosure of such possibilities. The rigidity of the defence, the refusal to think about meaning, or about childhood experiences, the unavailability of symbolisation, are all features of the transsexual who believes that if only he/she were 'given' the body of the other sex then the true self will be realised. No other solution will suffice, the transsexual patient will proclaim (Volkan and Greer 1964, p.171). It would seem to follow that psychoanalytic psychotherapy has little to offer in these cases, indeed Stoller (1964a) commented that '...whatever one does is wrong' (p.117). He expressed more hope in the treatment of children (p.116). This was then borne out by Di Ceglie (ed) (1998) who connected 'atypical gender identity organisation' with psychological trauma, and gave detailed accounts of psychoanalytic psychotherapy, though no mention is made of abusive behaviour.

The viability of the treatment accounts that follow hung in the balance at times and it seemed that it was the gender issue that was creating such uncertainty. Each of these young patients presented their gender confusion fairly aggressively time and again, and I found myself wondering whether there could be anything useful or creative in the issue. However, Coates and Moore (1997, pp.294–5) found that in psychotherapy with traumatised children they frequently came across the transsexual fantasy as embodying reparative wishes; a good object had been split off from any destructive feelings and constructed as an all-gratifying maternal figure. In the case of the abused/abuser the boy's own body may have been the source of pain, except in so far as it is felt to be a sexualised part of the mother. Thus, the boy attempts to deal with his fears of abandonment, though mourning is made impossible. Giving up the fantasy that one could be either sex is also described by McDougall (1995, pp.xiv–xv) as a necessity in the establishing of a singular sexuality. This then is the therapeutic task, to facilitate the process of mourning, for the sex which the adolescent cannot be, and for the maternal love he never had. The difference between the two cases I have chosen, one with poor outcome and the other more hopeful, perhaps hinges on the relative strength of the young person in this regard.

CASE ILLUSTRATION I

Sam, small but overweight, neglected and abused since earliest childhood, rejected by numerous foster homes for his sexualised and aggressive behaviour, was referred aged 12 when his placement was in difficulty. A stable placement is usually seen as a necessary prerequisite for treatment, as noted for example by Horne (2001, pp.14–15); however it was thought in this instance that perhaps it could work the other way round, that the placement might be supported by therapy, especially if the therapist was working within the therapeutic community; but in this case it was not to be.

Both Sam's mother and his father seem to have been given to polymorphous perverse activity with him and his sisters. Not much is known about the parents since they evaded any contact with the authorities soon after they relinquished responsibility for their children. He was described as having severe learning difficulties, but his intelligence, as is so often the case, after only a few months of residential placement, came to seem nearer the normal range. Instead of learning he had been compulsively repeating his traumatic abuse. His adaptation to the gross abuse of his early childhood came to the notice of the police and social services before he was ten when already he had developed a compulsive pattern of molesting little boys. The professionals responsible for him were extremely worried, not only about his continuing risk to the public, but also about his own future, which seemed increasingly fixed in the form of an aggressive child molester. The transsexual wishes served also to further bewilder the adults trying to provide for him.

If, as Freud (1923, p.32) said in *The Ego and the Id*, character is based on series of identifications, then what possible hope could there be for someone with Sam's background to become anything other than completely rejected by society? However, the acting out drew attention to his situation, and again Winnicott's (1958a) notion of the positive function of the Anti-Social Tendency comes to mind. By so compulsively abusing others Sam could achieve two aims: as well as avoiding the powerlessness of being the victim, he could also demonstrate to parental figures somewhere the extent of abuse perpetrated on him.

In our first meeting he proclaimed to me proudly that he had come to the residential unit because he 'sucked little boys' dicks!' and then somewhat more sadly, that he had nowhere to live. He was however much more defensive when it came to the question of current abusive behaviour toward adults and other young people. His first statement I took to be a sort of challenge to see how I might react. Would I be shocked and unable to help him? Would I be excited by his graphic words? Or would I be able to respond in a way that said no to the abuse of a child. This was but the opening of a series of salvos; he needed to know what he must do to be rejected.

There was a temporary calming down of his disruptive and oppositional behaviour in the unit, which lulled staff (including the therapist) into thinking that perhaps the therapeutic space was what he had needed. Before long, however, his testing out was back in full force; he was violently disruptive in education and residential work. He created scenes that reflected the persecutory anxieties of his inner world. He was extremely provocative to the other boys, continuing his attacks into meetings called especially to deal with his behaviour. Later he would be full of remorse and it still seemed that the possibility was there for him to become aware of the effect he had on others. For a while he appeared to have made some moves toward changing his abusive patterns of behaviour.

I would hear about him marching about the unit, verbally abusing everyone, just as he sometimes did with me. Some of the obscenities hurled as missiles against all and sundry provide clues as to the nature of the inner adaptation he must have made at stages of the abuse. These are some examples:

(to other boys), 'Your mother is a fat cunt! …You fucked your mother, your mother sucked your dick off and ate it!'

(to staff), 'You've got big tits!' Or, 'Show me your prick!'

Also at this stage his desire to be a woman was expressed aggressively and sexually. Even to strangers he would say, 'Come on you want to fuck me, don't you? When I've got a cunt you will fuck me!'

What can be inferred from this about his inner world? What might the relationship have been like with the mother? What was her actual involvement in the sexual abuse of the boy? His hatred of the female seemed based not only on a fear of her abusive power over him but was fuelled by an incorporation of that power. She had, it seemed, completely overwhelmed him so that his masculinity was in effect destroyed. Her own sexual abuse as child was known, though we can only speculate on the way in which her destiny was being played out in her son. He became perhaps the violent and orally overwhelming mother, embodying also a distorted masculinity in his sexual aggression to other children. It is as if he was trying to reverse the mastery that his mother had exerted over him.

The perversion of motherhood is about the complete control of another being (Welldon 1988, p.81). What possibilities of masculine identification would Sam have? If in normal development we expect the boy to make use of some 'disidentification' from mother (Greenson 1968), we can see that in Sam's case there would be no pathway open for him to even begin this process. There was no father to offer alternatives to the perverse and undifferentiated bond with mother. Instead, he would be forced back on to the remnants of gratification in the early experience with mother, only to be confronted with the reality that for her he was an erotic extension of her own body.

What had happened to Sam's mind? At times his behaviour seemed 'mindless'. His speech and action was so filled with preoccupations with the body there seemed no room for anything else. Winnicott's (1949) *Theory of Mind and its Relation to the Psyche* shows how mind develops its primary function to cover self against trauma, a way of knowing being a cure for the erratic mothering. For Sam the need to know in this way was expressed in his choice of gender identity. He was protesting against that which he could not trust, his own body. His mind was stuck, so it appeared, at the stage of trying, and failing, to comprehend the body's experience. There was little or no satisfaction in the body, instead an all-consuming rage against it and the mother. Castrating himself would be both an act of triumph, as he takes over the other's body, and despair, as he destroys his masculinity. Meanwhile the mind, unable to think about experience, and in its failure to repair the damage, had become itself a repetition of the trauma.

He made pictures that might in one view be taken as provocatively made pornographic scribbles, but in another as containing important information about his psychopathology. Mostly they were destroyed triumphantly and tantalisingly. I tried to distinguish some valid information from the aggressive content and understood them to be about the hated mother and about the acts of abuse. Coates and Moore (1997) in their study of the valuable properties of children's drawings discuss the age-appropriate level of symbolisation in the pictorial representation of traumatic experience (p.288). I began to see Sam's aggression in its sexualised form as attempts, albeit failed, to break free from the primitive consuming mother. It was as if he was saying, 'Not me, someone else has to be abused!' But my comments were easily felt by him to be more attacks. He would revert wildly to cries that he was a fat pig, bastard, crap, etc. I was careful and tried to provide containing responses with the aim of slowing this process down.

Sam undercut my usual way of dealing with juvenile sex offenders, and made me think about some of my assumptions. Using a masculine role model in a positive way helps most boys find the kind of paternal presence these boys have lacked and so desperately yearn for. On the basis of this emotionally containing relationship I would seek to guide the boy to a perception that his perverse psychopathology can be recognised for what it is, not denied but accepted as something that needs to be changed. This working alliance is based on the boy's need for a kind of father-figure who can make what has been unbearable at least possible to think about. As Valerie Sinason (personal communication) has said, 'the neutral stance of the therapist is interpreted by the abused child as a repetition of the hostility he has experienced before.' However, Sam's statements like, 'You must think I'm crap', or 'You must hate me' could also be taken more as sado-masochistic and painful protests than attempts at control. Interpretations of his need for someone who could value him were more helpful than feeding back to him the hatred that was pouring out. Or so I thought. Such comments at certain points in the treatment did lead to a degree of calm and some depressed acceptance of responsibility for the way in which he knew he had got people to hate him. As usual I tried to convey that, though I may have hated what he has done, and what was done to him, that was not the same as hating him. Naturally this involved more than just telling him. Normally if the work proceeds beyond initial stages it is often possible to give due credit to the commitment and courage that a young person may well have shown in facing up to painful issues. Thus, the boy finds, as it were, a good father, and therefore becomes able to face the bad. In Sam's case however this strategy was impossible.

It seemed increasingly to be the gender identity problem that blocked progress. I did not know whether I was talking to a male or a female. It was not that he was effeminate, he was far too aggressive for that. He was explicitly inviting me to have sex with him, as though he were female. I experienced his insistence to 'become a woman' as an intrusion into my being, an attempt to get into my heterosexuality. I began to feel a profound desire to be rid of him. Some self-analytical thought was required. Just as he was the sexual object for the parent so he would be bound, of course, to sexualise the emotional contact with a therapist. Why was the male/female abuser/victim in him so repellent that it threatened to disrupt my professional stance? He touched upon feelings in me about the distinction of femininity and masculinity, about the conflicts between them, and the sometimes uneasy compromises that have to be made in male/female relationships. Sam was so undifferentiated that this boundariedness of gender could no longer be maintained. He seemed the embodiment of a particularly violent primal scene and mother as all-destroyer.

A brief series of pictures from one session, which turned out to be the last but one, have survived. The session was stormy. He was shouting excitedly about becoming a woman.

'When I'm 18 I will do it! I'll have my prick cut off, and have a cunt instead! I've already got the tits!'

But looking at me as though expecting me to give a word of warning he sat and drew frantically. (Figure 8.1).

'Lesbians, that what I'll be, and get love!' (He drew the heart with an arrow.)

Figure 8.1

'But that's no good, women want a man, they want this!' (He scribbled aggressively.) (Figure 8.2).

Figure 8.2

I asked about the figure of eight shown inside the woman.

'Oh, that's her baby.' And, much less angrily, he drew another. (Figure 8.3).

Carefully he showed the inner baby, and there seemed to be a penis and so I asked if it were a boy.

'It might be a boy.'

I said, 'But the man seems to have got smaller?'

'He is going to be sucked up in there. He'll disappear, be with the baby and never seen again.'

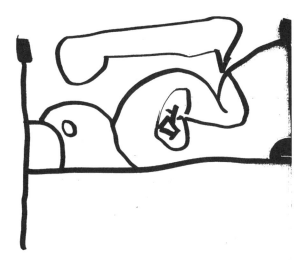

Figure 8.3

Crude as these pictures are (lack of features, limbs, etc.), I felt at the time that they were spontaneous expressions of some of the inner conflicts underlying Sam's pattern of sexual abuse. At least the trauma was being given some form. I began to think that we were now going to be able to start tracing back the transsexual 'solution'. At last perhaps there was an emotional connection with the idea of becoming a woman; it could be seen as an attempt to get the love he wants whilst avoiding the castrating power of woman. The transsexual wish seemed for Sam to be an expression of intruding into the primal scene with the aim of becoming a male/female in intercourse. This appeared to be a fantasy of being the baby inside, and in this way being a part of the intercourse. As the baby inside takes shape, so it seems the male outside is diminished, swallowed up. But at least perhaps the baby was where we could start from, or so I thought.

I had no idea of the resonance of some of this material by the time we met again for what was to be the final session. He said he thought he was now working in his therapy and wanted me to tell the residential staff that he was doing well now, but he went on to talk about hating a new arrival in his house, a boy he said was 'a baby, an idiot!' This new boy, 'Mark', was younger than Sam and similar in some ways, especially in the uninhibited verbal abuse that was flung sometimes at staff. I spoke to Sam about unwelcome aspects of himself that he saw in Mark and about his jealousy that Mark might receive the good things of which Sam could feel so deprived; especially now that he felt he had made a start in his therapy, he was fearing that I too would be more interested in this new baby. It seemed that these comments could be accepted and our conversation went on in a more sad way to a new disclosure, that he had been inserting sharp objects in his anus. It seemed that some bleeding was causing him to be anxious about this. There was an appropriate degree of shame in this, unlike the aggressive outbursts that I knew all too well. We talked about the meaning of what he was doing, and how it was something to do with him feeling that having things pushed into made him female, and he spoke about his dejection that he could never be male. However, I was also concerned about the self-injurious nature of this behaviour and he agreed that staff would have to know of this and some medical attention might well be needed. I was not surprised when I heard that a short time after this Sam had been extremely provocative to Mark, but was concerned to hear that he had seemed unable to stop and that the situation had escalated. There was a physically violent interchange with Mark. Sam then struck a female member of staff who had been remonstrating with him. Moreover, before this incident had been resolved, he exposed his penis to the new arrival. All of these actions, as Sam well knew, would constitute grounds for terminating his placement, especially if he refused to engage in any discussion or thinking about his behaviour. He seemed quite indifferent to this eventuality and accepted the fact that his local authority had no option other than to place him, as they did after a few days, in a secure unit.

His abrupt departure and the failure of our attempts to work with him naturally led to some questioning about the provision of treatment. I wondered if the sessions, by their analytic function, may have precipitated a decompensation of his ego functioning and self-control, rather than assist with the containment that had been so obviously needed. No, my colleagues assured me, his sexualised aggression had been consistently a management difficulty. Changes of any kind had always been a particular source of increased stress. To have protected him from change at all times would have been impossible. I had to accept that the attempted psychotherapy was probably less important than the unfolding of events in the therapeutic community. He had until the new arrival been the youngest in his house and had somewhat gloried in acting the the role of baby, something about which residential staff had felt uncomfortable. The task of giving up the illusion of being a baby would have required some mourning, and it was precisely the process of mourning, in all sorts of ways, that Sam found impossible to bear. By his actions, therefore, he induced in effect a violent separation, one that he could feel had been forced upon him. I saw him again only briefly because he refused a final session with me, instead erupting with rage and verbal abuse when I came across him in the corridor. Countertransference feelings of having been cheated, tantalised with positive thoughts of getting on well with the therapy and then abruptly let down, must have been, so it seems in retrospect, a result of a 'concrete' communication of his own experience of being excited and then dropped so many times.

CASE II 'RICK'

By contrast Rick's treatment could get under way, despite the disturbing similarities in background and psychopathology. Factors that contributed to the more optimistic picture arise mainly from his relatively benign family environment. His mother was able to provide a consistent attachment, and support treatment, confirming once again Bentovim's research finding that cases of young abusers are most hopeful when there is at least one long-term caring attachment relationship (Bentovim and Williams 1998, p.104). Because of this Rick could tolerate at least to some extent the psychological exploration of some of the effects his abuse and could make use of treatment in terms of his development, whereas Sam could let nothing in to his perverse world.

Referral

Rick M, aged 10, was brought by his mother to her general practitioner after she found that he was being sexually abused by a lodger, 'Brian'. Subsequently it was discovered that this had been going on for many years, since Rick had been at least two years old, perhaps earlier. Ms M felt acutely guilty at having allowed Brian to baby-sit. She had needed help with Rick, being a single parent who needed to work. In retrospect she could see there had been indications, including a genital infection when he was three, and on more than one occasion Rick had said that he did not want to be left with Brian, that Brian hurt him, but since she saw no visible injury she had thought Rick was 'just fussing'. She felt terrible that she had 'not noticed' these, and other signs, even though she knew that her lodger had a conviction for abuse of a young girl. She had thought this would mean that he would not be interested in a boy. Her 'blind spots', predictably, were connected to the fact that she herself had been the victim of sexual abuse as a young teenage girl. She had also been the victim of domestic violence from Rick's father before he had disappeared when Rick was three.

Her worries about Rick included his anal masturbatory behaviour, his sexual preoccupations, and increasingly getting younger children to join with him in sexual activities. There had also been behavioural problems for several years at school, with Rick being excluded from more than one. He was currently attending a special unit where he could have more supervision, but his teachers were still concerned about poor academic progress, sexualised aggression and deteriorating conduct. Perverse sexual development seemed to be developing; as well as soiling and smearing faeces, he was urinating in his room, sometimes on the carpet, or storing urine in cans in his room. He was masturbating with animals, showing his bottom to other children and instructing them in anal insertions. He had started fires in his room and, when challenged on any behaviour, he would throw tantrums, run off, or collapse in despair saying that he was dirty like Brian and should be killed. Ms M too felt in despair, blaming herself for all that happened and still feeling that Rick had not told her 'everything'. When first referred she was still reeling from the shock that Rick had been abused, orally, anally and genitally by Brian.

At the assessment stage Ms M described Rick's symptoms, which could be recognised as those of Post Traumatic Stress Disorder, as put in DSM IV (American Psychiatric Association 1991). There were signs of dissociation, hyper-arousal, and Rick showed great anxiety as he would not separate from his mother. One of her main anxieties was that her son might turn out to be an abuser, since he seemed so preoccupied with sexual matters and younger children. She was relieved when at last Rick agreed to be seen on his own, and she could have her own concurrent therapy sessions too. The following account does not include much information from her treatment but it will be obvious to the reader how crucial this was in contributing to Rick's therapy and development.

After an initial frozen anxiety in the room, Rick instituted games that left little space to talk or think about anything. Awkward as this might be for a therapist who wants to get to work, and engage with the problem, it is useful to note in passing that this beginning to treatment perhaps bodes much better than the initial contact with Sam, who revealed too much too soon. It is important to note also that an assessing therapist needs to have a different approach to a young person whose trauma is still very near the surface for them, where the abusing pattern is far from established, and who in any case is much younger than many of the other abused/abusers described elsewhere in this book. By means of his control of the session, Rick could keep emotional contact within tolerable limits and become relatively sure I was not going to be another abuser, nor that the therapy was going to be another deception. In this situation a therapist needs to be respectful of the capacity of the child to tolerate the emotional contact, which might easily feel like an intrusion, or indeed itself a sexual assault. I quickly learned that any mention of what had happened to him, or indeed about some of the things he had done, was unproductive.

It was not long, however, before Rick began to show some of the effects of the abuse he had suffered. Toys were for him, as for many children, natural or permissible part-objects, in other words, to be treated as cruelly as required, representing people but without consequences in reality, for the most part at least. 'It's only play...', or, 'Only a story...' was always a fall-back position if the meaning of the play became too close to painful experience. Again there is a contrast here with Sam, who used a medium that was much 'hotter', in the sense that the content and meaning of his pictures were hard to evade. Puppets were Rick's favourite for several weeks and even after that period Rick went back to them from time to time.

An Oedipal constellation of King, Queen, and 'Jokester' made up the main *dramatis personae*, with an occasional policeman and the gradually dominating presence of a crocodile. I glimpsed something of the terror and humiliation of the abused child, as Rick took the character of the King who bellowed at Jokester (played by me) that he should

'Kiss this dirty arse!…Clean out the toilets…Lie down there and let me sex you!'

Since we each had our hand each in our respective glove puppet this last demand felt too much for me to accept. I took it as an opportunity to talk about the need for safe boundaries here as anywhere. My response interrupted the flow of material, and produced manifestations of rage that I was beginning to expect. This came first via the Queen who imprisoned and demolished the King, and used the Jokester (whom I had taken for the son, but not a straightforward Oedipal rival) for her own greedy ends. He had to provide her with endless food, and gratify her desires to see 'the people', her subjects, robbed, tortured and killed for her amusement. Was this his conception of a mother who had regularly left him with the abuser? My tentative comments in this direction produced an extraordinary reaction; *he* was the Queen he asserted. Over the next few weeks began also to dress and act effeminately. I began to think he was showing me something not so much of his view of mother in reality but a female presence he could identify with as abuser rather than victim. However, this role was evidently causing some anxiety though he clearly loved being Queen; he handed over the Queen puppet to me and instead became the crocodile, who ate the King, the policeman (and his thousands of reinforcements). My task was to try and make the Queen safe from the crocodile.

It was around this time that Rick's play began to break down. Increasingly the stories were interrupted by his rolling on the floor, and lying still with his bottom pushed upward. I questioned aloud his actions, 'as though I would be interested in that part of you?' The situation was technically difficult because it seemed important both to acknowledge the communication and also to avoid giving him straight back the idea that he might wish to be abused. Although his invitation might appear real enough, I took it that he needed to know if sex with him was something *I* wanted. In many ways of course I made it clear that it was not, but it was far from a straightforward matter. He would dress up and mimic female qualities in mock allurement toward me. I felt I needed to respond in a realistic way, and discourage such behaviour; I wondered aloud why he needed to do this, and took every opportunity to positively connote the fact that he was really a boy. This was not entirely welcome. We went into a phase of considerable disruption of the sessions.

He got me out of the room and kept me in the corridor, since of course I would not attempt to force my way in against the chairs he put to keep me out. He got hold of my keys and threw them out of the window, made phone calls all around the clinic (before I removed the phone), shut me into the basement by holding the door closed at the top of the stairs as we came from the therapy room and so on, much to my embarrassment with colleagues. He would refuse to come into his session, run off and hide in the clinic corridors, and at other times refused to leave the session. Despite some fear of my retaliation, he was openly triumphant and gloried in his power over me. On occasions I probably showed my anger and spoke sharply to him, but gradually realised that there was something more than the desire to make me feel something of the powerlessness and humiliation of the abused child; he was also discovering in himself something like a masculine assertion. However, his power was, it seemed, making him anxious, as well as excited, and also I was hearing that disruptive behaviour was increasing at school. Eventually I felt I needed to draw a limit, and asked his mother to join us for a session to discuss what was acceptable in the clinic. This was useful in that he became tearful at some of the painful feelings he had been blotting out by his disruptive acting-out. With his mother there it seemed safer to refer to the abuse, and so we could agree that the sessions would resume.

The crocodile glove puppet became a main character, and could be both aggressor and victim. The crocodile, though male, was impregnated by the King, from behind, and was shown with several piglets in its belly. There was much more sadism in this sequence of play, with the crocodile smashing up the house, eating its own babies. It would be punished mercilessly, especially by the Queen, and there were several sessions of ritualised beating and hammering the puppet. The crocodile's crime, I began to see, was being both the abuser (since Rick was venting and verbalising some of his rage against Brian), and also the female identification of Rick as victim, who could be in fantasy a maternal figure who had the power of life and death. Indeed the Queen was then shown to give birth to a baby whose job it then was to kill the King his father. The 'female' crocodile seemed to come in and out of the play as and when needed to show the amount of rage possible in

him, though at other times the Jokester seemed a more adequate expression
of Rick's 'male' alter ego.

Against this background of sadistic and abusive relationships it seemed
that Rick was working through something of the confusion of his own
gender identity. The absence of a father had created a gap that had to be
filled somehow, even with a kind of 'female–male' that would take away the
terror of abandonment and helplessness. This underlying fear became more
obvious around break times with his resentment toward me for not giving
him enough toys, or time, or freedom and so forth. Talking about this need
for me to be there as and when it might suit him, rage and despair when I
was not, and so on, seemed to calm him and so there were periods of constructive play, literally as well as metaphorically. However, co-operative play
inevitably tended to bring us together, which produced it own anxieties. For
instance, the truck he had built, and the caravan I had constructed at his
request out of Lego bricks, were going to take two families on holiday, until
on the road they were waylaid by bandits who massacred both families. The
mess incurred by the event meant that the play material was hurled all over
the room. I took it that the hoped-for family (with me) could not be allowed
to exist. This seemed a precursor to a series of games that became violent.
From seemingly innocent games with rolled-up paper balls, Rick managed
to vent some of his aggression, whereupon I had to draw limits.

On these occasions there was also an element of sexual seductiveness as
he would slip away inviting me to grab him, or inviting me to retrieve
something from his lap. On one occasion he was angry that I said we could
not go into the garden:

'But those people are out there. How come they are allowed out there?'

I said that it was tough that adults seem to be able to do whatever they
want.

'Oh, but you're not allowed to rape a boy!'

'Do you really think that I want to do that?'

'You might! How do I know?'

Indeed, I thought, how could he know that? (Though he does here
seem to know that he is a boy!) I spoke about his testing me as coming out of
a need for safety, as distinct from some examples of his behaviour which
were in the nature of pre-emptive strikes. I clarified that he now knew he
was a boy, without having to be abused or abusive. Nonetheless, on some of
these occasions, especially at certain points such as the last session before a

break, or following a cancelled session, he would be impossible to reach and, when he flounced out of the room he would pass me such a cold look of icy contempt I felt that I did not know him at all. He would go to his mother in the waiting room and look back at me sometimes in a way that made me feel that I was the abuser.

About this time I began to fear for my own position. In this situation of open conflict between us I became aware that Rick had a very powerful weapon if he were to make an allegation that I had touched him, sexually or aggressively. Child protection procedures would have to be gone through, my innocence could hardly be proved, since no-one sees what goes on in the therapy room. Having the usual police check would mean nothing. Even if I could demonstrate my innocence I imagined that 'mud would stick', and that professionally I would be ruined. My nightmarish scenario was not diminished by reading an account of a psychotherapist who had been falsely accused (Ironside 1995) and who described a 'catastrophic' experience (p.195). I envisaged that even though no-one who knew me would believe I had done anything, nevertheless there could be no real protection against a malicious accusation and its consequences. Might I be disgraced, or even imprisoned, for something I had not done? I found myself picking up on media accounts of genuine miscarriages of justice, and wondering if I could really go on working with Rick. Should I stop working with this child as I had been, behind a closed door? Video taping every session seemed impractical, and would in any case have meant the virtual destruction of the psychotherapy as it had been set up. It would have seemed that I could no longer see myself as trustworthy. I discussed all this with colleagues, both with peers and went for extra supervision. No-one of course had the means to remove risk if I was to go on working with Rick, but sharing my anxieties helped me realize the countertransference meaning of what had been induced in me. One senior colleague, Dorothy Lloyd-Owen, pointed out that, since I had seen such a number of these boys, what was it about this one that had so alarmed me? I may not have been very receptive to her question at the time, but the comment made me realise that my concrete reactions to this stage of the therapy needed some rethinking. Anne Alvarez helped me to preserve my role with my patient, and specifically how to communicate with him about his inner reality, rather than being deflected by my own anxieties. What I had been getting was a little bit more than a glimpse of what the terrified child goes through. Like Sam, this boy was forcing me to question what I was doing as a psychotherapist. Perhaps complacently I had become accustomed to using a masculine identity as a kind of role model, providing an emotionally corrective experience that might bypass some of the worst of the traumatic damage experienced by this child. I considered how Rick's abuse had begun probably before he had speech, and that perhaps this terror that was put in me was Rick's only way of communicating what was still inside him. The professional annihilation I feared was merely my equivalent of the constant fear that Rick had endured. The 'powerful weapon' that I imagined Rick had was something he had taken from the phallic power of the adult abuser. He could feel that having been my victim he could now become the abuser, and I, once the abuser, would now be the victim. I had been terrorised, fearful of being blamed, and silenced, just as he had been.

Some of this hostility, and pain, was played out in subsequent sessions where a more settled state of mind helped Rick to focus his communications instead of feeling he had to disrupt sessions (and my confidence) to the point of almost destroying treatment. The intense conflicts went back to being shown in play material. Families of dolls, of animals, of robots, of cars, were carefully stood up together and then used for target practice with bricks flung at them, and the most explosive result was most delightfully welcomed by him. Becoming bored by this, as he was perhaps also by my interpretations that he felt that the abuse had destroyed his faith in his family, or that adults like myself needed to be able to stand up to his attacks, he moved on to allow more discussion of external reality. He confided in me about arguments at school, and about the times when he felt vulnerable and under attack. As I was perhaps counselling patience or making some ordinary comment like that, he remarked, 'but why do you allow children to hit you?' At a superficial level this made no sense to me since I had many times said he may not hit me, and indeed he had never seriously done so. On further discussion however it appeared that he was anxious about his attacks on me and perhaps sensed that he had pushed me close to my limits. This conflict between us was also about the question whether the sexual abuse by the lodger was really in fact Brian's fault, i.e. not Rick's own, as he feared. I let him know that I could see his concern, and that he needed to know that I could protect myself (though I did not introduce the subject of my own fears of allegations). So, clarifying the boundaries between us may also have met his complex feelings about Brian's abuse of him.

Something certainly seemed to have cleared from that time because our contact became very different. He brought a spinning top which produced quite a violent spin. I was asked to construct an enclosure out of bricks and he was fascinated to see the impact of his top as it struck back and forth. The delightful tension for Rick was to see whether the walls could stand up to the blows, or whether it was more exciting to see the bricks fly off when struck at random by the top. I felt that this was to do with his need to see if he could be contained, and if his violence, which so often he felt was out of control, could be made safe. The other side of the story was the pleasure at (symbolic) destruction of the containment offered by the therapy; but perhaps because it was symbolised, this material did not need interpretation. Our interaction in the sessions was now tolerable, instead of a constant battle for control. He could leave sessions early in protest at something I said, and return by agreement, rather than feeling that either one of us had had to submit to the other. He might still eye me carefully from time to time in order to be sure that I was not going to retaliate to some real or imagined attack on me.

Where then was the spinning top now safely contained, in his own mind, or in the session? As with Winnicott's (1971) theory of transitional space and transitional object, this is a paradoxical question because is not either/or, but both. The working-through of this abuser/victim dynamic was intricately bound up with the question of gender; it seemed that for Rick the danger of contact with me was that he would lose his masculinity. The lodger had fostered a perverse attachment so that Rick adapted to abuse by surmising that his (male) body became as if female, just as he felt made into something like a female by the abuser. The spinning top was an apt metaphor for his state of mind (and sometimes general hyperactivity) as he desperately attempted to repudiate the emasculation, and seduction, of the abuse. At the time of writing the spinning top seems to have come to rest, as Rick has, at least for periods of time, discovered a capacity to be in one place, and know himself to be male, rather than spinning between invented images of femininity.

DISCUSSION

Each of these boys' symptomatology may be understood as attempts to patch over fragmented sense of self. They might also be seen as 'brief communications from the edge' (Horne 2001), albeit that the plea to be heard and understood is heavily disguised. Both boys were at a stage of very early adolescence, or pre-adolescence, before the physical changes of puberty, yet with some of the precursors of the psychological changes that herald the development of adolescent identity. In different ways they were reacting to the expected demands of adolescence as if they were intolerable. Separation from childhood was experienced as annihilation, because there was no foundation for an adolescent identity except as victim or abuser. They were each in the process of disavowing their masculinity and opting instead for a path of perverse transsexual development. Perhaps not all transsexualism is perverse, but in the case of these abused/abusing boys it provided an avenue for gratifications that would inhibit healthy development.

To establish a realistic sexual identity (that is to say, based upon the actual body), bisexual fantasies have to be relinquished, or modified in some way (McDougall 1995, pp.5–6). Mourning, as noted above, is a necessary element in this process. Why was this so difficult in these cases? Both boys had reacted to their traumatic abuse by identifying themselves with the aggressor and adopting an abusive pattern of their own. In Rick's case the abuser was not female and so it was more of an active choice to portray himself as female. With Sam it was more of a compulsion. What they had in common was the need to find another as victim in order to avoid their own confusion and pain. What each brought to therapy was the need to continue the abuse of the other, to communicate their unwanted feelings in no uncertain terms. Part of this 'evacuation' into the other was the confusion about gender, which was manifested most clearly in the difficulty for the therapist in relating to the young patient. The therapist became seen as the partner in perversion as though he would be interested in the boy as 'female'. The therapist's interest in working with the child was interpreted as a sexual interest. At times the therapist did not know to whom he was talking. Was this a boy who thought he was a girl, or who was pretending he was female? If so, why would he use his male body to abuse other children? Or was he showing that neither male nor female could offer him any hope of safety?

Sam's case presents itself as the most hopeless, perhaps arising from the fact that the abuser was his mother and that in identifying with his aggressor he was relinquishing his masculinity. For both, however, maleness is equated with power, and femaleness with excitement. Underlying both these misconceptions is the experience that the body has been used as sexual object, and is no longer his own. If, as for Sam, there has been no renunciation of incestuous objects then an Oedipal rival is impossible to locate; no outside authority can be allowed to exist, hence his extremely defective socialisation. In the session material, such as it was, we were not able together to develop the 'symbolic organisation' around the important motifs (Coates and Moore 1997, p.307).

Rick, by contrast, was not compelled to destroy all his attachments. Although the damage caused by abuse was comparable with that of Sam, in terms both of the transsexual complication, and the abusiveness to other children, it seems that there was an overriding factor ultimately in his ability to mourn his losses. Probably the essential condition for this to happen was the containment of Rick's hostility through an adequate home environment. Thus, a separation from childhood and a developmental move was possible for him. It is also likely that his home situation would have broken down if he and his mother had not been helped to do some work on their shared trauma.

Sam externalised his difficulty with separation by engineering a precipitate departure, managing to leave behind intense feelings of failure in all the staff who had been involved with him. Being locked up was perhaps his only realisation of remaining the baby locked inside of mother, fantasising an all-inclusive, undifferentiated oneness. He could not afford, as Rick could, to engage in a struggle with (and sometimes against) a therapist, who might bring about an awareness of vulnerability, or loss. These cases exemplify a parallel process; just as the therapist is struggling to find an identity by which to relate to the patient, so the young person begins to uncover the damage done to the sense of who they are, and the uncertainty of who, or what, they will become.

CHAPTER 9

Paedophilia as a Perverse Solution to Adolescent Conflicts: The Case of Mr D

I dreamed that I was in a dark house looking for something, or someone. There was a movement in the shadows, someone was watching me. It was some sort of ghoul or zombie. His face seemed to be rotting. Then I saw that there were others looking at me with dead eyes and moving slowly towards me. I woke up terrified.

INTRODUCTION

Most paedophiles, according to a survey quoted by Howitt (1995, p.71) will admit to having been first aware of sexual impulses toward children by the age of 20. It is also reported (Elliott *et al.* 1995) that offending behaviour frequently starts in adolescence. Although the foundations of perverse psychopathology may be laid much earlier, it does seem clear that the trajectory of sexually perverse behaviour begins in these formative years. The 'fixed paedophile profile' takes shape in adolescence whilst a less serious 're-active' form may crop up in adult years (Groth 1978). There is naturally less therapeutic optimism in the treatment of adults who are confirmed in their paedophilic orientation, whilst the younger person, it is hoped, because of their incomplete sexual development may be guided into more socially acceptable behaviour. Adolescents however are typically volatile and unpredictable; they may well refuse treatment, or if there is compliance, it may well not arise from an awareness of needing help or a desire for self-knowledge. An adult who is committed to his treatment may not only benefit from this process but can provide a great deal of useful information about the development, function and meaning of those patterns.

The main developmental function of adolescence, in the psychoanalytic conceptualisation of Laufer and Laufer (1984, p.10) is the establishment of the 'final sexual organisation' of the adult personality. This has been the mainstay of the views put forward in this book. In the case of an adult then the question immediately arises as to whether that sexual orientation is indeed 'final' and whether or not change is possible. The various tasks of adolescence, changes in relation to family, to the individual's peer group, to their own body, and moving away from previously incestuously tinged childhood relationships, all have to be integrated with remnants of infantile conflicts, but in the context of a mature body with adult physical development. When that final sexual organisation is established, there seems to be no room for compromise, which may have been possible earlier in adolescent development (Laufer and Laufer 1984, p.189) The following case description and discussion asks whether an adult with a history of deviant sexual development might retrace his steps in order to correct these sexually perverse patterns; and if not, if the sexual orientation *is* fixed, whether at least some therapeutic gains are possible.

Mr D, aged 29, sought treatment because of a fear of breakdown, connected with the stress of leading a secret sexual life seducing pubertal boys, whilst outwardly maintaining a respectable veneer. In the years since adolescence the elements of his perverse behaviour had become increasingly bizarre, and dangerous; some of his underage victims had got together and were blackmailing him. He had been offered psychoanalytic treatment after an 'indecent exposure' offence some years before, as a 19-year-old. (In fact the offence involved the attempted assault of an eleven-year-old boy.) Mr D dropped out of that treatment after a few months. He felt he had not been helped by the neutral non-directive and interpretative stance of the therapist. He told me that he had concealed from his former therapist his fascination with sucking boy's penises. Unable to speak about this, he felt abandoned by the silence of the analyst. Intense shame at his secret caused him to break off treatment. Some ten years later he experienced an initial relief as he tearfully shared his current difficulties. We established an agreement that he would stop his sexual abuse of children, and undertake intensive (three times a week) psychotherapy. Thus, Mr D took the opportunity of exploring in detail and in depth the underlying reasons for his sexual predilections.

A recurrent theme was the distortion of his adolescent development. He described intense social anxieties that could be mollified only by a sexual fascination with boys beginning puberty. Neither the pre-pubertal child's body, nor the fully developed adult body, whether male or female, was of interest to him. He found himself aroused and attracted only to the young male body at the point of change. 'It's as though I am stuck in a time warp.' Not all paedophiles of course show this characteristic. Nevertheless, this particular deviation in an individual's sexual development raises questions about adolescent developmental tasks and whether it is possible for someone to locate the point of arrest, and through therapeutic work to resume the development of a more healthy and fulfilling sexual identity.

CONFIDENTIALITY AND A SETTING FOR TREATMENT

Adult work is technically different from adolescent psychotherapy, and because of the greater equality of status, the therapist must adopt a different stance. There is a different kind of professional responsibility in the therapist. Confidentiality of treatment is a more vexed issue with adults. For a young person being looked after by social agencies and brought for help, it is appropriate that the therapist should have freedom of communication with other professionals who may have parental responsibility, when anticipating instances of possibly dangerous or abusive behaviour. The rights of the patient can be balanced against his need to be kept safe from the consequences of his own actions. The situation is less clear with an adult who is seeking help. A therapist cannot ignore or condone offences against children, but there is also an ethical argument against breaking the confidentiality that is essential to effective treatment. Various aspects of these questions are explored in a recent collection of articles edited by Cordess (2000). One of those contributions, by McClelland and Hale, proposes that different levels of disclosure should be required for different professionals and propose a means of balancing of arguments for and against breaking confidentiality in a 'Disclosure Test' (p.51). This has yet to be agreed by statutory agencies.

Whilst there is no absolute rule, and little in the way of precedent, there needs to be in each case an agreement that can become a contract that seems acceptable to each party. In this case Mr D agreed that psychotherapy would be offered on condition of his abstention from the sexual abuse of children. A diagnostic consultation for the patient with a senior practitioner, and ongoing supervision of the work ensured that the therapist would not be working in isolation and thereby run the risk of taking on excessive responsibility with this patient.[1] Indeed, Mr D seemed to feel encouraged and supported by the understanding that I would not be able to keep secret any information about the recurrence of his abuse of children. He altered his work so that he was no longer in contact with young teenagers. However, for the therapist to have revealed past crimes would have effectively barred Mr D from treatment. Being sufficiently convinced of Mr D's motivation to correct his behaviour and work on his difficulties, and adequately supported by a network of fellow professionals, both therapist and client can find enough containment to be able to work on otherwise very dangerous issues. Far from being neutral, the therapist speaks for, and thus comes to symbolise the existence of a real authority, that of the father who imposes limits on gratification; the therapist in this position will therefore also have to accept the consequences of this: not only gratitude but also resentment.

Paedophiles are well known for their skills in ducking and weaving in order to avoid responsibility for their actions (internally to negate the Oedipal father) and Mr D proved to be no exception. For example, he claimed early in the treatment to have been unaware until only recently of the illegality of sex with 12–13-year-old boys, and yet had clearly been operating as if he should not be found out. At times it appeared that the treatment was for him a device to avoid the full force of the law should charges be brought against him, and that his therapy was a means of avoiding change rather than producing it. Such undermining would destroy the work if there were no basic framework centred on a notion of real change. Fundamental to the structure of a working relationship is the location and limits of responsibility between therapist and client. The therapist has responsibility naturally for the direct work with the client, to avoid false solutions, and to maintain the focus on the presenting problem, but this may reach the point of having to act if therapeutic work fails to prevent dangers to children. A clear agreement at the beginning of treatment defines the responsibility of both therapist and client and creates a boundary between the two, thus preventing the kind of merging and boundarylessness that perversity brings. Work on this at the early stage produced an important insight for Mr D that, '…the person I lie to most of all is myself'. Many times we referred back to this important self-perception.

Telling the story in its different versions has been developed into a model for therapeutic work (White and Epston 1990; White 1995). Narrative therapy has also been proposed as an effective way of dealing with sexual abuse and abusing (Etherington 2000). This model can be contrasted with one for abusers that is more directive, and emanates from the therapist's version, as it were, of the story; Wyre 1987 and Wyre and Swift 1990 prefer to challenge an abuser's justifications, in order to break down his denials, no matter how well hidden. This cognitive behavioural model goes on to provide prescriptions for 'relapse prevention'. Instead, the narrative model proposes that the client needs to tell his own story, to rewrite it, and thus find a new way of being. This model of 'narrative therapy' has something in common with the principles of psychoanalytic psychotherapy, although the narrative therapists mentioned above are also critical of the paradigms of psychoanalytic psychotherapy. The model of perverse psychopathology, it is said, threatens to take away authorship of the client's own experience, and the therapist is set up in an all-knowing and therefore all powerful, and possibly abusive, position.

Alternatively, as I hope to show here, a psychodynamic approach to Mr D's personal history both makes sense of his otherwise bizarre behaviour and opens up pathways towards change. In an equal, honest and open interaction with the therapist the client begins to see that taking responsibility is not the equivalent of custodial sentence, or a softer option, but a way forward to change. The quest for understanding must not be confused with a desire to condone or excuse. The psychodynamic therapist need not be straitjacketed by a supposed 'analytic' neutrality because it is not possible to be neutral on questions of child abuse. The quest for meaning in perverse behaviour arises from both the therapist's and the client's shared awareness of the necessity for change. The aim is not so much to explain the behaviour by interpretations based on psychological theory, but to use the client's stories to illuminate and change previously repetitive patterns. The therapist in this view need not repudiate the role of the authoritative father, just as another transference, that of the castrating mother cannot be avoided. Consistent interpretations of the working relationship with the therapist, based on an agreement about its limits, ensure that these roles are understood rather than enacted, or unthinkingly repeated.

THE INITIAL PICTURE OF SADO-MASOCHISM

Mr D sought help after a series of what were described to his doctor as panic attacks. He experienced a rising feeling of terror, for 'no apparent reason'. With tightness in his chest, dizziness, nausea and feelings of terror, he thought he was going to die. When he mentioned to his doctor that he thought also that he had a sexual problem, perhaps he was 'gay', he was not sure, he was referred for psychological help. Upon further exploration of the context of these panic attacks it became clear that they occurred when Mr D had impulses to abuse boys, in situations where he might be caught. He admitted that he had been entrapping pubertal boys for sexual activities for some years, exploiting his position as a youth worker. He was relying on inducements, payments and seduction with drugs and alcohol rather than overtly violent means of coercion. The 'fun-seeking' image he had promulgated for some time was beginning to break down and the underlying abusive nature of his acts was becoming inescapable; some of his victims had got together to threaten him with violence and exposure. Also the sexual activities themselves had been changing; whereas he used to set up 'mugging' games in which boys would take his money for touching genitals and being touched, Mr D found himself more recently paying boys to physically abuse him, including beating his genitals, bondage, particularly of testicles, and on some occasions driving a nail through his foreskin onto a table. Complex scenarios, 'sexual situations', as he called them, had been staged by him with boys in which he would be robbed, tied up and beaten, but as they became real and he found he did not have control, he had become frightened.

A common theme through these sado-masochistic scenarios, which was explored during the first months of psychotherapy, was the interplay of power relations. Through various means he would play at being under the power of the other, and foster the illusion that his partner was in control. This was most blatantly evident in a game in which he would give his partner the key to a padlock that had been locked over his testicles. The boy was given to think that only he had the key, and that when they met again, Mr D would be released. However Mr D was quietly triumphant and excited in the knowledge that he himself had another key. Through this and many other devices Mr D would keep a sense of control. He would have led his victim into something that the boy was not aware of, usually a first sexual experience, whilst giving him the illusion that he had taken advantage of Mr D. These games, the rules of which were the subject of the most intense efforts, were the end points to much manoeuvring, wooing or courtship by Mr D. It was only boys disinclined to homosexuality who would be of interest. Any sign of effeminacy or homosexual interest would deter Mr D. He delighted in turning a boy away from heterosexuality. The pinnacle of his achievement would be to persuade the boy to allow fellatio, the performance of which Mr D considered himself able to give more pleasure than could any woman. A more hidden aim, which emerged in our work together, was in being able to induce a sense of disappointment in a boy, that sex with a female would not be as pleasurable as it had been with him. But the more knowing a boy was, the more experienced in sex with either males or females, then the less desirable would that boy be.

FAMILY BACKGROUND

Mr D was born the only child of an upper-middle-class, relatively aged and academic couple. Whilst his mother and father were not abusive or blatantly neglectful in a material sense Mr D experienced them as remote and preoccupied in their own concerns. During the course of examining his childhood, however, an underlying difference emerged between his view of mother and father. Mother was perceived as immensely powerful and controlling whilst father, though offering some hope of separateness and life, was extremely distant and ungratifying. During the early months of therapy he had a conversation with his mother whilst looking at some old family photos. She said that she felt he had turned away from her by the beginning of school age and that he had gone into a shell, from which he never returned. However, Mr D was living with his parents up until a year after his treatment began. He described his childhood as happy at school, but there was 'nothing at home'. Both his parents worked long hours. He was vaguely aware of something disagreeable, and piecing together half-overheard conversations deduced that his mother really detested the sexual demands of his father. He saw the father as humiliated and banished to his study and unable to be potent with Mr D's mother in any way. Mr D grew up fearful of his mother's control, but at times joined with her in contempt for the father.

For as long as he could remember he felt he needed to be secretive and to conceal all his activities for fear of detection. Less conscious but equally real was the fear of being taken over by these activities. He yearned for closeness with father but perhaps gave up hope of anything more than he could expect. Mr D would liven up considerably when talking about his school days, his friendship and activities with boys. In this context he could be the centre of attention. He loved the 'camaraderie' (a favourite phrase) at school and college, but by then he was leading a double life.

In his own early adolescence something occurred that may have had traumatic impact. Symptoms of what turned out to be appendicitis were ignored by the parents and developed into peritonitis. Mr D described one sleepless and extremely painful night in hospital where he felt he could not ask for help from the nursing staff. When his parents visited the next day he first of all hid himself and then showed a face grimaced in pain, anger and rejection of his parents who were startled. But then he smiled, relaxed and gave them a 'happy, good face'. He remembered distinctly their relief when they were shown the acceptable side of him. Meanwhile he had successfully concealed his pain and rage. Some of these contradictions were evident in the interactions with me; always jovial when meeting me and parting, this covered up a state of mind in which eventually he came to admit that sometimes he felt abandoned, desperate that he had little in his life except the pleasures that he felt I was now removing.

THE SCENARIO OF SEXUAL PERVERSION

Mr D had a very wide circle of friends and colleagues and spent a great deal of energy being helpful, kind, and someone that everyone appreciated. But no sexual relationship could incorporate loving or warm feelings. The dream reported at the head of this chapter, communicated in the first few weeks of treatment, was a stark portrayal of Mr D's inner world, populated as it was by the corporeal relics of hate that had been expressed toward the body of his erotic choice. There were some friendships that had survived, though they were based on denial of the earlier sexual component. A boy's athleticism, physical beauty and newfound potency were what Mr D prized above all else. Intelligence, personal charm and creative potential were adornments and felt to be valuable extras but not essential. Size of penis was the subject of endless fascination. Many boys had been seduced by Mr D who were 'lacking in that department' but usually these sexual partners were dropped after a sexual encounter. As much as Mr D gloried in the young male body, he disparaged his own. His own penis he felt was too small, and there seemed to be no pleasure in his own physicality; he was slow to become aroused, and immensely disgusted if he should ejaculate. Indeed, it would only be by being tied up and brought to orgasm 'involuntarily' by a partner that this would happen. This would signify the end of any pleasure. The pursuit of the boy and the breaking-down of the boy's resistance to the idea of sex contained most of the excitement. The contrast between his idealisation of the young male body and the contempt for his own was a striking realisation for Mr D in the early months of treatment, as was the issue of power between himself and his young victims. It was with a sense of dawning amazement that Mr D realised that he was virtually stealing a body of which he might be proud instead of his own which he had to reject. Mr D was not conscious however of envying the boy since immediately the 'sexual situation' was over, i.e. when the boy had ejaculated, usually into Mr D's mouth, then all the faults in the boy, his selfishness, deceptiveness, greed, manipulativeness and so on, would be overwhelming to Mr D who would then have to break off contact.

On one occasion, shortly before seeking help, Mr D was left naked in a hotel room handcuffed and terrified that the boys would not return. He was filled with self-loathing and disgust since his paid sexual partners had brought him to orgasm and then left him 'in a mess'; but reflecting on these 'madnesses' he realised that he had also become more worried by the increasing use of drugs and alcohol leading to a sense of disorientation and fear of loss of control. Discussing these issues led to a better sense of reality, as Mr D was able to see the cyclical pattern; periods of self-disgust and abstinence led to a build-up of tension, idealisation of a young male, in whose image he wanted to see himself, followed by the creation of a new yet more dangerous scenario of sado-masochistic encounter. He admitted to having seriously contemplated suicide during the downward spiral of this pattern of events.

The first few months of therapy brought a sense of hope and the possibility of renewal. Mr D admitted that he had been turning a blind eye to his own addictive behaviours in previous years. Acutely aware of how able he was to lie to himself, he had been forced at this point to admit that he was in a complete dead end and that he would have to stop. He was thus more realistically determined to change his ways, not out of professed concern for others, but for his own survival.

Generally he would express great appreciation of me as a 'sympathetic ear' for things he had never spoken about before, but at certain times something quite different would be glimpsed; there would be traces of pleasure at the idea of shocking me, and triumph at doing things like giving money to young men who would then allow sex, activities which, although just within the law, nevertheless, as he well knew, were essentially, that is internally, at the same level of perversion. His quiet satisfaction at my helplessness, as he saw it, was the external sign of his determination not to change.

STUCK BETWEEN HOMO- AND HETEROSEXUALITY

My interpretations about the importance of power and control in his sexuality were refuted by his insistence on the erotic. He became preoccupied with women and by the fact that he had no desire for them. Mulling over the process of development of his sexual identity in his own adolescence he considered what had happened to his heterosexuality. He had been out with a number of girls. Being good-looking and charming there was no difficulty in attracting females. He wanted to 'have sex', and did so around the age of 18, with a young woman, in order he said, not out of any great wish to do so, but to 'see what all the fuss was about'. He was quite frankly disappointed. There was little or no enjoyment and it seemed a chore. By that point he had already had a number of sexual experiences with boys, one older than himself who initiated him at the age of 13, and then with boys younger than himself. These consisted of mutual masturbation and beginning to experiment with oral sex, which was later to be the much preferred activity. By the time he was 19 he was completely fascinated by the physical changes of male puberty. He had also by this point organised a network of contact where boys would come to him for money. He used to inspect the penis and if it were too small he would tell them to come back in a few months time when to his great joy the penis was bigger. Then he would be fascinated to stimulate this penis rather than have any involvement with his own. He persisted with girlfriends for a time though often became infuriated by them because of their expectations of his time and attention. Above all he hated the sense of being controlled, and in our discussions Mr D could link these with similar feelings of fear and hate that he had had as a child about his mother. After many more months it was possible for Mr D to make the connection between this sense of control he perceived in the female with his own sense of deprivation and experience of the mother as withholding.

Through this work we could also understand something of his revulsion at the idea of homosexuality. For some years he had presented an image of heterosexuality to the world, imagining that he was hiding a homosexual identity, telling himself that he was just 'doing things with boys'. But the homosexuality was just another layer of deception. He would console himself that his shameful secret was 'being gay', despite the fact that he had no sexual interest in men. He had continued to live with his parents, with visits from boys only when they were out of the house. Mr D wondered whether he had turned to boys as a way of not admitting his sexuality. He justified the abuse of young people as a necessary means of covering up the shameful sense of who he was. He realised that he confused being homosexual with being female and therefore hateful. The sexual contact with boys seemed to be a way of trying to confirm his masculinity, and paradoxically disowning homosexual desires. In the second year of treatment he was prepared to have this strategy more deeply questioned. He asked himself – if he were homosexual then why was at no stage an adult homosexual relationship satisfactory? His sexual relations had always been with prepubertal boys. The few encounters he had had with homosexual men were greeted with sheer distaste. As an experiment at about two years into the therapy he went to a 'gay sauna' but was horrified to see a man penetrating another in anal intercourse. He had to rush away from the situation. The horror seemed to be about fear of attack and led us to an awareness of his criterion for sexual excitement, that of a sense of being in power and control. He reminisced that at the age of 15 he had told his parents about his homosexual fears, and they had sent him to the doctor 'to get a pill'. The issue was never spoken about again, but remained a source of grievance, that he had never been understood.

At times in these discussions it seemed that I as the therapist was being invited to compensate for the parents' rejection, by accepting his homosexuality, and become a mother who would allow him to separate. But this was a fantasy designed to fend off anxieties about the paedophilia. Similarly, Mr D's protestations that he was 'clean' (i.e. staying away from abusing boys), whilst at one level being reasonably valid and convincing, nevertheless were also duplicitous in that the fantasies, and orientation, remained unchanged. I was being put in a position of the mother who has the wool pulled over her eyes. He began to be much more specific about occasions in which he was tempted to get talking to the newspaper boy, for example, or a boy wandering on the street. On one occasion he said that my face floated into his mind and deterred him from going ahead with the contact he was developing with a group of boys. It seemed that I was functioning as a kind of superego for him, but one whose control was somewhat precarious. On some occasions I had to be placated and on others hated. As our discussions continued over the months, it seemed that I was moving towards being perceived also as having ego functions. He would take my lead in examining the meaning, for example, of an apparently innocent impulse to strike up conversation with this or that boy in a shop, or on the street. (These would initially have been put as evidence that he could now have contact with boys without risk. More than once I drew a comparison with the alcoholic who now was giving himself permission to have a drink.) He was more able to think through the possible consequences of his actions, now that he was more aware of their meaning. However, double meanings, and deceptions were still rife, for instance his protestations that I had helped him so much, how his life was totally changed, no longer having to live in torture and fear, closely followed by accounts of perverse behaviour albeit within legal age limits.

There was a combination of triumph as well as shame as he revealed that from time to time he was paying young men for sex, 'over 18!' he hastily assured me. These were not the type of younger boys that he would have targeted previously, he insisted, but were lower-class, immature young men, in need of money, a job, somewhere to live. They would be involved with drugs and petty crime, and Mr D would take care to present himself as a force for good, someone who was trying to raise these boys up from their lowly position to something more respectable. The promised elevation of course never occurred, and gradually Mr D could see that these partners were being employed to enact fantasies arising from the insoluble problem of being neither heterosexual nor homosexual. The anger and dissatisfaction however was that these were far from the ideal male of his imagination. He had got rid of the 'toys', i.e. whips, locks, straps and other sado-masochistic equipment, but retained the essential feature of deceiving partners that they were the ones in control. It was painful for him to realise that their sexual contact with him was based on a need for money. His feelings of helplessness about this contrasted enormously with the satisfaction of actually being in control of the 'sexual situation'. Thus, in relation to me he could also maintain the sense of being in control as well as the pretence of being under mine.

I began to see the sexual scenarios created by Mr D as less the acting-out of erotic fantasies than providing information about the emotional trauma behind Mr D's sexual compulsions. He felt devastated by the rejection, as would inevitably happen, from the young man of his desires. These sexual encounters seemed more likely to occur around break times in the therapy. The sessions came to concentrate much more on the emotional needs that lay behind the sexual acting-out. As well as being the mother who could be duped, I felt myself now to be more the father from whom he needed understanding and guidance. It was as though I should be able to rescue Mr D from his dirty, messy dangerous feelings. In this uneasy balance Mr D seemed contained, both in his triumph over me and in the desperate need for help.

Pain was a crucial factor in the management of this uneasy balance between separation and closeness. Sucking the penis of a paid partner who was on top of him, Mr D would feel consumed with pleasure, but also be in terror of suffocation and being crushed. He would only rarely have an erection during these sexual encounters, but would masturbate later at the thought of the pleasure that he had given the partner, who was now gone. The excitement was at the thought of the power of the other man's penis. Being anally penetrated left him with a similar sense of having acquired the potency of the partner. Then Mr D began to experiment with these sexual situations and reported to me that, unusually, he himself had penetrated another man's anus. There was great excitement when he saw his penis disappear between the buttocks of the other man. However, there was no pleasure in his penis, but instead pain, which became unbearable. He discovered that he preferred being buggered and began to experience anal orgasms. In this way Mr D it seemed was inventing new games, playing with the anxiety-laden fantasy of losing his own penis and then possessing the penis of the other in his anus. This seemed to be attempting to fend off castration anxiety by identification with the powerful penis of his partner, but because his anal possession has turned the powerful phallus into faeces it seemed that Mr D could never escape the emptiness of having neither his own penis nor that of another. The use of pain seems crucial here because it has the function of being able to control the object in an omnipotent way. 'You've taken my penis, you've given me pain,' he seemed to be saying to his partner, 'therefore you owe me your powerful penis, and I will turn it into shit'. In this way Mr D seemed to be triumphing over terrors of castration terrors of abandonment by the father. The price of this triumph however was his masculinity that left him defenceless against the deeper terror of annihilation by mother.

THE PERVERSION FENDS OFF THE DEATH OF THE FATHER

After about two years of therapy Mr D's aged father fell ill and within three months had died. Mr D senior's health had been failing for some years and Mr D's anticipation of this outcome emerged as an important factor in his seeking help. He had become closer to his father, communicating more than before. Mr D's main dread was being 'left alone with mother'. However, a few weeks before the inevitable result of his father's terminal illness, Mr D met Craig, just 18, for whom he was suddenly filled with great desire. The funeral, which Mr D had so dreaded, faded into insignificance beside his preoccupation with Craig. Although he was of the legal age of consent, Craig provided many opportunities for Mr D to exploit. From a deprived background with no parents, money, accommodation or work opportunities Craig needed Mr D. He was unattached, immature, promiscuous, but above all, heterosexual, which evoked Mr D's desires to corrupt and deflect Craig from women. Mr D set himself the task over the next few months of trying to inveigle Craig into a 'sexual situation', and so was able, despite my efforts, almost entirely to deny the effects of his father's death.

It seemed to me from tales of their encounters that Craig was stringing Mr D along and playing hard to get so that Mr D's offers of money, help, etc. were redoubled. But Mr D could not hear my interpretations on this since Craig was so idolised. Craig was regarded as an innocent, unfortunate in his neediness and especially gifted in his abilities, which remained undefined. As long as I was being seen as representing his own superego, ineffective, and silenced, derived from the mother who would deprive him, then I could be ignored. Craig was also identified with the deprived and the idealised self. He was oblivious to my interpretations about his need to corrupt that ideal self. On a trip abroad Mr D succeeded in getting Craig drunk enough to accept fellatio. This happened a few more times over the next few months, but always surreptitious and never acknowledged. Mr D reported his blissful feelings when he felt that Craig, though pretending to be asleep, was occasionally more active in his enjoyment at having his penis sucked. Mr D even managed, after great efforts, to get Craig to allow anal intercourse. It was perhaps this that finally overstrained the relationship. But Craig's heterosexual identity needed to be reasserted and so he would provocatively bring young women back to Mr D's flat, where he had moved in, to have sex loudly, and much to Mr D's disgust. One of Craig's girlfriends, said Mr D, 'might as well have her head cut off for all the interest Craig has, apart from her body'. On more than one of these occasions Mr D found himself a voyeur to Craig's sexual intercourse and reported that he was both excited at the sight of Craig's buttocks moving in intercourse and also humiliated that he was excluded. Dreams occurred about this time which very much mirrored this pattern; there would be a third person hiding in the background, looking on at an object of Mr D's desire. This enabled some useful work to be done on the infantile excitement of being a voyeur in the primal scene. This seemed to have been connected with memories of parents' sexual problems. It was possible therefore for Mr D to see both the hatred and the excitement of the parental intercourse that he had recreated by bringing Craig into his flat.

As the relationship with Craig went downhill Mr D could accept that he had as always been lying to himself that there ever could have been a relationship that could work. As Craig's drunken fights in pubs and occasional threats of violence to Mr D himself became inescapable, Mr D had to agree that there was something corrupting and destructive in his own involvement with Craig. He decided that the relationship should have to peter out. Whilst presented to me on the one hand as a positive and good thing to do, it was clear that Mr D had also lost interest in Craig. Mr D had to dismantle all the many ways in which he had made Craig dependent. This meant giving up the illusion that this was a relationship between adults. Some of the anger and bitterness towards Craig was also expressed towards me, though in roundabout form. I would be regaled with tales of 'straight' men, tantalised by the idea of forbidden sex with younger women, but resigned to the dullness of sex with a fat, middle-aged, and bossy wife; these were subtle and sometimes more obvious attempts to make me feel that I was the one deprived of pleasure in life and excluded from exciting sexual relations. My comments on this process produced a realisation in Mr D that he was the one after all struggling with these anxieties despite his efforts to disown them.

GIVING UP THE PAEDOPHILIC SOLUTION

A plateau was reached after about two years of treatment with the depressive realisation that giving up the relationship with Craig meant giving up the object of his sexual desires in the form of the immature young male of his fantasy. This was felt to be extremely difficult because for Mr D there was as yet nothing to take its place. He threw himself into his work where he was now engaged in projects with older adolescents both male and female. There were a few flirtations, never consummated, and every few weeks the tensions within him would rise until he felt that he was compelled to re-establish contact with one or other of the young men with whom he occasionally paid for sex. However, the pleasure had gone out of these encounters, partly because he now could see through his own delusion, that he was so desired. Now he realised that there was really nothing of the love that he had so idealised and imagined. Whilst expressing great relief that he was no longer abusing children, and feeling protected from the worst of his sado-masochistic practices, there was nevertheless a vague bitterness toward me. The old triumph that he used to express at the miserable marriages that he saw around him in his friends was replaced by a gloomy despondency that for him the object of desire was truly unattainable. He considered the possibility of sexual relations with the women he occasionally met or with 'older' (i.e. mature) men, but none of them appealed. Whereas he had many friends from different walks of life, these were social contacts that could never be considered as sexual connections. He felt the irony acutely that just as he had learned to take some pleasure in his own body and get a sense of potency and effectiveness in himself, so he lost touch entirely with the possibility of a partner. Whilst expressing appreciation for me keeping him on the 'straight and narrow', the question seemed to hang oppressively in the sessions: 'Is this all there is?'

As he questioned whether there was any hope of change, it seemed to me that Mr D was seeking to retain his essential paedophilia as a state of safety in order to protect himself from anxieties arising from any other kind of sexual orientation. In this way too he was keeping me at a distance. Having defined my role and my function for him, which was to make safe (and secretly actually preserve) the internal paedophilia, he was now closing down the possibility of further change. At this point he began to wonder whether the therapy should stop but was immediately brought up against the possibility that he could revert to his old ways. He knew he could not go on seducing boys but nor could he give up the desires. Several missed sessions seemed to be attempts to solve the problem of not being able to continue and not being able to stop. I said that he seemed to feel that it was I who had taken away his pleasure; was I simply leaving him with the fear of becoming more depressed and lonely? His response was to say submissively, 'Well, that's just how it has to be.' I felt that I had now become a kind of implacable father who castrates him. Important external changes had been achieved but little internal change in terms of his sexual orientation, and the evidence for this was the lack of movement in terms of a more satisfactory sexual relationship.

For several months we were on a plateau of attenuated depression. The ploy of sexual games had been given up to a considerable extent but these meant the surfacing of depressive anxieties and pain. There were many bleak periods in these sessions. Hopelessness was mitigated by a gallows humour, that he was 'just impossible to please', but behind this mournful presentation I felt that I too was being experienced as impossible to please; he imagined that I would 'let him go', i.e. end his treatment only when he had achieved a 'normal sex life', though no such agreement had of course been made. This situation as he had set it up suited the perversion perfectly since, knowing he would never be 'normal', it gave him the freedom to gratify his desires with male prostitutes. It also distanced the need to think about ending therapy. However, his treatment did end, but before describing that process, this is perhaps a suitable point to discuss some of this clinical material.

DISCUSSION: THE FUNCTION OF THE PERVERSION

Given the risks to the perpetrator of this form of anti-social activity, especially in the current climate of hatred and vigilante action against paedophiles, there must be some very powerful purpose served by its persistence. From Freud's (1909) case of the 'Rat Man' onwards, the sense of compulsion, or addiction has been observed as one of the essential features of perversion (Goldberg 1995, pp.176–7). McDougall (1986) extends the metaphor of addiction, drawing attention to the need for 'people as addictive substances' (p.68). Mr D had been driven to specific sexual behaviours in the sexual scenarios developed as an adolescent which then became fixed as an adult. Disentangling the unconscious reasons for those 'choices', and tracing them back to the points at which they were first made, was a process that gave some hope to Mr D that he might change. However, the sense of a really free choice was curtailed by his need for me to be a coercive and depriving maternal presence. Nonetheless, it was felt to be a revelation, and a liberation, when he could see how the question of control was an integral part of the sexual scenarios that he created. He came to accept how invested he was in the control of others as a form of sexual coercion. An important emotional insight was the realisation that the coercion of others resulted from his inner sense of being controlled by his own desires and frustrations. This led to the next step of discovering the reasons behind the need for such control.

Since it was in adolescence that the sense of compulsion first became familiar to Mr D, it is there perhaps that the origins of these problems may be found. Laufer and Laufer (1984) describe a form of 'premature foreclosure' that some adolescents adopt in order to defend against primitive anxieties stirred up by sexual maturation.

> The developmental process has ended prematurely, with the integration of a distorted body image and the ability to ward off any...doubt in the solution found. There is an absence of anxiety. The main means of sexual gratification has been established without the adolescent's having been able to allow for any change of earlier solutions to conflict... (Laufer and Laufer 1984, p.181)

The young people included by these authors in this category are those who have chosen perverse and addictive behaviours, over and above human relationships. The overriding need is to avoid breakdown, of the kind that was beginning to catch up with Mr D. The perverse behaviours developed in *early* adolescence by Mr D seem to suggest this developmental arrest. The feared breakdown is an 'unconscious rejection of the sexual body' (p.22) in which the ego is passive in the face of demands from unconscious sexual fantasy. With some relenting of Mr D's sense of compulsion and of his need to coerce others, we were able to work on the meaning of the 'sexual situations' that were the result of such intense efforts. McDougall (1986, pp.245–63) describes 'neo-sexualities' as invented scenarios in which the rules of sexuality and procreation are rewritten in accordance with the infantile requirements of the perverse structure. In Mr D's case the drama centred on the erect phallus, the idealisation of which could fend off the fear of impotence, inadequacy, castration; but this idealisation only thinly covered its opposite – hence Mr D's horror at the 'mess' he felt left with when a sexual partner brought him, usually against his conscious will, to orgasm.

The attraction to the young male body was, after Mr D's adolescent development, fully established as a sexual orientation but had its roots in infantile frustrations and primitive (infantile) sensual experience. Oral and anal desires and fears proliferate around the central phallic orientation. His oral pleasures were manifold, not only in sucking the penis but also his delight in talking, laughing, making others laugh, drinking, drugs, and a fascination with perfect teeth. These pleasures produced triumph over the depriving mother, the reversal of an orally depriving breast. His compulsion to fellatio may have originated in a fantasy of being in control of the nipple, the reverse of which was his horror of a nipple that is felt to be like his own penis, limp, small and ungiving. He could thereby fend off that anxiety of oral deprivation by finding (creating), a powerful nipple-penis, harnessing its power and making it one that could not only feed, but fill him up and choke him, even kill him if he were not able to induce it to ejaculate. Sucking the penis became an obsession and is evocative of an infantile desperation to feed from a nipple, albeit with an aim which is very different from that of the feeding infant. Instead of obtaining nourishment, the perverse intention is consciously to give pleasure, but unconsciously to gain control, corrupt and turn away the heterosexual rival.

Interpretations along these lines led to a reduction of the compulsion both in behaviour and in fantasy. However, as acting-out reduced, Mr D became more aware of despair at his sense of deprivation and inadequacy.

Thus, disentangling the perverse structure revealed an underlying depression. As our work went on, a transference developed in which Mr D seemed to be experiencing something very unexciting, almost as if a limp kind of food was being provided by me. A period of frequent absences demonstrated his need to avoid such frustration and the associated anxieties at this time. Nevertheless, the process of accepting these interpretations reduced the need for triumph over the internalised mother and the prevention of her intercourse with father. Mr D went on to experiment with other forms of sexual behaviour and his discovery of an anal orgasm seemed to be a recurrence of an infantile idea that he could take over mother's vagina. As soon as this appeared, however, Mr D had to disown it and to veer away from that homosexual form of sexual expression. Obsessional traits in his own character were mobilised – cleanliness, controllingness, all powerful aspects of mother's perceived character, and employed to prevent him pursuing anal sex. Undertaking a colonic irrigation at this time seemed to be about a wish to clean out perverse fantasies whilst at the same time indulging a masochistic surrender to deep penetration.

Women were perceived as all like mother, feared and hated because of their need to be in control. McDougall (1986) describes the pervert's terror of mother as a 'chasm', a void in which he will be annihilated (pp.99–102). Here the therapeutic value of his awareness of his need to control was indispensable. His early relationships with women foundered largely because he felt their needs and demands to be intolerable. It was as if he needed to get away in order to preserve some sense of being himself. Boys were immensely more exciting and he would go to endless lengths to satisfy their desires, but only in so far as he felt himself to be in the powerful position of hunter, seducer or leader. Games of allowing the other to think he was in control when really Mr D was 'calling the shots' (a favourite phrase), were crucial. Instead of feeling controlled by a girlfriend (equivalent to mother), with a young male he could feel that he had the powerful penis under his control, i.e. become himself the all-powerful mother. An important part of disentangling this compulsion was Mr D's growing awareness that he had in fact embodied many of the hated characteristics he felt about his mother, his ability to organise events of all kinds, to run things, to nag and control people. He even found himself talking and acting like the mother he so hated and despised. The ever-present feature always was the need to be in control in order to defend against crushing low self-esteem. He now could see that in order to neutralise the mother as castrator he had commandeered her power. Finding out about this process led to the difficult stage of confronting the opposite of triumph, that of shame.

THE PERVERSE STRUCTURE AS AN ATTEMPT AT SOLVING THE PROBLEM OF EMOTIONAL INTIMACY

Much of the clinical material points toward difficulties in separating from mother as the central issue. Tremendous relief was experienced in moving out of the parental home. Glasser (1988) showed how the annihilatory anxieties associated with sexual perversion can be understood as structured around the 'core complex' (p.125). He postulates that the capacity for emotional closeness and intimacy has been damaged by early experiences that threatened to engulf, dominate and control the developing infant. Glasser suggests that one of the infant's responses to these early threats to emotional, psychic, and, in some cases, physical survival is to mobilise a particular form of sexualised aggression that has as its aim, not the removal or the destruction of the threat, but to retain at a safe distance the parental object on whom of course he depends. This covert aggression, originally self-preservative, is turned into sado-masochism because of the conflation of love and hate. Sadism expresses the need to keep control, whilst masochism not only provides a cover but also, if the object is perceived as needing the child to suffer, serves the need to preserve attachment relationships. 'Thus the pervert is able to engage the object in sadomasochistic terms...(which) keeps the object at a safe distance – a distance which precludes trust and intimacy' (Glasser 1988, p.126). Much of these dynamics emerged in the transference. Mr D's pseudo-servitude to me was based on the idea that as the cruel mother I had power over him; but also he knew he had the capability of turning the tables and of pulling the wool over my eyes, as he had done so much with his mother. As father I was despised and jeered at, in hidden ways, as for example, the poor unfortunate heterosexual married to a fat, unappealing and controlling wife. The phallus in all its glory, his adoration as well as humiliation before it, was also his triumph over the feared and hated mother. This was achieved not in identification with father but by means of the perverse solution. In the absence of an effective father the young Mr D arranged his own omnipotent controls to fend off unbearable feelings in relation to mother.

OBSTACLES TO AN ADULT SEXUAL IDENTITY

The phallus could not become the equivalent of father's genital because infantile impulses, oral and anal, conspired to corrupt and destroy. Both orifices were invested each in particular ways with magical properties akin to worship of the penis, but it was anality that was at the core of the destruction of the phallus. The fascination and again triumph with the anus was expressed in many ways, for example, in response to seeing Craig bend over in a pub, he could say secretly to himself, 'I've been there.' Secrecy was an important ingredient because he would no longer feel excluded from the excitement of the hidden, and then revealed, phallus. In his adolescence the development of his sexual body was felt to be terrifying to him and he turned to other boys for consolation, but in so doing Mr D constructed a scenario in which father's anus has substituted for mother's vagina and is despised by the boy. The loss of both incestuous objects of desire is mollified by the glorification of the boy-man's penis. Mr D could feel that he was master over the process of sexual development where before he felt he had had no control. In this way the perverse solution was an attempt to compensate for the perceived lack of father and to bypass the difficulty of coping with envy and rage with mother. The secrecy was at the same time a reversal of the experience of being excluded from the secret relationship of his parents. Obsessional traits defended against anal preoccupations and emotional investment. Above all, Mr D needed to feel that he had the secret of sexuality, the secret that there is no difference between the sexes and no dependence on an object of desire for satisfaction (McDougall 1986, p.267). The fear in the adolescent Mr D of the vagina is overlaid by turning to the penis of other boys, but the fear returns because the anus is then contaminated with terrors of mother's vagina. With his mouth the infant Mr D fantasises his conquest of the terrifying mother, but the anus demolishes father's phallus, with devastating results on the psyche.

Relinquishing the quest for the adored phallus was felt to be equivalent to annihilation. In his treatment Mr D came across the inevitable challenge to his sexuality and had to question the illusion of making the penis the solitary and self-sufficient tower, as it were, of his defensive system. The union of penis with vagina was contemplated with horror, and indistinguishable from anal intercourse. Only the penis stimulated by mouth was exciting. There was little sense of the penis as belonging to a person as such, or being anything other than an object in itself, and for only itself. Hence,

the fascination with the young male body, to be grasped before its possession by another (female). With each new conquest of a young boy there was
the promise of a consummate experience, of being completely overwhelmed by the phallus. But with each partner there was disappointment,
followed by contempt.

Could the father, either as a real person, or as a psychic entity have
provided an alternative to the world of perverse actions? Ruszczynski
(2001) shows how the misrepresentation of reality is central to the perverse
state of mind, and he goes on to draw in the significance of the role of the
father. Ruszczynski quotes Glasser (1995, p.409), who pointed to the resolution that would, if allowed, be provided by father as an alternative object
above and beyond the 'irreconcilable conflict of the core complex'. Seen as
weak and ineffective, however, the father was not felt to be a viable alternative for the young boy. The masculinity of father could not be introjected as
a symbolic entity, a process that might have provided the boy some hope of
independence; instead, that quality of maleness was grasped at, literally and
gobbled up in a concrete or physical manifestation. But this phallus was not
seen as really masculine. Mr D fought shy of a homosexual identity seeing
himself as 'between male and female'. The phallus for him had to have
immature, feminised qualities, like his choice of sexual partner with the
smooth skin, the pretty face. Thus, the perverse solution had the effect of
'undifferentiating' male and female and thereby diminishing anxiety about
relating to someone who is different, which would give rise to conflicts
about closeness, about separation and loss of his incestuous objects. The
intended 'solution' however left aside the question of the development of
Mr D's own masculinity. The omnipotent fantasy barely patched over an
impotent inner reality.

ENDING PHASES OF TREATMENT

Having a male therapist might have facilitated the process of finding some
positive masculine ideal within himself, but it was difficult to see this as real.
As treatment wore on, Mr D became disenchanted, embittered even, and
there was a certain grim satisfaction as he said, 'Well, there is no cure, is
there, for people like me, how can there be? There's nothing you can do,
we've understood everything, there's nothing more to say…' However, if I
was perceived as someone who might yet have something to say about his

retreat to a comfortable fatalism, then he would prefer a masochistic submission to me as mother rather than accept me as a sort of father who might be acknowledged as not only right but having some emotional contact with him. The experience of having triumphed over me as mother led inevitably to mourning the loss of father. Looking back, he could see how the infatuation with Craig was as much determined by defiance of me as by a need to reject the internal parents. It was as if he was again saying: 'if I can get nothing from either parent, then I will get it from this boy!' The analytic process was hated, just as I had to be, because it would mean the giving-up of his source of gratifications and defences against breakdown. The sense of humiliation to my power was palpable, because he would report to me his continued abstinence as though it were my demand; yet his perversion could always reassert itself by the occasional use of male prostitutes, without physical masochism, but which would always confirm his masochistic triumph at being deprived of what he called 'love'.

Thus, we remained on a plateau in the third year of treatment, which felt like a kind of wasteland. I was beginning to feel that perhaps the therapy had been no use. It was as if I too had to mourn his failed development as Mr D accepted the impossibility of his desires. Thus, his disappointment with the therapy was a means of working through the loss of an idealised state that before had driven his perversion; but it is only in retrospect that it seems that his incestuous parental ties were perhaps to some extent resolved in the transference. At the time it felt like we were simply stuck. Each session seemed to close the therapy with feelings of deprivation and loss. The sessions became more difficult for Mr D to bear, since they drove in on him each time the need for separation and the impulse to enact this by prematurely ending treatment was intense.

The flat depressed tone of the final months of treatment was not driven by rage and hate. Whereas he had been in a state of prolonged, or delayed, adolescence, he was now withdrawing into something perhaps more akin to Winnicott's (1965) notion of adolescent 'doldrums' in which nothing appears to be happening, but internal changes may be taking place (p. 246). There was little acting-out, but instead a withdrawal of emotional investment in the world, not totally in work or social spheres but certainly in the sexual arena. Young men who would have been targeted in the past, were thought about by Mr D during this time with wistful yearning, painfully conscious that these were images of what he once would have grasped, corrupted and destroyed. Thus we ended on a sad but cordial note. It seemed that we had achieved as much as possible. The sexually perverse orientation had remained essentially unchanged, but there was now sufficient ego strength for Mr D to confine his acting-out to the occasional use of male prostitutes which, though undesirable, was infinitely less damaging than the abuse of children. Thus, it was a great surprise when I heard some 18 months after the end of his therapy with me, that he was in a homosexual relationship of a much healthier kind than he had thought possible. Meeting him and discussing this in a follow-up session it seemed that his judgement was correct; certainly there was little evidence of abusiveness or exploitation in the contact he described, albeit with an adult younger than himself. This situation made it possible for us to negotiate over the writing-up of his treatment. He said that he felt sufficiently 'past all that' to let it go and hoped that this account I had written might help others who feel they are stuck in their situation.

CONCLUSION

In treating cases of adolescent foreclosure the question is whether separation-individuation might be reworked. For development to proceed there need to be choices and opportunities that remain available for the young person to deal with emotional pain rather than closing down in favour of false, i.e. in this case perverse solutions. For Mr D this meant mourning the loss of his idealised childhood, which was symbolised by his paedophilia. We discovered how he had short-circuited his adolescent development and retained incestuous fantasies that were recreated in perverse behaviour. He had remained in a hostile dependency with mother and a triumphant eroticised contempt of father. The treatment provided a means of revisiting some of these infantile areas, and to an extent reliving them in the transference, since at times I became for him the mother who had the wool pulled over her eyes, and at other times the father who could annihilate or be annihilated. As the pain, anger and sense of grievance surfaced in the therapy, these were examined. By this means Mr D seems slowly to have been able to reclaim a body that was felt as his own rather than having been stolen from mother. Working this through in the transference resulted in a degree of detachment from me as maternal enemy. The ambivalent paternal transference that developed served to contain the rage and despair that was fuelling his addiction to perversity. He came to see the falsity of his perverse solutions, and his adherence to the incestuous parents of his imagination. Finally it was interesting to note that he could move to an adult sexual relationship only after leaving therapy. Whether this unresolved transference means a significant lack of therapeutic gain remains to be seen. Separating from perverse desires, and from the therapist who knew about them, has enabled something close to an adolescent maturation finally to begin.

NOTE

1   My thanks are due to Dr Rob Hale for the diagnostic assessment and to Mrs Dorothy Lloyd-Owen for supervision of the work described here.

CHAPTER 10

Reflections on the Supervision of Psychotherapy with Young Abused/Abusers

Anne Alvarez

INTRODUCTION

Kingsley Norton (1997) has pointed out that the dilemma for those who wish to help the self-harming person is that the self-harmer is both victim and perpetrator. He draws attention to the danger of extreme polarisations in our response. The same, I think, is true of most young abusers, and one could argue that some degree of polarisation or split is by definition inevitable. It is natural, I think, to swing between sympathy for the victim and horror, outrage or disgust for his or her perpetrating phantasies or acts. It is probably well-nigh impossible to hang on to such divergent sets of feelings at the same time. The supervisor's task is as nothing to that of the therapist but is – and, by definition, must be – disturbing too. His or her position is, however, a step removed both from the sense of tragedy and from the shock which many of these patients evoke in us, and this is an advantage, for two reasons: first, the supervisor may be available as a vehicle for the sharing, or even the necessary projection of at least some of the disturbance aroused in the therapist; second, the supervisor from his vantage point may find it easier to see the health which lies hidden within the pathology of the young abuser – the non-abused and non-abusive parts of his personality. A danger, however, is that the supervisor may wish to rush to 'teach' the therapist to see the latter or to see tiny developmental moves in the direction of health in a manner that is premature – premature in the sense that the supervisor may not have left the therapist room or time to process – and also to share – the degree of disturbance such patients regularly evoke. Therefore, although I now wish to draw attention to certain issues which I think are relevant to work with these patients, I hope this will not sound like a manual or a recipe book or an intellectualisation of a problem which is frightening and disturbing for everyone.

SOME DISTINCTIONS BETWEEN DEVIANCE, DISORDER AND DEFICIT IN PERSONALITY DEVELOPMENT

Deviance: The perpetrator

In addition to the many disturbing and painful emotional states that traumatised people are prey to – the depression and despair, self-hatred and revenge – an additional problem in the treatment of young abusers is often the factor of addiction to the abusive behaviour as well as the possible perverse excitements accompanying the acts or phantasies. The experience of their own abuse may have led originally to a desperate need to find someone else to be the victim and only incidentally to identify with the abuser; but the chronicity of their own attempts to evacuate the experience into someone else may have led to a further development, a more established characterological identification with the abuser, and, furthermore, the addiction to abusive acts. That is, the victim may become perpetrator not only for defensive reasons but also because he or she is addicted to or excited by the acts. This raises very particular problems for the psychotherapist accustomed to dealing with patients of a more neurotic or even borderline level of illness, where more ordinary explanatory interpretations may have been helpful. When the perpetrator has gone on to become a predator with psychopathic characteristics, the technical and emotional countertransference problems are especially difficult, and the therapist finds that explanatory interpretations fall on very stony ground. It is important, therefore, that the therapist shows that he can understand that the patient is

not frightening children because he needs to but because he likes to. He may
not be producing shock in his therapist because he needs to project and
communicate his own unacknowledged feelings somewhere but because by
now he likes shocking the therapist as witness to the phantasy. It may
become evident that the patient finds this fun and exciting. Or, worse, the
therapist may need to understand that the patient is excited by the idea of
killing a child or raping a child and that ordinary pleasures and ordinary
excitements are not available to him or her. It is unfortunately all too easy for
therapists and supervisors to hasten to find psychoanalytic explanations for
why a patient might be having such a phantasy or intention and to use such
explanations – however accurate from the point of view of original etiology
– to evade the full horror of the patient's current phantasies. The explana-
tion – that the patient was abused himself – may not account fully for the
fact that now he or she is no longer simply preoccupied with evacuating the
experience into someone else – he has become identified with the original
perpetrator and addicted to and/or excited by this activity. It has now
become part of his character structure. Disorder has become deviance. I
have stressed the distinction between the desperate vengeful hatred of
certain borderline paranoid patients, and the cold addiction to violence in
the psychopathic child in previous papers (Alvarez 1995, 1997), but it is
important to stress that many cases are mixed and the person may move
back and forth between either of these states of mind. It is important, I
think, for therapists to recognise the difference, and our patients are relieved
when we do.

Meloy, a psychologist who has had a long and intensive experience with
violent inmates in prisons in the San Diego area in California, has made a
similar distinction between what he calls 'affectively evoked aggression' –
aggression evoked by the perception of threat – and 'predatory aggression'
which is directed towards the destruction of prey, usually for food gathering
in sub-human species (Meloy 1996, p.25). The latter involves minimal
autonomic arousal and vocalisation. 'When a household cat is cornered and
threatened, the neurochemical set produces a display of affective aggression: hissing, hair standing on end, dilating pupils, active clawing, arching
back. When the same cat is stalking a bird in the back-yard, predatory
aggression dominates: quiet stalking of the prey, the absence of ritualistic
display, and focused attention on the target.' He states that predatory
aggression is the hallmark of the psychopath. (He is careful to distinguish

between the severe end of a continuum of psychopathy and the milder end where he thinks people tend to be treatable.) Meloy suggests that the anecdotal descriptions (p.70) by workers in forensic treatment and custody settings of certain patients or inmates' eyes as 'cold, staring, harsh, empty, vacant, and absent of feeling' and the consequent feeling of eerie fear which they evoke should be taken very seriously. He points out that this experience of chilling fear does not seem to arise with even very dangerous explosive combative patients. I have had the experience in supervision, of hearing therapists apologise for these feelings in ways that I know I myself have done when denial was operating, and it is important for the supervisor to take the therapist's feelings very seriously and, of course, for the therapist to feel free to talk about such feelings.

Parallel to his distinction between affective aggression and predatory aggression, Meloy makes a distinction between aggression in the borderline personality and in the psychopath: he talks about the nature of the internal object involved in moments of aggression. In both types of patients there may be an internalised predatory stranger (Meloy links this with attachment problems and stranger anxiety); in the borderline, the predatory stranger is introjected but not necessarily identified with. (John Venables, one of the boys involved in the murder of James Bulger, seemed much more frightened of his mother than of the detectives interviewing him (Morrison 1997, p.132). In the psychopathic patient, the stranger object becomes central to the child's self-esteem, fear is projected into others, and the child becomes identified with the aggressor. The introject has seeped into more and more of the personality, and protest is stifled. Either kind of patient is living in a paranoid world where he is always looking over his shoulder. The problem is that, in the later stages, the child may begin to accept this paranoid world, even to like it. At this stage of chronicity, one may be mistaken in looking for desperate motivations as triggers for apparently terrible acts. Much more ordinary motivations and milder frustrations can trigger them if the child has moved from a paranoid to a psychopathic state of mind.

Neville Symington (1980) in his discussion of responses evoked by the psychopath, warns against the tendency to condemn, to collude with, or to deny the reality of the psychological states of mind we are confronting, I think it does require a certain stamina, steadiness of eye and emotional courage to avoid and to overcome these three responses and to manage to examine honestly what one is seeing and hearing in the sessions of people who have become hardened and whose feeling self has frozen over. It is easier for workers to bear it when the patient is disturbed by the violence of his phantasies than when he or she says casually, or excitedly, that he or she cannot stop thinking about strangling little necks. This is very difficult for the listener to bear alone. Even for therapist and supervisor together, the work is chilling, and I have often wondered whether such work might not be nearly intolerable for workers with young children.

Deviance arising from disorder – the traumatised victim

Many chapters in this book will address this issue and this element in the personality of young abusers. The treatment situation may come to represent the trauma. Hatred, revenge, desperation or persecution may lead the patient to project powerful feelings of fear or disgust or sexual arousal into the therapist. As I indicated above, it is important for the therapist to try to distinguish when this involves a desperate and very primitive form of projective identification for purposes of communication (Bion 1962; Joseph 1978), and when it is being done more coldly and casually. This is not to suggest that the problem in the countertransference of processing the former type of projective identification is easy. Feelings of impotent rage on behalf of the patient as victim, and about the cycle of abuse and violence which has been set up, can flood both therapist and supervisor and lead to despair.

At times, where some capacity for reflection is present in the patient, he or she may be able to accept the type of explanatory interpretation which shows him or her that the therapist is being made to experience something which originally belonged to the patient, either in the past or in the present. At other more desperate moments, however, such a return of projections back to the patient would overload an already overwhelmed psyche and it would be important instead for the therapist to contain the experience within himself, and simply to describe to the patient what it seems that he, the therapist, should be feeling and not to remind the patient that the feeling really belongs to him or originates with him (Joseph 1978; Steiner 1993). At other moments, the thought might be more thinkable (Bion 1962), if the therapist simply describes the experience in terms of what it might be like for some imaginary someone to have it. Sometimes this keeping of the experience somewhere in the middle of the room, as it were, helps the patient to think and to avoid the claustrophobia and over-heated atmosphere that transference interpretations of a certain kind can increase for patients for whom emotional closeness is so confused with sexual encounters. This latter level of purely descriptive work would also be important with patients who have witnessed much abuse and whose identification with an abusive situation function as what Gianna Williams (1997), has called a 'foreign body'. Their violence often erupts as if from nowhere but may be experienced by them as necessary, inevitable and deeply familiar. The patient may feel himself to be enacting a drama in a somewhat depersonalised state, especially if the experience took place at a pre-verbal stage: interpretations, therefore, addressed to the 'you' of ordinary conscious self-identity might miss their mark. It can often be better simply to describe the fact that something seems to have to happen to someone and to acknowledge the compulsive feel of the phantasy.

Deficit in the development of the normal part of the personality

It may be important to draw attention to a third factor in work with these very disturbed young people who are the subject of this book. Deviance and disorder may be accompanied by delay and deficit in any or all aspects of the personality: in ego function in the self, its sense of identity and its capacity to love, to enjoy, and to feel self-respect. There is also likely to be deficit in the inner representation of decent, protective and encouraging superego figures. In other words, the positive side of the patient's personality may be just as underdeveloped as the traumatised and persecutory side is overdeveloped. Where there has been neglect as well as abuse, the young person may experience great despair about his own capacity to give pleasure in any manner which is not sexual and for that matter, his capacity to have pleasure which is not of an overtly sexual kind. Many of these children have never had the experience of their parents as playmates. This may be a dangerous generalisation on my part, but in my experience many of the depressed or abusive mothers in these damaged families have had little capacity to play with their infants or toddlers in ways that are now known to be so important for emotional and cognitive development (Murray and Cooper 1997); also, few of their fathers have had the interest, or opportunity, at an earlier stage, to engage in ordinary rough-and-tumble play. It is an interesting discovery that it is not always so much a question of these patients giving up excitements, but of their exchanging purely and compulsively repetitious sexual excitements for other, more ordinary, forms of excitements. The problem of regulation of excitement, or of how to express love and affection in non-abusive ways is often overwhelming

Technical implications

Identifying the level of symbolisation. First, it is important for the therapist to understand not only the content of phantasy, but also a second dimension – that is, the level of symbolisation at which a piece of play or phantasy is being expressed (Segal 1957; Winnicott 1971). If an abused adolescent boy who has always chosen, either openly or more disguisedly, to exhibit his bottom to his therapist (because of his conviction that that is all an adult could possibly be interested in about him) now begins instead to play a more simple peep-boh game, where he jumps out from behind a curtain, it might be important *not* to interpret sexual seductiveness or excitement but, instead, to comment on the fact that the boy needs to be sure that the therapist is surprised and delighted to find him once again after, for example, the break between sessions. Attention only to deep symbolic sexual content may lead the therapist terribly astray into almost abusive interpretations. These young people have a deep and, given their experience, realistic conviction that no one is interested in them in their own right – only as sexual objects. Teasing games of an ordinary kind – ordinary, that is, for a three-year-old – may begin to emerge in a 15-year-old, but whatever the accompanying sexual charge, these might, in this patient population, need to be seen in their non-sexual but nevertheless exciting, other light. It is difficult too, but nevertheless very important, for the therapist to be able to find the more ordinary glimmerings of an ordinary capacity for liking, pleasure, enjoyment and even excitement (which may be hidden and disguised within much stranger and more apparently perverse forms) and to amplify these.

The transitional area. Sometimes it may be even harder to see that there is a question not so much of a change in the content of the play, as of a change in the form, with in fact very little change in the content. The usual sadistic phantasy, for example, or the same drawing, may be described or drawn in a slightly lighter tone or with less intensity or in a more communicative, less absorbed manner – a possible move from the concrete level of experience, or from what Segal (1957) called the 'level of symbolic equation' to what

Winnicott (1971) called the 'transitional area'. The pressure from the Post Trauma Stress Disorder may be beginning to lighten and thoughts may be becoming slightly more thinkable. The therapist may be so accustomed to the relentless repetition of the perverse themes that only in telling them to the supervisor, or on reflection, may he or she notice the lighter quality or tiny changes in the theme. One patient commented that he had been watching a lot of horror films lately: in another patient, this might have been nothing more than a repetition of a usual compulsion; but for him it was a move beyond and outside his usual very private phantasies to something held within – and limited to – its frame, vaguely shared and even part of the shared public culture (however limited a culture). When the patient himself commented how strange it was how much he liked such films, a little of the observing witnessing ego (Sinason 1992) was finally able to be present and not totally engaged in the abuse.

Recognising real love. A third problem is that the recognition of tiny signs of real love or affection or trust may be so hidden within or obstructed by the more abusive relationships that they can be very easy to miss. In John Woods' Chapter 4, the therapist knew – and the patient, Andrew knew that he knew – that Andrew and his sister had had regular sexual relations for the benefit of their parents and parents' friends, and that he still had sexual phantasies about her. It was extremely important for Andrew that, at the moment when he was complaining of not being able to see his sister, his therapist commented that he really loved her. Such patients, as implied in their lack of experience with ordinary emotional relationships and play experience, have little capacity to modulate states of excitement and arousal, and such comments, rather than increasing excitement, can, at certain stages of the work, reduce it. It can also provide a precious and moving moment where the young person feels someone can find something good and valuable in him. These young people are not simply abused and traumatised: many are also deprived of an opportunity to express love.

Disidentification. Fourthly, it is important for the therapist to be alert to signs of what Sandler (1988) has called the process of 'disidentification'. For the more psychopathic patients, or for those with 'foreign body' type of unconscious identification with the abuser, it will be an important step when some realignment begins. A very traumatised boy who had witnessed much violence and, at aged two, seen his alcoholic mother die in front of him, returned from his three-week summer break from therapy and insisted to his therapist that there were no cars in the box of toys he had always used in his sessions with her. She showed him that his usual cars were still there. He replied, 'Oh no, those cars were from a long time ago with another lady.' This gives an indication of how faint and remote was his memory of his almost year-long intensive treatment with her. The process of building up a mind capable of memory, internal representations of good and reliable objects, in patients so fragmented and with such profound ego deficits is painfully slow. Yet only when some faith and trust in a good object and good self is established can the disidentification with abusive objects even begin to get going. One horribly abused boy, after some period in therapy began to have dreams in which terrible things were being done to a child. The beginnings of some degree of symbolisation which signals the process of recovery from trauma seemed to be under way, but neither the child, as he recounted the dreams, or any figure in the dreams, seemed to evidence shock or protest over the cruelty. Finally, he had a dream in which some adults were looking on 'astonished' at what was being done to the child. His internal objects had not yet acquired the capacity to feel outrage, or to try to rescue the child, but his therapist and I felt that astonishment was at least a start, and might lay the ground for eventual shock and outrage. (Often such children act to impress and shock us as a way of checking whether or not everyone accepts such abuse as normal.) It is interesting that when John Woods' patient Andrew first included the witch mother in his drawing of a fierce dragon which stood for himself, she first only appeared hidden in the scales (Chapter 4). The next picture showed her astride him, and Andrew commented that the dragon had no power of its own. However terrible a depiction this was of his feeling of possession by his abusive parents, it was nevertheless being depicted, and there was finally some differentiation between the two figures. Such fleeting moments of disidentification are extremely painful, however, because the young person may get a full sense of the terrible damage done to him. In the next moment, Andrew first wanted to attack his therapist, then to kill a beautiful child. The therapist told him that this was because he realised that the beautiful child in himself had been killed and abused, and now he wanted it to be done to someone else. Andrew in fact, even at his most affectionate, had rarely been able to approach someone or to present himself with confidence: he felt he had to placate and cling, and drew himself as an ugly spider, for example. Gradually, as his belief in himself and in good objects grew, he seems to have been able to accept interpretations about how he attacked his own goodness.

Idealisation and the ideal object. Excessive idealisation of the therapist may be a further issue connected with the growth of hope and trust. Andrew often told his therapist that he was attempting to live more responsibly only for him, and a patient of mine recovering from a paranoid state after years of abuse began singing very sentimental popular love songs to me. It is easy to feel that one's task is to facilitate de-idealisation and integration, but I have come to think that these initial idealisations, however sentimental or even creepy their tone, may involve precious experiments and adventures in finding an ideal object – experiments which may have been denied the patient at early infantile levels.

CONCLUSION

Most professionals involved in the care or treatment of young abusers acknowledge the need for good communication and shared experience. The therapist is impelled at times to be preoccupied by outside events and the supervisor, more protected from these, may be able to help the therapist to attend more to the processes within the here and now of the session, to the tiny shifts and even developments in the transference. Given the pressures on therapists and the responsibilities they carry, there can be a great urgency to work fast, to solve problems, to show the patient his defences against his trauma, his denials and resistances and the reasons for his vicious projections. Yet the chronicity of the trauma and of the likely characterological problems implies the necessity to rein in the impulse to understand and instead, to 'stand' what one is hearing or seeing (Joseph 1978). The work has to be delicate and tentative towards the traumatised healthy victim but alert and vigilant in regard to the perpetrator. Slow careful description of fleeting or budding feeling states of a normal kind needs just as much attention as do the pathological and highly disturbing states. Regarding the latter, therapist and supervisor may both have to experience the horror and the fear evoked about the fate of the patient's possible future victims as bravely as possible. There is no cause for over-optimism in the face of such damage to the personality, yet the occurrence of another offence need not necessarily imply total failure of the therapy. The task of repair is enormous but not impossible.

Anne Alvarez is Consultant Child and Adolescent Psychotherapist at the Tavistock Clinic, London.

References

Adshead, G. and Mezey, G. (1993) 'Ethical issues in the psychotherapeutic treatment of paedophiles; whose side are you on?' *Journal of Forensic Psychiatry 4*, 2, 361–368.

Agazarian, Y. (1994) 'The Phases of Group Development.' In V. Schermer and M. Pines (eds) *Ring of Fire; Primitive Affects and Object Relations in Group Psychotherapy.* London: Routledge.

Alvarez, A. (1995) 'Motiveless malignity; problems in the psychotherapy of psychopathic patients.' *Journal of Child Psychotherapy 21*, 2, 167–182.

Alvarez, A. (1997) 'Projective identification as a communication: its grammar in borderline psychotic children.' *Psychoanalysis Dialogue 7*, 6, 753–668.

American Psychiatric Association (1991) *The Diagnostic and Statistical Manual of Mental Disorders IV* (DSM IV). Washington, DC: APA.

Anastasopoulos, D. (1998) 'Shame in psychotherapy with adolescents.' *Journal of Child Psychotherapy 23*, 1, 103–123.

Araji, S.K. (1997) *Sexually Aggressive Children.* Thousand Oaks, CA: Sage.

Astor, J. (1988) 'Adolescent states of mind found in patients of different ages seen in analysis.' *Journal of Child Psychotherapy 14*, 1, 67–80.

Bailey, T. (2002) 'Outcome research and an evidence base in child psychotherapy.' *The Bulletin of The Association of Child Psychotherapists*, Issue 126, October 2002, p.3–6.

Baker, L. and Gibson, R. (1995) 'Social Work with Abused and Abusing Youth, (S.W.A.A.Y.); Statement of Purpose.' Unpublished document.

Balbernie, R. (1994) 'There is no such thing as an abused child, but there is phantom hybrid of the mind.' *British Journal of Psychotherapy 11*, 1, 20–31.

Balbernie, R. (1999) 'Profile of a potential abuser.' *British Journal of Psychotherapy 16*, 2, 160–172.

Bandura, A. (1986) *Social Foundations of Thought and Action.* New Jersey: Prentice Hall.

Barratt, G. and Segal, B. (1996) 'Rivalry, competition and transference in a children's group.' *Group Analysis 29*, 1, March 1996, 23–35.

Barwick, N. (2000) *Clinical Counselling in Schools.* London: Routledge.

Bateman, A. (1998) 'Thick- and thin-skinned organisations and enactment in borderline and narcissistic disorders.' *International Journal of Psychoanalysis 79*, 1, 13–26.

Bateman, A., Brown, D. and Pedder, J. (1996) *Introduction to Psychotherapy.* London: Routledge/Taylor Francis Group.

Becker, J. (1990) 'Treating adolescent sexual offenders.' *Professional Psychology Research and Practice 21*, 362–365.

Becker, J and Abel, G. (1985) 'Methodological and ethical issues in evaluating and treating adolescent sexual offenders.' In E.M. Otey and G. Ryan (1985) *Adolescent Sex Offenders; Issues in Research and Treatment.* National Institute of Mental Health No. (Adm) 85 13960 Rockville MD: DHHS, 109–129.

Becker, J. and Kaplan, M.S. (1988) 'The assessment of adolescent sexual offenders.' In *Advances in Behavioral Assessment of Children and Families 4*, 97–118.

Beckett, R. (1999) 'Evaluation of Adolescent Sexual Abusers.' In Erooga, M. and Masson, H. (eds) (1999) *Children and Young People Who Sexually Abuse Others.* London: Routledge, 204–224.

Behr, H. (1988) 'Group analysis with early adolescents.' In *Group Analysis 21*, 2, 119–130.

Benjamin, H. (1966) *The Transsexual Phenomenon.* New York: Julian Press.

Bentovim, A. (1995) *Trauma Organised Systems.* London: Karnac Books.

Bentovim, A. (1996a) 'Systems theory.' In C. Cordess and M. Cox (eds) *Forensic Psychotherapy: Crime, Psychodynamics and the Offender Patient 1*, 107–115.

Bentovim, A. (1996b) 'The trauma organised system of working with family violence.' In C. Cordess and M. Cox (eds) *Forensic Psychotherapy: Crime, Psychodynamics and the Offender Patient 2*, 291–311.

Bentovim, A. (2000) 'Working with victimisation experiences, a therapeutic manual.' Unpublished.

Bentovim, A. and Williams, B. (1998) 'Children and adolescents victims who become perpetrators.' *Advances in Psychiatric Treatment 4*, 101–107.

Bernard, F. (1985) *Paedophilia; A Factual Report.* Rotterdam: Enclave.

Bion, W.R. (1962) *Learning from Experience.* London: Heinemann.

Birksted-Breen, D. (1996) 'Phallus, penis-as-link and mental space.' *International Journal of Psychoanalysis 77*, 649–658.

Bleiberg, E., Jackson, L. and Ross, J.L. (1986) 'Gender identity disorder and object loss.' *Journal of the American Academy of Child and Adolescent Psychiatry 25*, 1, 58–67.

Blos, P. (1962) *On Adolescence.* Mass. USA: Free Press Books.

Bollas, C. (1989) *Forces of Destiny.* London: Free Association Press.

Bollas, C. and Sandelson, D. (1995) *The New Informants; Betrayal of Confidentiality in Psychoanalysis and Psychotherapy.* London: Karnac Books.

Britton, R. (1998) *Belief and Imagination; Explorations in Psychoanalysis.* London, New York: Routledge.

Butler, J. (1990) *Gender Trouble – Feminism and the Subversion of Identity.* Stamford CA: Stamford University Press.

Calder, M.C., with Hanks, H. and Epps, K.J. (1997) *Juveniles and Children who Sexually Abuse; A Guide to Risk Assessment.* Lyme Regis: Russell House Publishing.

Campbell, B., Castledine, A. and Jones, J. (2002) *And All the Children Cried.* London: Consortium Books.

Campbell, D. (1994) 'Breaching the shame shield; thoughts on the assessment of adolescent sexual abusers.' *Journal of Child Psychotherapy 20*, 3, 309–326.

Campbell, D. and Hale, R. (1991) 'Suicidal Acts.' In J. Holmes (ed) (1991) *Textbook of Psychotherapy in Psychiatric Practice.* London: Churchill Livingstone.

Canham, H. and Emanuel, L. (2000) 'Tied together feelings; Group psychotherapy with latency children.' *Journal of Child Psychotherapy 26*, 2, 281–302.

Carlson, S. (1990) 'The Victim/Perpetrator; Turning Points in Therapy.' In M. Hunter (ed) (1990) *The Sexually Abused Male.* Lexington: Lexington Books.

Clulow, C., Schmuli, A., Vincent, C. and Evans, C. (2002) 'Is empirical research compatible with clinical practice?' *British Journal of Psychotherapy 19*, 1, 33–44.

Coates, S. and Moore, M.S. (1997) 'The complexity of early trauma, representation and transformation.' *Psychoanalytic Enquiry 17*, 3, 286–311.

Connor, T.A. (1996) 'Ethical and clinical issues in involuntary psychotherapy.' In *Psychotherapy 33*, 4, 587–592.

Cordess, C. (ed) (2000) *Confidentiality and Mental Health.* London: Jessica Kingsley Publishers.

Cordess, C. and Cox, M. (eds) (1996) *Forensic Psychotherapy: Crime, Psychodynamics and the Offender Patient.* London: Jessica Kingsley Publishers.

Crittenden, P.M. (1997) 'Toward an Integrated Theory of Trauma.' In D. Cichetti and S.L. Tooth (eds) (1997) *The Rochester Symposium on Developmental Psychopathology.* New York: University of Rochester Press.

Cunningham, C. and MacFarlane, K. (1991) *When Children Molest Children.* Brandon VT USA: Safer Society Press.

Dalal, F. (1998) *Taking the Group Seriously.* London: Jessica Kingsley Publishers.

Davies, R. (1996) 'The Inter-disciplinary Network and the Internal World of the Offender.' In C. Cordess and M. Cox (eds) *Forensic Psychotherapy; Crime, Psychodynamics and the Offender Patient.* London: Jessica Kingsley Publishers.

Davies, R. (ed) (1998) *Stress in Social Work.* London: Jessica Kingsley Publishers.

Del Balzo, Voand Judge, T. (1998) 'Towards socialisation; the seriously disturbed adolescent in group psycho-therapy.' *Group Analysis 31*, 2.

Di Ceglie, D. (ed) (1998) *A Stranger in My Own Body.* London: Karnac Books.

Dockar-Drysdale, B. (1968) *Therapy in Child Care.* London: Longman.

Doherty, K. and Anderson, I. (1998) 'Talking about rape.' *The Psychologist*, December 1998, 583–587.

Dwivedi, K.N. (1993) *Group Work with Children and Adolescents.* London: Jessica Kingsley Publishers.

Edgcumbe, R. and Burgner, M. (1975) 'The phallic-narcissistic phase.' *The Psychoanalytic Study of the Child 30*, 161–180.

Elliott, M., Browne, K. and Kilcoyne, J. (1995) 'Child sexual abuse; What offenders tell us.' *Child Abuse and Neglect 19*, 5, 579–594.

Erikson, E. (1963) *Identity, Youth and Crisis*, Faber and Faber.

Erooga, M. (1994) 'Where the Professional Meets the Personal.' In T. Morrison, M. Erooga and R.C. Beckett (eds) *Sexual Offending Against Children*. London: Routledge.

Erooga, M. and Masson, H. (eds) (1999) *Children and Young People Who Sexually Abuse Others*. London: Routledge.

Etherington, K. (2000) *Narrative Approaches to Working With Adult Male Survivors of Sexual Abuse*. London: Jessica Kingsley Publishers.

Evans, J. (1988) 'Research findings and clinical practice with adolescents.' *Group Analysis 21*, 2, 103–114.

Evans, P. (1997) 'Journeys in the labyrinth; some difficulties in the psychotherapy of severely traumatised adolescent.' *Journal of Child Psychotherapy 23*, 1, 125–143.

Finkelhor, D. (1984) *Child Sexual Abuse: New Theory and Research*. New York: Free Press Books.

Fishman, C. (2001) 'Working with the paedophile patient.' Unpublished paper from Tavistock/Portman Conference.

Fonagy, P. (1999) 'Male perpetrators of violence against women: An attachment theory perspective.' *Journal of Applied Psychoanalytic Studies 1*, 7–27.

Fonagy, P., Moran, G.S. and Target, M. (1993) 'Aggression and the psychological self.' *International Journal of Psychoanalysis 74*, 3, 471–485.

Fonagy, P. and Roth, A. (1996) *What Works for Whom; A Critical Review of Psychotherapy Research*. New York: Guilford Press.

Fonagy, P. and Target, M. (1996a) 'Playing with Reality.' *International Journal of Psychoanalysis 77*, 2, 217–233.

Fonagy, P. and Target, M. (1996b) 'Personality and Sexual Development.' In C. Cordess and M. Cox (eds) (1996) *Forensic Psychotherapy: Crime, Psychodynamics and the Offender Patient*. London: Jessica Kingsley Publishers.

Fonagy, P. and Target, M. (1998) 'An Interpersonal View of the Infant.' In Hurry (ed) *Psychoanalysis and Developmental Therapy*. London: Karnac Books.

Foulkes, S.H. (1964) *Therapeutic Group Analysis*. London: Allen and Unwin. Reprinted London: Karnac 1984.

Foulkes, S.H. (1974) 'My philosophy in psychotherapy.' In Selected Papers (1990). London: Karnac Books.

Foulkes, S.H. (1975) *Group Analytic Psychotherapy*. London: Gordon and Breach Reprinted London: Karnac Books 1986.

Foulkes, S.H. and Anthony, E.J. (1957) *Group Psychotherapy; the Psychoanalytic Approach*, Penguin London: Karnac 1984.

Freud, A. (1936) *The Ego and the Mechanisms of Defence*. London: Hogarth 1968.

Freud, S. (1896) 'Further Remarks on the psycho-neuroses of defence.' *Standard Edition 3*. London: Hogarth Press, 159–183.

Freud, S. (1897) 'The aetiology of hysteria.' *Standard Edition 3*. London: Hogarth Press 1962.

Freud, S. (1905) 'Three essays on the theory of sexuality.' *Standard Edition 7*. London: Hogarth Press 1962.

Freud, S. (1909) 'Notes upon a case of obsessional neurosis.' *Standard Edition 10*. London: Hogarth Press 1962.

Freud, S. (1911) 'Formulations on the two principles of mental functioning.' *Standard Edition 12*, London: Hogarth Press 1962.

Freud, S. (1911) 'On the universal tendency to debasement in love.' *Standard Edition 11*, London: Hogarth Press 1962.

Freud, S. (1914) 'Remembering, repeating and working through.' *Standard Edition 12*. London: Hogarth Press 1962.

Freud, S. (1915) 'Mourning and melancholia.' *Standard Edition 14*. London: Hogarth Press 1962.

Freud, S. (1919) 'A child is being beaten.' *Standard Edition 17*. London: Hogarth Press 1962.

Freud, S. (1920) 'Beyond the pleasure principle.' *Standard Edition 18*. London: Hogarth Press 1962.

Freud, S. (1923) 'The Ego and the Id.' *Standard Edition 19*. London: Hogarth Press 1962.

Friedrich, W.N. (1995a) *Psychotherapy with Sexually Abused Boys*. London: Sage.

Friedrich, W.N. (1995b) 'Managing Disorders of Self-regulation in Sexually Abused Boys.' In M. Hunter (ed) *Childhood Survivors and Perpetrators of Sexual Abuse*. London: Sage.

Frosh, S. (1994) *Sexual Differences, Masculinity and Psychoanalysis*. London: Routledge.

Garland, C. (1982) 'Taking the non-problem seriously.' *Group Analysis 15*, 1, 4–14.

Garland, C. (ed) (1998) *Understanding Trauma*. Tavistock Clinic Series.

Gilligan, J. (1996) *Violence: Reflections on our Deadliest Epidemic*. New York: Puttnams. London: Jessica Kingsley Publishers 2000.

Ginott, H. (1961) *Group Psychotherapy with Children*. New York: McGraw-Hill.

Glaser, D. (2000) 'Child abuse and neglect and the brain – A review.' *Journal of Child Psychology and Psychiatry 41*, 1, 97–116.

Glasser, M. (1964) 'Aggression and Sadism in the Perversions.' In I. Rosen (ed) (1964) *Sexual Deviation*. Oxford University Press.

Glasser, M. (1988) 'Psychodynamic aspects of paedophilia.' *Psychoanalytic Psychotherapy 3*, 2, 121–135.

Glasser, M. (1995) '"The Weak Spot" – some observations on male sexuality.' *International Journal of Psychoanalysis 66*, 405–14.

Glover, E. (1936) *On the Early Development of Mind.* New York: International Universities Press 1970.

Goldberg, A. (1995) *The Problem of Perversion.* New Haven. Yale University Press.

Golding, W. (1954) *The Lord of the Flies.* Faber London: Penguin 1967.

Goldner, V., Penn, P., Scheinberg, M. and Walker, G. (1990) 'Love and violence.' *Family Process 29*, 343–365.

Greenson, R. (1968) 'Dis-identifying from Mother; Its Special Importance for the Boy.' In D. Breen (ed) (1993) *The Gender Conundrum.* London: Routledge.

Griffin, S., Williams, M., Hawkes, C. and Vizard, E. (1997) 'The professional carers group; supporting group work for young sexual abusers.' *Child Abuse and Neglect 21*, 7, 681–690.

Groth, N. (1978) *Sexual Assault of Children and Adolescents.* Lexington: Lexington Books.

Grotsky, P., Camerer, M. and Damiano, T. (2000) *Group Work with Sexually Abused Children.* London: Sage.

Gunn, J. and Taylor, P. (1995) *Forensic Psychiatry; Clinical, Legal and Ethical Issues.* London: Butterworth Heinemann.

Hackett, S. (1999) 'Empowered Practice.' In M. Erooga and H. Masson (ed) (1999) *Children and Young People who Sexually Abuse Others.* London: Routledge.

Hall, Z. and Sharpe, J. (2000) 'Group analytic psychotherapy for male survivors of sexual abuse.' *Group Analysis 34*, 2, 195–209.

Hawkes, C., Jenkins, J. and Vizard, E. (1996) 'The Roots of Sexual Violence in Children and Adolescents.' In V. Varma (ed) (1996) *Violence in Children and Adolescents. London: Jessica Kingsley Publishers.*

Henry, R.M., Wesley, N., Jones, A., Cohen, M. and Fairhall, C. (1997) 'AIDS and the unconscious: Psychodynamic groupwork with incarcerated youths.' *Journal of Child Psychotherapy 23*, 3, 373–398.

Herman, J.L. (1992) *Trauma and Recovery.* New York: Basic Books.

Hoag, J. (1997) 'Evaluating the effectiveness of child and adolescent group treatment.' *Journal of Clinical Child Psychology 26*, 3.

Hodges, J., Lanyado, M. and Andreou, C. (1994) 'Sexuality and violence; preliminary research hypotheses.' *Journal of Child Psychotherapy 20*, 3, 283–308.

Hoghughi, M.S. (ed) with Bhate, S.R. and Graham, F. (1997) *Working with Sexually Abusive Adolescents.* London: Sage.

Hopper, E. (1997) 'Traumatic experience in the unconscious life of groups.' *Group Analysis 30*, 4, 439–470.

Hopper, E. (2001) 'The social unconscious.' *Group Analysis 34*, 4, 9–27.

Horne, A. (1999) 'Sexual Abuse and Sexual Abusing in Childhood and Adolescence.' In A. Horne and M. Lanyado (eds) (1999) *The Handbook of Child Psychotherapy.* London: Routledge.

Horne, A. (2001) 'Brief communications from the edge.' *Journal of Child Psychotherapy 27*, 1, 3–18.

Horne, A. and Lanyado, M. (eds) (1999) *The Handbook of Child and Adolescent Psychotherapy*. London: Routledge.

Howitt, D. (1995) *Paedophiles and Sexual Offenders Against Children*. Chichester: Wiley.

Hunter, M. (1990) *The Sexually Abused Male 2*. Lexington: Lexington Books.

Hurry, A. (ed) (1998) *Psychoanalysis and Developmental Therapy*. London: Karnac Books.

Ironside, L. (1995) 'Beyond the boundaries; the patient, the therapist and an allegation of sexual abuse.' *Journal of Child Psychotherapy 21*, 2, 183–206.

Jacobs, E., Harvill, R. and Masson, R. (1988) *Group Counselling*. California: Brookes/Cole Publishing.

Joseph, B. (1978) 'Different Types of Anxiety and their Handling in the Clinical Situation.' In E. Spillius and M. Feldman (eds) (1989) *Psychic Equilibrium and Psychic Change: Selected Papers of Betty Joseph*. London: Routledge.

Jukes, A. (1994) *Why Men Hate Women*. London Free Association Books.

Kahn, T.J. (1990) *Pathways; A Guided Workbook for Youth Beginning Treatment*. Brandon VT: Safer Society Press.

Keenan, B. (1993) *An Evil Cradling*. London: Vintage.

Keenan, M. (1998) 'Narrative therapy with men who have sexually abused children.' *Irish Journal of Psychology 19*, 1, 136–151.

Kennedy, R., Heymans, A. and Tischler, L. (eds) (1986) *The Family as Inpatient*. London: Free Association Press.

Kinston, W. and Bentovim, A., (1980) 'Creating a Focus for Brief Marital and Family Therapy.' In S.H. Budmann (ed) (1980) *Forms of Brief Therapy*. New York: Guilford Press.

Klein, M. (1935) 'A contribution to the psychogenesis of manic-depressive states.' In *Love, Guilt and Reparation*. London: Hogarth 1975, 262–89.

Klein, R.H. and Schermer, V.L. (2000) *Group Psychotherapy for Psychological Trauma*. New York: Guilford Press.

Kohon, G. (1999) *No Lost Certainties to be Recovered*. London: Karnac Books.

Kolvin, I. (1981) *Help Starts Here*. London: Tavistock.

Koss, M.P., Tromp, S. and Tharan, M. (1995) 'Traumatic memories, empirical foundations, and clinical implications.' *Clinical Psychology; Research and Practice 2*, 111–32.

Lanyado, M., Hodges, J., Bentovim, A., Andreou, C. and Williams, B. (1995) 'Understanding boys who sexually abuse other children.' *Psychoanalytic Psychotherapy 9*, 3, 231–242.

Laub, D. and Auerhahn, N. (1993) 'Knowing and not knowing massive trauma; forms of traumatic memory.' *International Journal of Psychoanalysis 74*, 2, 287–302.

Laufer, M. and Laufer, E. (1984) *Adolescence and Developmental Breakdown*. New Haven: Yale.

Lousada, J. (2000) 'The state of mind we are in.' *British Journal of Psychotherapy 16*, 4.

Masson H. and Erooga, M. (1999) 'Children and Young People who Sexually Abuse
     Others: Incidence, characteristics and causation.' In M. Erooga and H. Masson
     (eds) (1999) *Children and Young People Who Sexually Abuse Others.* London:
     Routledge.

McClelland, R. and Hale, R. (2001) 'The Doctor–Patient Consultation and Disclosure.'
     In C. Cordess (ed) (2001) *Confidentiality and Mental Health.* London: Jessica Kingsley
     Publishers.

McDougall, J. (1972) 'The primal scene and sexual perversion.' *International Journal of
     Psychoanalysis 53*, 3, 371–384.

McDougall, J. (1986a) *Theatres of the Mind.* London: Free Association Press.

McDougall, J. (1986b) 'Identifications, neo-needs, and neo-sexualities.' *International
     Journal of Psychoanalysis 67*, 1, 19–31.

McDougall, J. (1995) *The Many Faces of Eros.* London: Free Association Press.

Meloy, J.R. (1995) *The Psychopathic Mind.* London: Aronson.

Meloy, J.R. (1996) *The Psychopathic Mind: Origins, Dynamics and Treatment.* London:
     Aronson.

Milton, J. (2001) 'Psychoanalysis and cognitive behaviour therapy – Rival paradigms
     or common ground?' *International Journal of Psychoanalysis 82*, 431–446.

Mollon, P. (1998) *Remembering Trauma.* London: Whurr 2002.

Moore, S. and Rosenthal, D. (1993) *Sexuality in Adolescence.* London: Routledge.

Morrison, B. (1997) *As If.* London: Granta.

Murray, L. and Cooper, P. (1997) *Postpartum Depression and Child Development.* New
     York: Guilford Press.

Naglieri, G. (1996) 'Counter-transference in adolescent group psychotherapy.' *Group
     Analysis 29*, 1, 97–105.

Nijenhuis, E.R.S. and Van der Hart, O. (1995) 'Forgetting and Re-experiencing
     Trauma.' In J. Goodwin and R. Attias (eds) *Splintered Reflections; Images of the Body in
     Treatment.* New York: Basic Books.

Norton, K. (1997) 'Managing self-harm.' *Henderson Hospital 50th Anniversary Conference.*
     Unpublished. London: Regents College.

O'Connor, H. (2001) '"Will we grow out of it?" – a psychotherapy group for people
     with learning disabilities.' *Psychodynamic Counselling 7*, 3, London: Routledge
     Taylor and Francis.

Offer, D. (1991) 'Adolescent development; A normative perspective.' in S. Greenspan,
     G. Pollock (eds) (1991) *The Course of Life 4,* 181–200. Madison, Connecticut:
     International Universities Press.

Page, M. (2001) *Two Way Street; Communicating with Disabled Children and Young People.*
     Video pubished by NSPCC and Joseph Rowntree Foundation.

Pelzer, D. (1995) *A Child Called 'It'.* London: Orion Books.

Perelberg, R. (1999) 'The interplay of identifications and identity in the analysis of a
     violent young man.' *International Journal of Psychoanalysis 80*, 1, 31–45.

Perry, B.D. (1997) 'Incubated in Terror: Neuro-Developmental Factors in the Cycle of Violence.' In J. Osofsky (ed) (1997) *Children in a Violent Society.* New York and London: Guilford Press.

Perry, B.D., Pollard, R.A., Blakley, T.L., Baker, W.L. and Vigilante, D. (1995) 'Childhood trauma, the neurobiology of adaptation, and "use-dependent" development of the brain. How states become traits.' *Infant Mental Health Journal 16,* 271–289.

Pines, M. (1999) *Circular Reflections.* London: Jessica Kingsley Publishers.

Pinter, H. (1984) *One for the Road.* London: Methuen.

Pithers, W.D. Gray, A., Busconi, A., and Houchhennns, P. (1998) 'Children with sexual behaviour problems: Identification of five distinct types and related treatment considerations.' *Child Maltreatment 5,* 4, Brandon Press, VT USA, 384–406.

Print, B. and O'Callaghan, D. (1999) 'Working in groups with young men who have sexually abused others.' In M. Erooga, and H. Masson (eds) *Children and Young People Who Sexually Abuse Others.* London: Routledge.

Reed Business Information http:/www.community care.co.uk 16/11/01.

Reid, S. (1999) 'The Group as a Healing Whole; Group Psychotherapy with Children and Adolescents.' In A. Horne and M. Lanyado (eds) (1999) *The Handbook of Child and Adolescent Psychotherapy.* London: Routledge.

Rosen, I. (1964a) 'Integrating the general psychoanalytical theory of perversion.' In I. Rosen (ed).

Rosen, I. (1964b) *Sexual Deviation.* Oxford: Oxford University Press, 1996.

Rowland, M.D., Henggeler, S.W., Gordon, A.M., Pickrel, S.G., Cunningham, P.B. and Edwards, J.E. (2000) 'Adapting multi-systemic therapy to serve youth presenting psychiatric emergencies; Two case studies.' *Child Psychology and Psychiatry Review 5,* 1, 30–43.

Royal College of Psychiatrists (2000) *Good Psychiatric Practice: Confidentiality; Council Report CR85.*

Ruszczynski, S. (2001) 'Perversions and perverse states of mind.' Unpublished paper from Tavistock/Portman Conference.

Ryan, G. (1998a) 'The relevance of early life experiences to the behaviour of sexually abusive youth.' *Irish Journal of Psychology 19,* 1, 32–48.

Ryan, G.D. (1998b) 'Treatment of sexually abusing youth; the evolving consensus.' *Journal of Interpersonal Violence 14,* 4, 422–434.

Ryan, G.D. (1989) 'Victim to victimiser.' *Journal of Interpersonal Violence 4,* 3, 325–341.

Ryan, G.D. and Lane, S. (1991) *Juvenile Sexual Offending.* Lexington: Lexington Books.

Sanderson, C. (1991) *Counselling Adult Survivors of Child Sexual Abuse.* London: Jessica Kingsley Publishers.

Sandler, J. (1988) *Projection, Identification, Projective Identification.* London: Karnac Books.

Scheidlinger, S. (1972) 'Adolescent Group Therapy.' In Wolman (ed) *The Handbook of Child Analysis.* New York: Van Nostrand.

Schore, A. (1996) 'The experience of dependent maturation of a regulatory system.' *Development and Psychopathology 8*, 59–87.

Schore, A. (2001a) Paper and discussion at Conference on Attachment, Trauma and Dissociation, London, July 7th and 8th, 2001: unpublished.

Schore, A. (2001b) 'Minds in the making.' *British Journal of Psychotherapy 17*, 3, 299–328.

Segal, H. (1957) 'Notes on symbol formation'. In *The Work of Hanna Segal*. New York: Aronson.

Segal, H. (1991) *Dream, Phantasy and Art*. London: Tavistock/Routledge New Library of Psychoanalysis.

Sermabakian, P. and Martinez, D. (1994) 'Treatment of adolescent sexual offenders.' *Child Abuse and Neglect 18*, 11, 969–976.

Shengold, L. (1989) *Soul Murder*. New York: Fawcett Columbine.

Shevrin, H. (1996) *Conscious and Unconscious Processes; Psychodynamic, Cognitive and Neuropsychological Convergence*. New York and London: Guilford Books.

Sinason, V. (1986) 'Secondary mental handicap and its relationship to trauma.' *Psychoanalytic Psychotherapy 2*, 2, 131–154.

Sinason, V. (1992) *Mental Handicap and the Human Condition*. London: Free Association Books.

Sinason, V. (1996) 'From Abused to Abuser.' In C. Cordess and M. Cox (eds) *Forensic Psychotherapy; Crime, Psychodynamics and the Offender Patient*. London: Jessica Kingsley Publishers..

Skynner, A.C.R. 'Reflections on the Family Therapist as Family Scapegoat.' In J. Schlapobersky (ed) (1985) *Explorations with Families*. London: Routledge.

Slavson, S. R. (1943) *Introduction to Group Psychotherapy*. New York: International Universities Press.

Sperling, M. (1959) 'A Study of Deviate Sexual Behaviour in Children by the Method of Simultaneous Analysis of Mother and Child.' In L. Jessner and E. Pavenstadt (eds) *Dynamic Psychopathology in Childhood*. *USA: Grune and Stratton*.

Stacey, R. (2001) 'What can it mean to say that the individual is social through and through?' *Group Analysis 34*, 4, 457–471.

Steiner, J. (1993) *Psychic Retreats; Pathological Organisations in Psychotic, Neurotic and Borderline Patients*. London: Routledge.

Stoller, R. (1964a) 'The gender disorders.' In Rosen, I. (1964b) *Sexual Deviation*. Oxford: Oxford University Press, 1996.

Stoller, R. (1964b) 'The hermaphroditic identity of hermaphrodites.' *Journal of Nervous and Mental Diseases 139*, 5, 453–457.

Stoller, R. (1975a) *The Transsexual Experiment*. London: Hogarth.

Stoller, R. (1975b) *Perversion: The Erotic Form of Hatred*. New York: Pantheon.

Stoller, R. (1979) *Sexual Excitement; the Dynamics of Erotic Life*. New York: Pantheon Books. London: Karnac Books 1986.

Stoller, R. (1985) *Observing the Erotic Imagination.* London: Yale University Press.

Swenson, C.C., Henggeler, S.W., Schoenwald, S.K., Kaufman, K.L. and Randall, J. (1998) 'Changing the social ecologies of adolescent sexual offenders.' *Child Maltreatment 5*, 4, 330–338.

Symington, N. (1980) 'The response aroused by the psychopath.' *International Review of Psychoanalysis* 3, 291–298.

Teicholz, J. G. and Kriegman, D.(1997) *Trauma, Repetition and Affect Regulation: The Works of Paul Russell.* New York: The Other Press.

Thomason, P. (2001) *Before It's Too Late; Focused Work with Sexually Abusive Adolescents.* London: Pavilion.

Timimi, S. (2002) *Pathological Child Psychiatry and the Medicalisation of Childhood.* London: Brunner Routledge.

Tonnesmann, M. (1980) 'Adolescent re-enactment, trauma and reconstruction.' *Journal of Child Psychotherapy 6*, 23–44.

Trowell, J. (1998) 'Child Sexual Abuse and Gender Identity Development.' In Di Ceglie (ed) *A Stranger in My Own Body.* London: Karnac Books.

Van der Kolk, B.A. (ed) (1987) *Psychological Trauma.* Washington DC: American Psychiatric Press.

Vizard, E. and Usiskin J. (1999) 'Providing Individual Psychotherapy for Young Sexual Abusers of Children.' In M. Erooga and H. Masson (eds) *Children and Young People who Sexually Abuse Others.* London: Routledge.

Volkan, V. and Greer, W. (1964) 'True Transsexualism.' In Rosen (ed) *Sexual Deviation.* Oxford: Oxford University Press 1996.

Waddell, M. (2002) 'The psychodynamics of bullying.' *Free Associations 9*, 2 (No 50), 189–210.

Watkins, B. And Bentovim, A. (1992) 'The sexual abuse of male children and adolescents; a review of current research.' *Journal of Child Psychology and Psychiatry,* 197–248.

Welldon, E.V. (1988) *Mother, Madonna, Whore; The Idealisation and Denigration of Motherhood.* New York: Guilford Press.

West, J. (1997) 'Caring for ourselves; the impact of working with abused children.' *Child Abuse Review 6*, 291–297.

Westman, A. (1996) 'Co-therapy and "re-parenting" in a group for disturbed children.' *Group Analysis 29*, 1, 55–68.

White, M. (1995) *Re-authoring Lives; Interviews and Essays.* Adelaide: Dulwich Centre Publications.

White, M. and Epston, D. (1990) *Narrative Means to Therapeutic Ends.* New York: Norton.

Williams, G. (1997) *International Landscapes and Foreign Bodies.* London: Duckworth.

Willis, S. (1988) 'Group-analytic drama; A therapy for disturbed adolescents.' *Group Analysis 21*, 2, 153–165.

Winnicott, D.W. (1947) 'Hate in the countertransference.' *Through Paediatrics to Psychoanalysis*. 1975, 194–203.

Winnicott, D.W. (1949) 'Mind and its relation to the psyche-soma.' *Through Paediatrics to Psychoanalysis*. 1975, 243–254.

Winnicott, D.W. (1952) 'Anxiety associated with insecurity.' *Through Paediatrics to Psychoanalysis*. 1975, 97–100.

Winnicott, D.W. (1958a) 'The anti-social tendency.' *Through Paediatrics to Psychoanalysis*. 1975, 306–315.

Winnicott, D.W. (1958b) 'The capacity to be alone.' *The Maturational Processes and the Facilitating Environment*. 1965, 29–36.

Winnicott, D.W. (1959) 'Classification; is there a psychoanalytic contribution to psychiatric classification?' *The Maturational Processes and the Facilitating Environment*. 1965, 124–139.

Winnicott, D.W. (1960) 'Ego distortion in terms of true and false self.' *The Maturational Processes and the Facilitating Environment*. 1965, 140–152.

Winnicott, D.W. (1960) 'Counter-transference.' *The Maturational Processes and the Facilitating Environment*. 1965, 158–165.

Winnicott, D.W. (1963a) 'Psychotherapy with character disorders.' *The Maturational Processes and the Facilitating Environment*. 1965, 203–216.

Winnicott, D.W. (1963b) 'Hospital care supplementing intensive psychotherapy in adolescence.' *The Maturational Processes and the Facilitating Environment*. 1965, 242–248.

Winnicott, D.W. (1965) 'Adolescence; struggling through the Doldrums.' *The Family and Individual Development*.

Winnicott, D.W. (1968) 'The use of an object and relating through identifications.' *Playing and Reality*. 1971, 86–94.

Winnicott, D.W. (1971) 'Transitional objects and transitional space.' *Playing and Reality*. 1971, 1–25.

Wood, A. (2001) 'Randomised trial of group therapy for repeated deliberate self-harm in adolescents.' *Journal of American Academy of Child and Adolescent Psychiatry 40*, 11, 1246–1253.

Woods, J. (1992) 'Omnipotence versus therapeutic responsiveness in group-analytic therapy.' *Group Analysis 25*, 3, *183–193*.

Woods, J. (1993) 'Limits and structure in child group psychotherapy.' *Journal of Child Psychotherapy 19*, 1, 63–78.

Woods, J. (1996) 'Handling violence in child group therapy.' *Group Analysis 29*, 1, 81–98.

Woods, J. (1997) 'Breaking the cycle of abuse and abusing.' *Clinical Child Psychology and Psychiatry 2*, 3, 379–392.

Woods, J. (1999) 'Book reviews.' *Clinical Child Psychology and Psychiatry 4*, 2, 281–300.

Woods, J. (2001) *The End of Abuse; A Playreading in Three Parts.* London: Open Gate Press.

Wyre, R. (1987) *Working with Sex Abuse.* London: Perry Publications.

Wyre, R. and Swift, J. (1990) *Women, Men and Rape.* Sevenoaks: Hodder and Stoughton.

Yalom, I. (1970) *The Theory and Practice of Group Psychotherapy.* New York: Basic Books 1985.

Zaphiriou Woods, M. (2003) 'Developmental Considerations in an Adult Analysis.' In V. Green (ed) *Emotional Development in Psychoanalysis, Attachment Theory and Neuroscience; Creating Connections.* London: Routledge.

Zinkin, L. (1983) 'Malignant mirroring.' *Group Analysis 16,* 113–125.

Zulueta, F. de (1993) *From Pain to Violence; The Traumatic Roots of Destructiveness.* London: Routledge.

Subject Index

Author Index